中英对照·双语典藏

走遍万水千山

游记篇

Travelling Over Mountains And Rivers

丛书主编/戴艳萍　主编/王欣　副主编/王宁 王丽丽

希望这些散文能让你领略到大自然的美妙，体味各地风土人情的别致，品读作者独特的艺术匠心和人生智慧，还能感受到英语是如何在各位语言大师手下妙笔生花，展示其特有的文字魅力的。

如果你想感受自然，请读一篇游记，
它会让你融入自然，敬畏生命。
如果你想缓解压力，请读一篇游记，
它会让你放松身心，心如止水。
如果你想平和心境，请读一篇游记，
它会让你净化心灵，感悟人生。

大连理工大学出版社

图书在版编目(CIP)数据

走遍万水千山：游记篇：英汉对照 / 王欣主编.
— 大连：大连理工大学出版社, 2012.8
　　（触动心灵的经典）
　　ISBN 978-7-5611-7187-5

　　Ⅰ.①走… Ⅱ.①王… Ⅲ.①英汉—汉语—对照读物
②游记—作品集—世界 Ⅳ.①H319.4:I

中国版本图书馆CIP数据核字(2012)第182794号

大连理工大学出版社出版
地址：大连市软件园路80号　　邮政编码：116023
发行：0411-81708842　邮购：04411-84703636　传真：0411-84701466
E-mail: dutp@dutp.cn　　DRL:http://www.dutp.cn
辽宁星海彩色印刷有限公司印刷　　大连理工大学出版社发行

幅面尺寸：168mm×235mm　　　印张：13.5　　　字数：230千
印数：1~6000
2012年8月第1版　　　　　　　2012年8月第1次印刷

责任编辑：张　钰　　　　　　　　　　　责任校对：程欢欢
封面设计：王付青

ISBN 978-7-5611-7187-5　　　　　　　　　定　价：25.00元

前言
preface

　　游历是古人的一种求知方式，也是提升修养的途径。孔子周游列国而博闻，司马迁遍历天下而著《史记》；杜甫颠沛流离知人间疾苦，写下忧国忧民的旷世绝唱；李白将一生赋予秀美山水，在壮美的意境中抒发豪情壮志。正如严复所言："大抵少年能以旅游观览山水名胜为乐，乃极佳事。因此不但怡神遣日，且能增进许多阅历学问，激发多少志气，更无论太史公文得江山之助者矣。"游历可以开阔视野，洗涤心境；磨炼意志，涵养心性，古今中外，莫不如是。

　　但一生太短，俗事太繁，奔波于尘世的我们，想有时间、有能力走出喧哗，在春暖花开时，面朝大海浩瀚；或在千里冰封时，漫步林海雪原，在自然天地间找回迷失到现实中的自我，这也许是一种不算奢侈但难以实现的愿望。我们不妨在倦意来袭时，或人生失意时，幽窗开卷，领略一番纸上山水，或许我们可以放下思想上的重负，忘记烦恼和忧愁。本书选取欧美名家游记原文，分成七个部分，每一部分都有一个明确的主题，有对国家、城市的概况介绍，也有对街头巷尾的细致描写，还有对自然美景的尽情歌颂。古人"读万卷书，行万里路"，本书则能让你足不出户，就能徜徉于万里之外的尼罗河畔，欣赏河面的涟漪起伏，聆听流水的潺潺之美；也能将你置身于孟买的街头，感受城镇的喧嚣与沉寂；还能让你真切体验泛舟水上的乐趣与超凡经历。

　　如果你想感受自然，请读一篇游记，它会让你融入自然，敬畏生命。

　　如果你想缓解压力，请读一篇游记，它会让你放松身心，心如止水。

　　如果你想平和心境，请读一篇游记，它会让你净化心灵，感悟人生。

　　这三十余篇名家美文，篇篇都尽显大家风范，篇篇都是人类的共同财富，是诸位作家将历史的足迹和大自然的神奇承载于文字之中，呈现在读者面前的瑰宝。让读者不仅能领略大自然的美妙，体味各地风土人情的别

致，品读作者独特的艺术匠心和人生智慧，还能感受到英语是如何在各位语言大师手下妙笔生花，展示其特有的文字魅力的。让读者在领略各地美景风采的同时，扩大知识面，提高文化素养，促进英语水平的整体提升。

让我们一起去分享这些历久弥新的经典篇章，一同去领略托斯卡纳的烂漫山花，墨尔本的欧陆风情，代托纳海滨的波澜壮阔以及圣安德鲁斯的沧桑变化吧！

本册书主编为王欣，副主编为王宁、王丽丽，参与本书编写的还有：王婧、许剑楠、王星宇、刘晓琳、余双全、周迈、汪露秋、项丹凤、王晓英、庄欣、孙礼中、刘瑜、宋沈黎、李雪等老师，在此表示感谢。

编者
2012年8月

Contents

目录

【闲庭信步　品别样风情】

Alhambra ·························· 3
阿尔罕伯拉官

Reflections in an English Inn ·············· 10
在英国小酒馆的沉思

Bombay Scenes ·················· 15
孟买街头景色

In and about the City ·············· 22
城里城外

【跋山涉水，叹壮丽神奇】

Flowery Tuscany ················ 30
如花的托斯卡纳

Niagara ······················· 37
尼亚加拉瀑布

Stonehenge ···················· 43
巨石阵

The Call of the Mountains ·········· 49
山谷的呼唤

目录

The Nile ································ 55
尼罗河

On the Beach at Daytona ············· 61
代托纳海滩

【悠悠泛舟，品岸边风光】

Rafting down the Neckar ··········· 69
内卡河上木筏行

The Flowing Canal ················· 75
奔腾的运河

To Rome by Pisa and Siena ·········· 82
经比萨和锡耶纳到罗马

Kayaking the Fjords of New Zealand ········· 89
泛舟新西兰峡湾

【异域情怀，国各有别】

A Glance at the Country ············· 97
匈牙利一瞥

Rural Life in England ··············· 104
英国的乡村生活

Spain ···························· 112
西班牙之旅

Kenya: Patchwork of Experiences ········· 119
肯尼亚——缤纷印象

【多彩都市，各具风姿】

First Impressions of the
Capital of Vienna ·········· 126
首都维也纳第一印象

Paris — The Beautiful City ·········· 132
美丽之城——巴黎

Zurich ·········· 138
苏黎世

Here Is New York ·········· 144
这里是纽约

【缤纷城市，缤纷印象】

A Guest's Impression of
New England ·········· 152
新英格兰的访客印象

Cracow ·········· 158
克拉科夫

Edinburgh ·········· 163
爱丁堡

Florence Eighty Years Ago ·········· 170
八十年前的佛罗伦萨

Geneva ·········· 177
日内瓦

目录

Marseilles ··· 184
马赛

St. Andrews ·· 190
圣安德鲁斯

Venice ·· 197
威尼斯

Sight-seeing in Melbourne ······························· 203
观光墨尔本

闲庭信步
品别样风情

Alhambra
阿尔罕伯拉宫

Reflections in an English Inn
在英国小酒馆的沉思

Bombay Scenes
孟买街头景色

In and about the City
城里城外

Washington Irving

华盛顿·欧文

华盛顿·欧文(1783~1859)，出身于富商家庭.曾任美国驻伦敦使馆秘书和美国驻西班牙公使，是美国最早的浪漫主义作家之一，他以笔记、小说和传记而闻名，是第一位获得国际声誉的美国作家。欧文汲取欧洲文化和欧洲文学的精华，创造了自己独特的风格，其文笔清新、自然、诙谐、富于乐感，在短篇小说等诸多方面为独立的美国文学做出了巨大的贡献。他的主要作品有《纽约外史》(*A History of New York, 1809*)、《见闻杂记》(*The Sketch Book, 1820*)、《草原漫游记》(*A Tour on the Prairies, 1835*)等。

Alhambra

We found ourselves in a deep narrow ravine[1], filled with beautiful groves, with a steep avenue, and various footpaths winding through[2] it, bordered with stone seats, and ornamented[3] with fountains. To our left we beheld the towers of the Alhambra beetling[4] above us; to our right, on the opposite side of the ravine, we were equally dominated by rival towers on a rocky eminence[5]. These, we were told, were the Torres Vermejos, or vermilion[6] towers, so called from their ruddy hue. No one knows their origin. They are of a date much anterior to the Alhambra; Some suppose them to have been built by the Romans; others, by some wandering colony of Phoenicians[7]. Ascending[8] the steep and shady avenue, we arrived at the foot of a huge square Moorish[9] tower, forming a kind of barbican[10], through which passed the main entrance to the fortress.

Within the barbican was a group of veteran[11] invalids[12], one mounting guard at the

阿尔罕伯拉宫

我们已置身于狭长幽深的峡谷中，周围环绕着美丽的树林，陡峭的林荫道和各种各样的羊肠小径蜿蜒其中，两边是石椅，几处喷泉点缀其间。在左边，我们望得见阿尔罕伯拉宫的高楼屹立上空；右边，在山谷的对面，在高高的山岩上同样有几座高塔，俯视着我们。据说这就是由于颜色朱红而得名的朱砂塔。没有人知道它们的来历，大概它们的年代比阿尔罕伯拉还要久远得多——有人认为是罗马人建造的；另外有些人又说是到处漂泊的腓尼基殖民者所筑。爬上陡峭的浓荫密布的道路，我们来到一座宏大的摩尔式方塔脚下，这种塔其实是一种碉楼，通向城堡的主要道路就经由这里。

碉楼内是一批老弱残兵，

---

1 ravine [rə'viːn]　 *n.* 峡谷
2 winding through 　= following a curving course　蜿蜒
3 ornamented ['ɔːnəmɛntid]　 *adj.* 装饰，点缀，这里是过去分词作定语
4 beetle ['biːtl]　 *vi.* = overhang，突出，此处译为"屹立"
5 eminence ['ɛmɪnəns]　 *n.* 高处，凸起部分
6 vermilion [və'mɪlɪən]　 *adj.* 朱红的，涂朱红色的
7 Phoenician [fi'niʃɪən]　 *n.* 腓尼基人
8 ascending [ə'sɛndɪŋ]　 登上，攀爬，此处为现在分词结构作状语
9 Moorish ['mʊərɪ]　 *adj.* 摩尔式的
10 barbican ['bɑːbɪkən]　 *n.* 碉楼
11 veteran ['vɛtərən]　 *adj.* 老练的，这里指"年老的"
12 invalid [ɪn'vælɪd]　 *n.* 病人，残疾者

portal, while the rest, wrapt in[13] their tattered[14] cloaks, slept on the stone benches. This portal is called the Gate of Justice, from the tribunal[15] held within its porch during the Moslem domination, for the immediate trial of petty causes — a custom common to[16] the Oriental nations, and occasionally alluded to[17] in the sacred Scriptures: "Judges and officers shalt[18] thou make thee in all thy gates, and they shall judge the people with just judgment..."

After passing through the barbican, we ascended a narrow lane, winding between the high walls, and came on an open esplanade[19] within the fortress, called the Place of the Cisterns, from great reservoirs[20] which undermine it, cut in the living rock by the Moors to receive the water brought by conduits[21] from the Darro, for the supply of the fortress. Here, also, is a well of immense depth[22], furnishing the purest and coldest of water — another monument of the delicate taste of the Moors, who were indefatigable[23] in their exertions[24] to obtain that element in its crystal purity.

有一个站在门前守卫，其余的裹着破旧的斗篷，在石凳上睡觉。这地方叫做公正门，因为在伊斯兰教教徒统治期间，门廊内设有法庭，以便随时审问小案件——这是东方国家的一种风俗，《圣经》中偶尔也曾提到过："你们要在各城门设立审判官和官长，他们应按公正的判断审视百姓……"

经过这座外堡之后，我们爬上一条狭窄的小路，在高墙之间蜿蜒前进，来到城堡内的一片广场上，这儿叫做蓄水池城区，因为当初摩尔人曾经劈开了山岩，在这下面辟出巨大的蓄水池，容纳由沟渠从达罗河引来的水，供给城堡使用。此外还有一口极深的井，供给人们最清洁、最清凉的饮水——这是另一项表现摩尔人高雅趣味的古迹，很能说明他们为寻找纯洁如水晶般的水源所尽的不屈不挠的努力。

---

13 wrapt in　= being covered in soft material 包裹
14 tattered ['tætəd]　adj.　（衣服等）破烂的
15 tribunal [traɪ'bjuːnl]　n.　法官席，法院，法庭
16 common to　= shared by two or more people共有的
17 allude to　=mention somebody or something briefly or indirectly 提及、暗指或暗示
18 shalt [ʃælt]　[古语] kshall 的第二人称单数形式
19 esplanade [,esplə'neɪd]　n.　平坦的空地
20 reservoir ['rezəvwɑ:]　n.　蓄水池
21 conduit ['kɒndjʊɪt]　n.　引水道，渠道
22 be of depth　= deep be of + n.结构等同于其形容词
23 indefatigable [ɪndɪ'fætɪgəbl]　adj.　不知疲倦的
24 exertion [ɪg'zɜː.ʃn]　n.　努力

In front of this esplanade is the splendid pile[25] commenced by Charles V.[26], and intended, it is said, to eclipse[27] the residence of the Moorish kings. Much of the Oriental edifice intended for the winter season was demolished to make way for[28] this massive pile. The grand entrance was blocked up[29], so that the present entrance to the Moorish palace is a simple and almost humble portal in a corner. With all the massive grandeur[30] and architectural merit of the palace of Charles V., we regarded it as an arrogant intruder[31], passing by it with a feeling almost of scorn, and rang at the Moslem portal.

While waiting for admittance, our self-imposed cicerone[32], Mateo Ximenes, informed us that the royal palace was entrusted[33] to the care of a worthy old maiden dame called Dona Antonia Molina, but who, according to Spanish custom, went by the more neighborly appellation[34] of Tia Antonia (Aunt Antonia), who maintained the Moorish halls and gardens in order and showed them to strangers. While we were talking, the door was opened by a plump

广场前面，有一座华丽的大楼，是由查尔斯五世着手建造的，据说这是他打算用来压倒摩尔人的王宫的。许多适合冬天居住的东方式大厦，都因为他要建造这个庞大的建筑物被拆毁了。宏伟的人口已被堵塞住了，因此现在要进摩尔人的王宫，就得穿过角落上一扇朴素的、甚至可以称得上是简陋的边门。不管查尔斯五世的这座宫殿多么宏伟、多么具有建筑方面的价值，我们总觉得它只是一个妄自尊大的闯人者，我们带着几乎可以说是蔑视的感觉经过那儿，到那座伊斯兰教宫殿的边门拉响了门铃。

在等待进入的时候，自告奋勇做向导的马提奥·雪门斯告诉我们，看管王宫的是一位可亲可敬的老妇人，名叫唐娜·安东尼娅·莫林娜（Dona，西班牙语，对"女人"的尊称），不过大伙都按照西班牙风俗，用比较亲密的"安东尼

---

25 pile[paɪl] *n.* 高大的建筑物
26 Charles V *v.* 查尔斯 V 世，是欧洲历史上重要的统治者之一。查尔斯五世作为西班牙帝王的同时，还统治着那不勒斯和西西里岛。他还当选为圣罗马帝国皇帝，是当时财富最多、势力最大的欧洲帝王。他在名义上或实际上统治的领土包括西班牙、德国、荷兰、比利时、奥地利、瑞士、大部分意大利、部分法国、捷克斯洛伐克、波兰、匈牙利和南斯拉夫，此外还有西半球的一部分地区
27 eclipse[ɪ'klɪps] *v.* 使……黯然失色
28 make way for = allow something or someone to pass 为……让路，给……腾出地方
29 block up 阻塞，挡住
30 grandeur['grændʒə] *n.* 庄严，伟大
31 intruder [ɪn'truːdə] *n.* 侵人者，干扰者，妨碍者
32 cicerone [ˌtʃɪtʃə'rəʊnɪ] *n.* 导游
33 entrust [ɪn'trʌst] *v.* 交托
34 appellation [ˌæpə'leɪʃ(ə)n] *n.* 称呼，名称

little black-eyed Andalusian damsel[35], whom Mateo addressed as Dolores, but who from her bright look and cheerful disposition evidently merited a merrier name. Mateo informed me in a whisper that she was the niece of Tia Antonia, and I found she was the good fairy who was to conduct us through the enhanted palace. Under her guidance we crossed the threshold[36] and were at once transported, as if by magic wand, into other times and an oriental realm, and were treading the scenes of Arabian story. Nothing could be in greater contrast than[37] the unpromising exterior of the pile with the scene now before us. We found ourselves in a vast patio[38] or court, one hundred and fifty feet in length, and upward of eighty feet in breadth, paved with white marble, and decorated at each end with light Moorish peristylos[39], one of which supported an elegant gallery of fretted[40] architecture.

Along the moldings of the cornices[41] and on various parts of the walls were escutcheons[42] and ciphers[43] and cufic[44] and Arabic characters in high relief[45], repeating the pious mottoes

娅姑姑"来称呼她，她把摩尔人的王宫中那些大厅和花园打理得井井有条，让外人参观。说着说着，门开了，走出来一位体态丰满、身材娇小、黑眼珠的安达路西亚姑娘，马提奥喊她陶洛丽斯，然而瞧她那伶俐可爱的相貌和欢欢喜喜的表情，显然该有个更悦耳的名字。马提奥悄悄告诉我她就是安东尼娅姑姑的侄女，将要领我们通过魔宫的那位善良的仙女。在她的引领下，我们跨过门槛，好像触发了魔棒，顷刻间置身于另一个时代，踏落在东方人的国土上，走进阿拉伯神话的奇景里。这座建筑不起眼的外观和我们眼前的情景对比起来，真是再也没有比这更显悬殊的差别了。我们发现已经到了一个宽广的庭院里，庭院长150英尺，宽约80余英尺，白大理石铺地，四隅都装饰着优美的摩尔式圆柱，其中一隅的圆柱上还支撑着一座刻有花纹的楼台。

沿檐板的花边、四壁，尽是各种饰有花纹的盾、符号和

35 damsel ['dæmz(ə)l]　n.　少女，姑娘
36 threshold ['θreʃhəuld]　n.　门槛
37 nothing could be in greater contrast than　这里是用形容词比较级结构表达最高级
38 patio['pætɪəu]　n.　庭院
39 peristylos[ˌperɪ'staɪləs]　n.　四周有柱廊的建筑物
40 fret [fret]　v.　以刻出的或锯出的图案装饰
41 cornice['kɔːnɪs]　n.　飞檐
42 escutcheon[ɪ'skʌtʃən]　n.　饰有纹章的盾
43 cipher['saɪfə]　n.　这里指符号
44 cufic ['kjuːfɪk]　adj.　古阿拉伯字母表的
45 in high relief　=with the background cut out deeply/shallowly　深浮雕

of the Moslem monarchs[46], the builders of the Alhambra, or extolling their grandeur and munificence[47]. Along the center of the court extended an immense basin or tank, a hundred and twenty-four feet in length, twenty-seven in breadth, and five in depth, receiving its water from two marble vases. Hence it is called the Court of the Alberca (from albeerkan, the Arabic for a pond or tank). Great numbers of goldfish were to be seen gleaming through the waters of the basin, and it was bordered by hedges of roses.

Passing from the Court of the Alberca under a Moorish archway, we entered the renowned Court of Lions. No part of the edifice gives a more complete idea of its original beauty than this, for none has suffered so little from the ravages[48] of time. In the center stands the fountain famous in song and story. The alabaster[49] basins still shed their diamond drops, the twelve lions which support them, and give the court its name, still cast forth crystal streams as in the days of Boabdil. The lions, however, are unworthy of their fame, being of miserable sculpture, the work probably of some Christian captive[50]. The court is laid out in flower-beds, instead of its ancient and appropriate pavement of tiles or marble, The

古阿拉伯字母以及用深浮雕雕刻的阿拉伯文字，记录着伊斯兰教诸王——阿尔罕伯拉宫的那些创建者的虔敬箴言或是赞扬他们的威望和德政的颂词。庭院中央是一个长124英尺，宽27英尺，深5英尺的大水池，承接着由两只大理石瓶流出来的水。因此，这地方被称为阿尔别尔卡院（阿拉伯文中池塘叫做阿尔别尔卡）。池中有无数金鱼游来游去，闪闪发光，池边围绕着一圈由玫瑰树丛攀成的短篱。

离开阿尔别尔卡院，从一条摩尔式拱廊下穿过去，我们就走进了著名的雄狮院。宫内没有任何地方能比这里更能使人完全领略阿尔罕伯拉宫昔日的优美了，因为它所遭受的时间摧残比全宫任何一处都小。院子中央有一个在诗歌和故事里盛传的喷水池。乳白石盘中喷洒着晶莹的水珠，那十二只托着石盘，并使这个庭院以此得名的狮子，还是和在波阿布狄尔时代一样，仍喷射着剔透的水流。其实，这些狮子都雕

46 monarch ['mɒnək] *n.* 统治者
47 munificence [mju:'nɪfɪsns] *n.* 宽宏大量，这里译为德政
48 ravage ['rævɪdʒ] *n.* 破坏，蹂躏
49 alabaster ['æləba:stə] *n.* 雪花石膏
50 captive['kæptɪv] *n.* 俘虏

alteration[51], and instance of bad taste, was made by the French when in possession of[52] Granada

From *Tales of the Alhambra* (1832)

刻得非常拙劣，大概是出于俘虏来的基督徒之手，哪里配得上这么大的名气。庭院内布置了许多花坛，取代了古雅且与之相称的花砖或大理石地板，这种俗不可耐的更改，是法军占领格拉达时的"杰作"。

---

51 alteration[ˌɔːltəˈreɪʃn] *n.* 改变
52 in possession of =having or controlling something so that others are prevented from using, 占有

含英咀华

阿尔罕伯拉，按照阿拉伯文的原意是"红宫"，原是摩尔族国王于13世纪在西班牙的格拉那达建造的一座辉煌宫殿。1826年，欧文到西班牙搜集了许多有关哥伦布的珍贵资料，游历了格拉纳达的名胜，并在阿尔罕伯拉宫逗留了将近3个月。这一切激起了他对研究西班牙历史的兴趣。1829年前后，他写了3部有关西班牙的著作：《哥伦布传》（*The Life and Voyages of Christopher Columbus*, 1828）、《攻克格拉纳达》（*The Chronicles of the Conquest of Granada*, 1829）和《阿尔罕伯拉》（*Tales of the Alhambra*, 1832）。在《阿尔罕伯拉》中他不仅描绘了阿尔罕伯拉宫地理的险峻悲凉、摩尔人的风俗人情及高深文化，更诉说了其故宫历史的沧桑和命运的变幻无穷。

William Cobbett
威廉·科贝特

威廉·科贝特（1762~1835），19世纪初英国最有影响力的政论家之一。他原本思想保守，但在法国大革命之后，奋起抨击政府，所写社论深得贫民之心。他没有进过学校，全靠自学成材。其作品文字十分动人，风格质朴有力，在19世纪初浪漫派极盛之时，独树一帜。《骑马乡行记》（*Rural Rides, 1830*）是他在 1821~1830 年间出游英格兰、苏格兰各地时对旅行所做的零星记载，但是文中并无多少风景描写，多是英国人民困苦生活的记录，是其众多作品中最受推崇的一部。

Reflections in an English Inn

East Everley (Wiltshire)

Sunday Evening, 27 Aug. 1826

Everley is but about three miles from Ludgarshall, so that we got here in the afternoon of Friday, and in the evening a very heavy storm came and drove away all flies, and made the air delightful. This is a real down-country. Here you see miles and miles square without a tree, or hedge[1], or bush. It is country of greensward. This is the most famous place in all England for coursing[2]. I was here, at this very inn, with a party eighteen years ago; and the landlord, who is still the same, recognized me as soon as he saw me. There were forty brace of greyhounds[3] taken out into the field on one of the days, and every brace had one course and some of them two. The ground is the finest in the world, from two to three miles for the hare to run to cover, and not a stone nor a bush nor a hillock[4]. It was here proved to me that the hare is, by far, the swiftest of all English animals; for I saw three hares, in one day, run away from the dogs. To give dog and hare a fair trial there should be but one dog. Then, if that dog got so close as to compel the

在英国
小酒馆的沉思

东伊弗雷（威尔特郡）

1826年8月27日星期日傍晚

因伊弗雷距路德格霄仅约3英里之遥，所以我们周五下午就到了这里。晚上下了场暴雨，赶走了所有的蚊蝇，空气也随之格外清新。这是一个真正的南部乡村。在这里，放眼望去一片空阔，方圆几里之内，没有树木、篱笆和灌木丛。这里绿地成茵，是全英国最负盛名的赛狗场。18年前，我曾随一个团体来过这里，就在这个小酒馆里；现在店主依然未变，一见我便认出来。在这期间的某一天，四十对猎狗被带到赛场上，每对狗占一个跑道，有一些占两个跑道。这片草地是世界上最棒的，即便让兔子跑上两三英里，中间也不会撞到石头、树丛和土丘。就是这里向我证明：兔子是目前为止英国所有的动物中速度最快的，因为有一天我

---

1 hedge [hedʒ]   *n.* 篱笆
2 coursing ['kɔːsɪŋ]   *n.* 这里指赛狗
3 greyhound ['greɪhaʊnd]   *n.* 灵提（一种赛狗）
4 hillock ['hɪlək]   *n.* 小山丘

hare to turn, that would be a proof that the dog ran fastest; when the dog, or dogs, never get near enough to the hare to induce her to turn, she is said, and very justly, to "run away" from them; and as I saw three hares do this in one day, I conclude that the hare is the swifter animal of the two.

This inn is one of the nicest, and, in summer, one of the most pleasantes, in England; for I think that my experience in this way will justify me in speaking thus positively. The house is large, the yard and the stables good, the landlord a farmer also, and, therefore, no cribbing[5] your horses in hay or straw and yourself in eggs and cream. The garden, which adjoins the south side of the house, is large, of good shape, has a terrace on one side, lies on the slope, consists of well-disposed clumps[6] of shrubs and flowers, and of short grass very neatly kept. In the lower part of the garden there are high trees, and, among these, the tulip-trees and the live-oaks. Beyond the garden is a large clump of lofty sycamores[7], and in these a most populous rookery[8], in which, of all things in the world, I delight.The village, which contains 301 souls, lies to the north of the inn, but adjoining its premises[9]. All the rest, in every direction, is bare down or open arable[10]. I

先后看见三只兔子在猎狗的追逐之下胜利逃脱。若要给猎狗和兔子一个公平的比赛，这里应该只有一条狗。然后若那条狗跑得离兔子太近而迫使兔子不得不转向，这将证明狗跑得最快；若那条狗或狗群没能跑得太近迫使兔子转向，就可以公正地称兔子"胜利逃脱"。而且在一天之内我先后看见三只兔子成功逃脱，我便得出结论，两者之中，兔子跑得更快。

这个小酒馆是全英国最好的，在夏季尤其令人心愉；因为我认为，我这方面的经历让我有资格如此肯定。屋子很大，院子与马房也不错。店主是一农户，因此，马可以痛快地吃草，你自己也可敞开肚皮享用鸡蛋和奶油。屋子南边是一个很大、修剪得很好的花园。花园的一边是排房。花园地处斜坡，园里是一丛丛布置得当的花与树木，以及一些修剪得很整齐的矮草。花园较低之处栽满高高的树木，其中有郁金香树和活橡树。花园外面

5 cribbing [krɪbɪŋ] *n.* 马咬秣槽，文中指马可以尽情吃草
6 clump [klʌmp] *n.* 树丛，植物丛
7 sycamore ['sɪkəmɔː] *n.* 大枫树
8 rookery ['rʊkərɪ] *n.* 白嘴鸦
9 premises ['prɛmɪsɪz] *n.* 房屋
10 arable ['ærəbl] *n.* arable land （可）耕地

am now sitting at one of the southern windows of this inn, looking across the garden towards the rookery. It is nearly sun-setting; the rooks are skimming and curving over the tops of the trees; while under the branches I see a flock of several hundred sheep coming nibbling their way in from the down and going to their fold. Now, what ill-natured devil could bring Old Nic Grimshaw into my head in company with these innocent sheep? Why, the truth is this: nothing is so swift as thought: it runs over a life-time in a moment; and while I was writing the last sentence of the foregoing paragraph, thought took me up at the time when I used to wear a smock-frock[11] and to carry a wooden bottle like that shepherd's boy; and, in an instant, it hurried me along through my not very short life of adventure, of toil[12], of peril[13], of pleasure, of ardent[14] friendship and not less ardent enmity[15]; and after filling me with wonder that a heart and mind so wrapped up in everything belonging to the gardens, the fields, and the woods should have been condemned to waste themselves away amidst the stench, the noise, and the strife[16] of cities, it brought me to the present moment, and sent my mind back to what I have yet to perform about Nicholas Grimshaw and his ditches !

11 **smock-frock** *n.* （欧洲农民干活时穿的）长罩衫
12 **toil** [tɔil] *n.* 苦工，累活。这里引申为"艰辛"
13 **peril** ['perəl] *n.* 危险
14 **ardent** ['aːdənt] *adj.* 热情的，热烈的
15 **enmity** ['enmət] *n.* 敌意，仇恨
16 **strife** [straif] *n.* 冲突，这里指城市的喧闹

是一大片枫树林，林中有很多白嘴鸦，能身处此景令我倍感愉悦。村里有301口人，都住在酒馆的北面，但都与酒馆紧邻。其余四面都是光秃秃的丘陵与开阔的耕地。我现在就坐在酒馆南面的窗户边，目光越过花园，眺望那些白嘴鸦。此时已近日暮，白嘴鸦在树梢飞上飞下；而在丛林间，我看见一群羊，有数百头之多，它们正从草地回到羊圈，边走边吃着草。现在，面对这些无邪的羊，有什么恶毒的恶魔能让我想起尼科·格林肖？然而事实是，思维的速度比什么都要快，它能在瞬间回顾你一生的经历。就在我写上一段中的最后一句时，思维一下子带我回到过去，那时我身披大衣，手提木瓶，就像个牧童；倏忽之间，它让我匆匆回忆起自己不算短暂的人生，充满冒险、艰辛、危险、乐趣、真挚友谊和仇恨。领略了这么多的奇妙，我的心灵在深深沉醉于花园、田野和树林之中的寸草寸木之后，竟然注定要浪费在恶臭、嘈杂和吵闹的城市里。它让我回到眼前，将我的思绪派到为对付格林肖和他操纵选举的诡计而不得不做点儿什么上。

My sons set off at about three o'clock today on their way to Herefordshire, where I intend to join them when I have had a pretty good ride in this country. There is no pleasure in travelling except on horse-back or on foot. Carriages take your body from place to place, and if you merely want to be conveyed they are very good; but they enable you to see and to know nothing at all of the country.

From *Rural Rides* (1830)

我的儿子们大约三点钟出发去荷伏特郡了，我在这个村里好好地遛一下马之后，会赶到那里与他们会合。只有骑马或步行，旅游才有乐趣可言。马车载着我们穿村过庄，你若仅仅是让它送你到某个地方，马车是很好的；但那样却不能让你欣赏、了解乡村的一切。

闲庭信步 品别样风情

含英咀华

本文摘自《骑马乡行记》，用词简洁，句式结构简单，语言浅显易懂，描写了英国乡村小酒馆的幽静雅致，表达了作者身处乡间悠然自得和深深沉醉于花园、田野和树林的寸草寸木之中的愉快心情。

Stephen Meredyth Edwardes

斯迪芬·麦勒迪斯·爱德华兹

斯迪芬·麦勒迪斯·爱德华兹（1873~1927），曾任职于印度内务部，他学识渊博，著作等身，涉猎广泛，尤以擅长印度历史著称，著有《印度莫卧儿王朝的统治》（*Mughal Rule in India, 1930*）、《巴伯尔，日记作者及暴君》（*Babur, Diarist and Despot, 1926*）、《孟买之行》（*By-Ways of Bombay, 1912*）等。

Bombay Scenes

The ebb and flow[1] of life remains much the same from day to day. The earliest street sound, before the dawn breaks, is the rattle[2] of the trams, the meat-carts on their way to the markets, the dust-carts and the watering-carts; and then, just as the grey thread of the dawn fringes the horizon, the hymn[3] of the fakir[4] rings forth, praising[5] the open-handed Ali and imploring the charity of the early-riser who knows full well that a copper bestowed[6] unseen during the morning is worth far more than silver bestowed in the sight of men.

So the morning passes into mid-day, amid a hundred sounds symbolical of the various phases of life in the western capital — the shout of the driver, the twang of the cotton-cleaner, the warning call of the anxious mother, the rattle of the showman's[7] drum, the yell of the devotee, the curse of the cart man, the clang of the coppersmith[8], the chaffering[9] of buyer and seller

孟买街头景色

日复一日，生活潮涨潮落、平淡无奇地持续着。在黎明破晓前，街上充斥着有轨电车的咯咯声，赶往市场路上的肉推车的嘎嘎声，以及垃圾车和洒水车的声音；当灰色的光线照亮地平线时，苦行者唱着圣歌向前走去，赞美慷慨大方的阿里，并恳求早起者的慈善，这些人清楚地知道早上不为人注意时施舍给人的铜钱的价值远远大于当着众人施舍的银子的价值。

因此，在西部之都，从早晨到正午，百余种声音喻示着人们生活的不同状态——司机的叫喊声，棉花清洁工的嘣琴声，焦虑的母亲的警告的呼唤声，街头演出人员的敲鼓声，皈依者的叫喊声，手推车者的

1　ebb and flow　兴衰,起伏。例如：The ebb and flow of politics in Washington goes on as usual. (华盛顿的政治风云一如既往，仍然变幻莫测。)
2　rattle ['rætl]　n.　咯咯声
3　hymn [hɪm]　n.　赞美诗，圣歌
4　fakir ['feɪkɪə]　n.　(伊斯兰教或印度教的) 托钵僧，苦行者
5　praising...in the sight of men　从句是由两个现在分词短语构成的，作状语表伴随，其中包含一个由"who"引起的定语从句，修饰前面的"early-riser"；定语从句中又包含一个宾语从句，宾语从句中的主语是"a copper"，谓语为系表结构即"is worth"
6　bestow [bɪ'stəʊ]　v.　= give，给予，赠给
7　showman ['ʃəʊmən]　n.　马戏团的老板，玩杂耍的
8　coppersmith ['kɒpəsmɪθ]　n.　铜匠
9　chaffer ['tʃæfə]　v.　= bargain，讲价，讨价还价

15

and the wail[10] of the mourner[11]. And above all the roar of life broods[12], the echo of the call to prayer in honor of[13] Allah, the All-Powerful and All-Pitiful, the Giver of Life and Giver of Death.

As the sun sinks low in the west, a stream of worshippers flows through the mosque-gates, gold-turbaned[14], shrewd-eyed Memon traders, ruddy Jats from Multan, heavily dressed Bukharans, Arabs, Afghans and pallid embroiderers[15] from Surat, who grudge[16] the half hour stolen from the daylight. At the main entrance of the mosques[17] gather[18] groups of men and women with sick children in their arms, waiting until the prayers are over and the worshippers file out; for the prayer-laden breath of the truly devout is powerful to exorcise[19] the demons of disease, and the child over whom the breath of the worshipper has passed has fairer surety of recovery than can be gained from all the nostrums[20] and charms of the Syed[21] and Hakim[22]. Just before and after sunset the streets wear their busiest air. Here

咒骂声，铜匠的叮当声，商贩与顾客之间的讨价还价声，哀悼者的恸哭声。在以上生活的嘈杂声中回荡着祈祷真神阿拉的呼唤，阿拉是全能全悲的化身、生与死的缔造者。

日薄西山时，礼拜者如泉涌般向清真寺的大门涌去：有戴着金黄色头巾、双眼精明的麦蒙商人，有来自木尔坦的脸色红润的加特人，有穿着厚重的布哈拉人、阿拉伯人、阿富汗人，还有来自苏拉特的肤色苍白的刺绣工，他们十分珍惜这来之不易的半个小时。在清真寺的主要入口处聚集着成群的善男信女，他们怀抱着有病的孩子，一直等到祈祷结束，做礼拜的人鱼贯而出；因为这些充满虔诚祷告的气息对驱除病魔有特效，祷告者的气息比在赛义德和医师那里得到的秘方和符咒更有效。日

---

10 wail [weɪl] *n.* 哀号声
11 mourner ['mɔːnə] *n.* 哀悼者
12 brood [bruːd] *n.* 窝，此处引申为"生活的圈子"，可不译出
13 in honor of 为纪念……
14 gold-turbaned ['gəuld 'tɜːbənd] *adj.* 缠金色头巾的
15 embroiderer [ɪm'brɔɪdərə] *n.* 刺绣工
16 grudge [grʌdʒ] *v.* 吝惜，此处是褒义词，= cherish意为"珍惜"
17 mosque [mɒsk] *n.* 清真寺
18 gather...file out 主句中的主语是 "groups of men and women"，谓语为 "gather" 前置，形成倒装句；从句中的 "waiting" 是现在分词，表伴随
19 exorcise ['eksɔːsaɪz] *v.* 除怪，驱邪，这里指 "驱除病魔"
20 nostrum ['nɒstrəm] *n.* 成药，所谓妙方
21 Syed *n.* 伊斯兰教教职称谓，原意为 "首领"、"先生"，转义为 "圣裔"
22 hakim [hæ:'kiːm] *n.* （伊斯兰教国家的）医师、学者

are millhands[23] and other laborers returning from their daily labors, merchants faring home from their offices, beggars, hawkers, fruit-sellers and sweetmeat-vendors, while crowds enter the cookshops and sherbet shops, and groups of Arabs and others settle themselves for recreation on the threshold of the coffee-sellers' domain[24]. There in a quiet backwater[25] of traffic a small crowd gathers round a shabbily-dressed Panjabi, who, producing a roll of pink papers and waving them before his audience, describes them as the Prayer-treasure of the Heavenly Throne ("Duai Ganjul Arsh"), Allah's greatest gift to the Prophet. "The Prophet and his children," he continues, "treasured this prayer; for before it fled the evil spirits of possession, disease and difficulty. Nor hath[26] its virtue faded in these later days."

During the hot months of the year the closeness of the rooms and the attacks of mosquitoes force many a[27] respectable householder to shoulder his bedding and join the great army of street-sleepers, who crowd the footpaths and open spaces like shrouded[28] corpses. All sorts and conditions of men thus take their night's rest beneath the moon, — Rangaris, Kasais, bakers, beggars, wanderers, and artisans, — the householder taking up a small position on

落前后街上充斥着一天中最繁忙的气息。结束了日常劳作的磨坊工人及其他工人正匆匆往回赶，商人也从办公室赶回家，乞丐、小贩、卖水果的和卖甜食的纷纷走进小饭馆和冰果子露店，成群的阿拉伯人和其他人在咖啡店门前消遣娱乐。在交通不那么拥挤的安静角落，一小群人聚集在一位衣衫褴褛的旁遮普人的周围。他手里拿着一卷粉红色的纸，在众人面前摇动，把它们描述成神圣王权的宝贵财富、真主阿拉送给穆罕默德的最好礼物。"穆罕默德和他的孩子们，"他继续说道，"珍惜这份祝福；因为在这之前你已摆脱了财富、疾病和困苦的恶魔。在以后的岁月里它的价值永不陨落。"

在每年炎热的月份里，房屋闷热、蚊子侵袭迫使很多有名望的人也不得不肩扛被褥加入到在街头睡觉的大军中，这些人就像裹尸布包裹着的尸体一样拥挤在人行道和空地上。各种各样的人都在月光下休息——染工、卡赛人、面包

23 millhand [ˈmɪlhænd] n. 研磨工人
24 domain [dəʊˈmeɪn] n. （个人或家庭的）地产，产业
25 backwater [ˈbækwɔːtə] n. 与世隔绝的地方，闭塞的地方。这里指街道上人较少、较安静的地方
26 hath （古）have 的第三人称单数，现在式，hath = has
27 many a = a large number of 许多
28 shrouded [ˈʃraʊdɪd] adj. 用裹尸布包着的

17

the flags[29] near his house, the younger and unmarried men wandering further afield to the nearest open space, but all lying with their head towards the north for fear of the anger of the Kutb or Pole star.

The sights and sounds vary somewhat at different seasons of the year. During Ramazan, for example, the streets are lined with booths and stalls for the sale of the rice-gruel or "Faludah" which is so grateful a posset[30] to the famishing Faithful, hurrying dinnerless to the nearest mosque. When the evening prayer is over and the first meal has been taken, the coffee-shops are filled with smokers, the verandahs[31] with men playing drafts, while the air is filled with the cries of iced drink sellers and of beggars longing to break their fast also. Then about 8 p.m., as the hour of the special Ramazan prayer draws nigh, the mosque beadle[32], followed by a body of shrill-voiced boys, makes his round of the streets, crying "Namaz tayar hai, cha-lo-o," and all the dwellers in the Musalman quarter hie[33] them to the house of prayer.

It is in the comparative quiet of the streets by night that one hears more distinctly the sounds in the houses. Here rises the bright note of the "shadi" or luck songs with which during the livelong night the women of the house dispel[34]

29 flag[flæg] *n.* （铺地板、路等的）石板
30 posset ['pɔsɪt] *n.* 牛乳酒
31 verandah [və'rændə] *n.* 游廊，走廊
32 beadle ['bi:dl] *n.* 小吏，此处意为"持杖官员"
33 hie [haɪ] *v.* 催促
34 dispel [dɪs'pel] *v.* 驱散，驱逐

师、乞丐、流浪者、工匠——每一户占据房子附近石板路的一小块地方，年轻人和未婚男女则漫步到稍远一点的空地上，但所有人都头朝北躺着，因为他们害怕北极星的威力。

四季变迁，风景和声音不尽相同。如在斋月期间，售货棚和货摊在街上排成一排，有卖米粥的，有卖"法露达"的，对于忍受饥饿之苦匆匆赶去最近的清真寺的信徒来说，它可是美味的牛奶酒。当晚上的祷告结束，吃完第一顿饭后，咖啡店里挤满了吸烟的人，走廊里坐满了玩跳棋的人，同时空气里充满了卖冰镇饮料的叫喊声和渴望开斋的乞丐的哭喊声。大约八点钟时，专门的斋月祷告即将到来，清真寺执杖官后面跟着一群嗓音尖锐的男孩，在穆斯林地区居民的催促下去祷告，在街上巡游，高呼"Namaz tayar hai, cha-lo-o"（伊斯兰教中祈祷时的欢呼）。

夜幕降临街道相对安静时，屋子里发出的声响清晰可闻。"夏迪"欢快的音符或幸运曲响起，屋里的女主人整夜用它来驱散聚集在出生、割礼或"比斯米拉赫"（伊斯兰教

the evil influences that gather around a birth, a circumcision[35] or a "bismillah[36]" ceremony. There one catches the passionate outcry of the husband vainly trying to pierce the deaf ear of death. Life in the city has hardened the hearts of the Faithful, and has led them to forget the kindly injunction[37] of the Prophet, which still observed in small towns or villages up-country: "Neither shall the merry songs of birth or of marriage deepen the sorrow of a bereaved[38] brother." The last sound that reaches you as you turn homewards, is the appeal of the "Sawale" or begging Fakir for a hundred rupees[39] to help him on his pilgrimage[40]. All night long he tramps through the darkness, stopping every twenty or thirty paces to deliver his sonorous[41] prayer for help, which don't ceases until the Muezzin voices the summons to morning prayer.

From *By-Ways of Bombay* (1912)

中吃饭前要祷告的话）仪式上的邪恶之气。与此同时，人们也能听到丈夫发出的激昂的尖叫声，似乎要刺穿死亡的聋耳朵。城市生活令信徒们的心变得异常冷酷，淡忘了穆罕默德善意的忠告，而这些忠告在小镇或村落里依然被人们铭记遵守：“不要以出生或结婚时的欢快歌声去加重失去亲人的兄弟的悲痛。”当你要回家时，最后听到的声音就是“萨瓦了”抑或行乞的苦行者为了朝圣乞求100卢比而发出的哀求声。整夜他都徒步走在黑暗中，每走20或30步就停一下，传出他响亮的祷告以求帮助，直到祷告时间的报时者召集清晨的祈祷者。

---

35 circumcision [ˌsɜːkəm'sɪʒn] *n.* [宗]割礼
36 bismillah [bɪs'mɪlə] *int.* [阿]以真主的名义，啊! 真主啊! （穆斯林誓语）
37 injunction [ɪn'dʒʌŋkʃn] *n.* 劝告，忠告
38 bereaved [bɪ'riːvd] *adj.* 丧失亲人的
39 rupee ['ruːpiː] *n.* 卢比，一卢比银币
40 pilgrimage ['pɪlgrɪmɪdʒ] *n.* 朝圣之旅
41 sonorous [sɒ'nərəs] *adj.* 洪亮的，响亮的

含英咀华

本文选自《孟买之行》，这篇选文并没有用华丽的词语描述孟买的美景，而是通过对声音、街道、行人的描写来展示这座城市的风土人情。文章按照一天中时间变化的顺序描写孟买街市的变化，体现出孟买是一个聚集了各种人种、国际色彩浓厚、堪称为民族大熔炉的城市。其中也有对人们做礼拜的场景的描述，展示了孟买的宗教特点——孟买有半数的居民信奉印度教，其他居民所信仰的宗教则包括了全世界几乎所有的宗教。在市内可以看到印度教庙、基督教大教堂、伊斯兰教清真寺还有佛教寺庙等，因而孟买素有"小印度"之称。

Charles Dickens

查尔斯·狄更斯

查尔斯·狄更斯（1812~1870），英国维多利亚时期的著名小说家，他的作品至今依然盛行，并对英国文学的发展产生了重要影响。他的成名作是1836年出版的《匹克威克外传》（*The Pickwick Papers, 1836*）；主要作品还有《雾都孤儿》（*Oliver Twist, 1837~1839*）、《老古玩店》（*The Old Curiosity Shop, 1840~1841*）、《大卫·科波菲尔》（*David Copperfield, 1849~1850*）等。狄更斯的文笔华丽，如诗一般美丽，但时常又语带幽默地讽刺英国的上流社会。

In and about the City

城里城外

So we go, rattling[1] down-hill, into Naples[2]. A funeral is coming up the street, toward us. The body, on an open bier[3], borne on a kind of palanquin[4], covered with a gay cloth of crimson[5] and gold. The mourners[6], in white gowns and masks. If there be death abroad, life is well represented too, for all Naples would seem to be out of doors[7], and tearing to and fro in carriages. Some of these, the common Vetturino vehicles, are drawn by three horses abreast, decked with[8] smart trappings and great abundance of[9] brazen ornament[10], and always going very fast. Not that their loads are light; for the smallest of them has at least six people inside, four in front, four or five more hanging behind, and two or three more, in a net or bag below the axle-tree[11], where they lie half-suffocated with[12] mud and dust.

我们飞速下山，来到了那不勒斯。公路上迎面走来了一支送葬的队伍。死者的遗体用深红色和金色的鲜艳彩布遮盖着，放在一个众人抬着的敞口棺材里。送葬者身着白色长袍，脸上戴着面具。在那不勒斯，如果有人去世，葬礼是很特殊的，因为所有的那不勒斯人都会走出家门，拥挤着坐在奔驰的四轮马车里。这些车中最普遍的是用三匹并排的马拉着的。这些套着精巧马套和大量奢侈装饰品的马跑得飞快。马的负重绝对不轻，因为即使是最小的马车，也至少会有六个人坐在里面，四个人坐在前面，四个或五个人挤在后面，

1 rattle ['rætl] v. make short sharp sounds quickly, 这里指迅速下山时车所发出的声音
2 Naples ['neɪplz] n. 那不勒斯，意大利南部港口城市，坎帕尼亚区首府，位于维苏威火山西麓、第勒尼安海的那不勒斯湾北岸
3 bier [bɪə] n. frame on which a coffin or a dead body is carried or placed before burial, 棺材架
4 palanquin [pælən'ki:n] n. 轿子，此处指"棺材"
5 crimson ['krɪmzn] n. 深红色
6 mourner ['mɔ:nə] n. 送葬者
7 out of doors = in the open air, 在户外
8 deck with = decorate with
9 great abundance of = plenty
10 ornament ['ɔ:nəmənt] n. 装饰（物）
11 axletree ['æksltri:] n. 轮轴
12 half-suffocated with = have difficulty in breathing, 窒息

Exhibitors of Punch[13], buffo[14] singers with guitars, reciters[15] of poetry, reciters of stories, a row of cheap exhibitions with clowns and showmen, drums, and trumpets, painted cloths representing the wonders within, and admiring crowds assembled without, assist the whirl and bustle. Ragged lazzaroni lie asleep in doorways, archways, and kennels[16]; the gentry[17], gaily drest, are dashing up and down[18] in carriages on the Chiaja, or walking in the Public Gardens; and quiet letter-writers, perched[19] behind their little desks and inkstands under the Portico of the Great Theater of San Carlo, in the pubic street, are waiting for clients.

Why do the beggars rap their chins constantly, with their right hands, when you look at them? Everything is done in pantomime[20] in Naples, and that is the conventional sign for hunger. A man who is quarreling with another, yonder, lays the palm of his right hand on the back of his left, and shakes the two thumbs — expressive of a donkey's ears — whereas his adversary[21] is goaded[22] to desperation. Two people bargaining for[23] fish, the buyer empties

两三个或更多的人坐在车轴下的网子里或袋子里，车下的泥土和沙尘使他们几乎窒息。

街头漫画者、弹吉他的歌手、朗诵诗歌的人、讲述故事的人，还有一大排小丑和表演者向路人推销着廉价展示品，其中包括皮鼓、小号、展示着内在奇迹的画有喷绘图案的布。旁边有许多围观的人，平添了几分眩晕和喧闹。衣衫褴褛的流浪汉懒洋洋地躺在商场门口、拱路旁或阴沟边。然而穿着体面的贵族们却坐在来来往往的四轮马车里，或者在公园里散步；那些街头替人写信的人，坐在圣卡罗大剧院门口旁，面前放着小桌子和笔墨，安静地等待着他们的顾客。

当你看着那些乞丐时，为什么他们总会不断地用右手敲着下巴？在那不勒斯，任何事都通过手势表达，那是饥饿的传统表达方式。在那边，有两

---

13 Punch [pʌntʃ] *n.* 潘趣（英国木偶戏 *Punch and Judy* 中的主角），此处引申为"街头漫画者"
14 buffo ['bufəu] *n.* 男低音歌手
15 reciter[rɪ'saɪtə] *n.* 吟诵者
16 kennel['kenl] *n.* （路旁的）沟渠，下水道
17 gentry ['dʒentrɪ] *n.* 贵族们
18 up and down = backwards and forwards，来来回回
19 perch [pɜ:tʃ] *v.* 位于
20 pantomime ['pæntəmaɪm] *n.* 手势
21 adversary ['ædvəsərɪ] *n.* 对手
22 goad [gəud] *v.* continually annoy a person，不断激怒某人
23 bargain for   discuss prices，讨价还价

an imaginary waistcoat pocket when he is told the price, and walks away without a word, having thoroughly conveyed to[24] the seller that he considers it too dear. Two people in carriages, meeting, one touches his lips, twice or thrice, and holding up the five fingers of his right hand, gives a horizontal cut in the air with the palm. The other nods briskly, and goes his way. He has been invited to a friendly dinner at half-past five o'clock, and will certainly come.

All over Italy, a peculiar shake of the right hand from the wrist, with the forefinger stretched out[25], expresses a negative — the only negative beggars will ever understand. But, in Naples, those five fingers are a copious language. All this, and every other kind of out-door life and stir, and maccaroni-eating at sunset, and flower-selling all day long, and begging and stealing everywhere and at all hours, you see upon the bright sea-shore, where the waves of the Bay sparkle merrily…

Capri — once made odious[26] by the deified beast Tiberius[27] — Ischia, Procida, and the thousand distant beauties of the Bay, lie in the blue sea yonder, changing in the mist and sunshine twenty times a day; now close at hand,

---

24 convey to　= make (ideas, feelings, etc.) known to another person，传达（思想、感情等）
25 stretch out　= extend，伸出
26 odious ['əudiəs]　adj.　可憎的，讨厌的，此处引申为"声名狼藉"
27 Tiberius [taɪ'bɪːrɪəs]　提比留（公元前42～公元前37，全名为 Tiberius Claudius Nero Caesar，公元1世纪14~37年间为罗马皇帝）

个人吵架，其中一个将右手掌放在左手背上，摇动两个大拇指做出类似驴耳朵的形状，再看另一方已经气得要发疯了。那边两个人在为一条鱼而讨价还价，得知价格后，买者做出掏空衣服口袋的动作，然后一句话不说转身离开了，这充分表达出他认为价格太贵了，然后一句话不说转身离开了。两个人坐着马车相遇了，其中一个摸了两三次自己的嘴唇，举起自己的右手手指，水平地向空中斩了一下，另一个人则爽快地点了点头，然后走了。那表示他被邀请在五点半参加晚宴，他答应一定会到。

在意大利，人们伸出食指，轻轻地以一种特殊的方式甩动右手腕，这表示拒绝——只有那些沮丧的乞丐才能明白。但在那不勒斯，五个手指可以表达很多种意思。明亮的海滨，波浪起伏，闪闪发光，在这里你可以看到所有这些生活场景。除了这些，还有其他各式各样的室外生活，在日落时吃通心粉；从早到晚卖鲜花；随时随地发生乞讨、盗窃……

卡普里——曾被神化的暴君弄得声名狼藉——伊斯基

now far off, now unseen. The fairest country in the world is spread about us. Whether we turn toward the Miseno[28] shore of the splendid watery amphitheater[29], and go by the Grotto of Posilipo to the Grotto del Cane and away to Baiae, or take the other way, toward Vesuvius[30] and Sorrento[31], it is one succession of[32] delights. In the last-named direction, where, over doors and archways, there are countless little images of San Gennaro, with this Canute's hand stretched out, to check the fury of the burning mountain, we are carried pleasantly, by a railroad on the beautiful Sea Beach, past the town of Torre del Greco, built upon the ashes of the former town destroyed[33] by an eruption of Vesuvius, within a hundred years; and past the flat-roofed houses, granaries[34], and macaroni[35] manufactures; to Castellamare, with its ruined castle, now inhabited by fishermen, standing in the sea upon a heap of[36] rocks.

Here, the railroad terminates[37]; but, hence

亚、普罗奇达岛和那千里之遥的海滨美景，静静地躺在这碧蓝的大海边，时而雾起，时而云开，一天中竟会变化二十次之多；置身于这一片变幻莫测之中，每当你觉得它们近在眼前，触手可及时，它们却远去了，无迹可寻了。世界上最明媚、最灿烂的国家在我们的身边漫天盖地地铺展开来。不管我们转向去宛如辉煌的水上竞技场的米塞诺岬，途经波西利波石窟到凯恩窟然后再到拜尔湖，还是另择佳径前往维苏威火山和索伦多，这些都带给了我们无限的快乐。在我们刚才提及的最后一条路线中，那里的房门和拱廊之上有无数的圣热内罗的小雕像，克努特伸出手来试图阻止火山的愤怒。我们在这美丽的海滩搭乘火车，经过拖勒·德·哥勒科，这是一座在一百年前被维苏威火山爆发摧毁又故地重建的小镇；接着，我们又驶过那些平顶的房屋、谷仓、通心粉工厂；然后到了卡斯泰拉马莱，这里能看到渔民居住的破旧的城堡，耸立在海边的一堆岩石上。

这里是火车的终点；但是我们可以骑马前行，沿着一系列迷人的海峡，顺着圣安吉

28 Miseno　米塞诺岬，位于意大利南部、那不勒斯西南部
29 amphitheater ['æmfɪθɪətə]　n.　圆形剧场
30 Vesuvius [vɪ'suːvɪəs]　n.　维苏威火山，位于意大利那不勒斯湾之滨，海拔1277米，是欧洲大陆唯一的活火山。它的火山口周边长1400米，深216米，基底直径3千米
31 Sorrento　索伦多，意大利西南部港口城市，位于紧靠那不勒斯海湾的一个半岛上
32 one succession of　= the coming of one thing or person after another in time or order，接连
33 destroyed　摧毁，此处为过去分词作定语
34 granary ['grænərɪ]　n.　谷仓
35 macaroni [,mækə'rəʊnɪ]　n.　[食]通心面
36 a heap of　= plenty，许多，大量
37 terminate ['tɜːmɪneɪt]　v.　终止

we may ride on, by an unbroken succession of enchanting bays, and beautiful scenery, sloping from the highest summit of Saint Angelo, the highest neighboring mountain, down to the water's edge — among vineyards, olive-trees, gardens of oranges and lemons, orchards, heaped-up rocks, green gorges in the hills — and by the bases of snow-covered heights, and through small towns with handsome, dark-haired women at the doors — and pass delicious summer villas — to Sorrento, where the poet Tasso[38] drew his inspiration from[39] the beauty surrounding him. Returning, we may climb the heights above Castellamare, and looking down among the boughs and leaves, see the crisp water glistening[40] in the sun; and clusters of[41] white houses in distant Naples, dwindling, in the great extent of prospect, down to dice. The coming back to the city, by the beach again, at sunset; with the glowing sea on one side, and the darkening mountain (Vesuvius), with its smoke and flame, upon the other, is a sublime conclusion to the glory of the day.

From *Picture from Italy* (1905)

洛，从最高峰自上而下陡降的美景——这邻近的最高峰，下至湖水边缘，葡萄园、橄榄树、柑橘与柠檬的种植园、果园、堆砌起来的岩石、绿色的峡谷将这群山点缀得像世外桃源，引人入胜，然后顺着白雪覆盖的山峰底部，穿过俊俏的、黑发少妇倚门相望的小镇——穿过充溢米香的夏日庄园——直至索伦多，连诗人塔索都从这庄园美景中得了灵感。回程中，我们爬上了卡斯泰拉马莱山，然后俯视千枝百叶，欣赏叮咚作响的泉水在阳光下熠熠生辉；那不勒斯一簇簇白色的房屋在视野里渐渐稀疏变小，最后消失在水天一线的无尽远方。在落日的余晖里，我们经由海滩回到了城市；一边是波浪起伏的大海，一边是连绵起伏的山脉（维苏威火山），烟火辉映，结束了光辉而有意义的一天。

---

38 Tasso 塔索，T. （Torquato Tasso 1544～1595）意大利诗人，文艺复兴运动晚期的代表人物，出生于富有文化教养的家庭。大学时期学法律，但十分热爱古典文化和哲学，跟人文主义者交往甚密。先受阿里奥斯托影响，用浪漫情调写骑士业绩的长诗。继又作为宫廷诗人写牧歌剧。代表作是叙事长诗《被解放的耶路撒冷》（1575）

39 draw inspiration from = get stimulation of the mind to do something beyond a person's usual ability, esp. creative ability in art, literature, music，从某事当中获得灵感

40 glistening 闪闪发光的，此处为现在分词作宾语补足语

41 cluster of = number of things closely together，此处指密匝匝的房子

闲庭信步　品别样风情

含英咀华

　　那不勒斯又称"那波利"，位于意大利南部，是坎帕尼亚区的首府。选文中狄更斯先从遇到的葬礼开始着笔描述那不勒斯的葬礼风俗，随后自然地引入了在那里所见到的人和景。他的描写侧重对人物的刻画，在读者眼前展现的是一个个活灵活现的人，包括"街头漫画者、弹吉他的歌手、朗诵诗歌的人、讲述故事的人、小丑和表演者"甚至是乞丐和街头的吵架者；而对于那不勒斯的秀美风景，作者却未使用大量的笔墨来描写。

跋山涉水
叹壮丽神奇

Flowery Tuscany
如花的托斯卡纳

Niagara
尼亚加拉瀑布

Stonehenge
巨石阵

The Call of the Mountains
山谷的呼唤

The Nile
尼罗河

On the Beach at Daytona
代托纳海滩

David Herbert Lawrence

大卫·赫伯特·劳伦斯

大卫·赫伯特·劳伦斯(1885~1930)，英国诗人、小说家、散文家。出生于矿工家庭，当过屠户、会计、厂商雇员和小学教师，曾在国外漂泊十多年，对现实持批判否定态度。他写过诗，但主要写长篇小说，共有10部，最著名的为《虹》（*The Rainbow, 1915*）、《恋爱中的女人》（*Women in Love, 1921*）和《查泰莱夫人的情人》（*Lady Chatterley's Lover, 1928*）。

Flowery Tuscany

如花的托斯卡纳

North of the Alps, the everlasting[1] winter is interrupted by summers that struggle and soon yield; south of the Alps, the everlasting summer is interrupted by spasmodic[2] and spiteful winters that never get a real hold, but that are mean and dogged. The in between[3], in either case, is just as it may be. But the lands of the sun are south of the Alps, forever.

In the morning, the sun shines strong on the horizontal green cloud-puffs of the pines, the sky is clear and full of life, the water runs hastily, still browned by the last juice of crushed olives. And there the earth's bowl of crocuses[4] is amazing. You cannot believe that the flowers are really still. They are open with such delight, and their pistil[5] thrust is so red-orange, and they are so many, all reaching out[6] wide and marvelous, that it suggests a perfect ecstasy of radiant, thronging movement, lit-up violet[7] and orange, and surging[8] in some invisible rhythm of concerted[9], delightful movement. You cannot believe they do not

阿尔卑斯山的北坡，冬季漫长，夏天如期而至却改变不了这里的寒冷；而其南坡，多数时间是温暖的夏季，偶尔也会有冬季的严寒，但不会持续太久。在南坡与北坡之间，哪种情况都有可能。但是，阿尔卑斯山的南面永远是阳光普照。

清晨，阳光肆意地照耀在松树上水平的绿色"云泡芙"上，天空晴朗，生机无限。河水湍急，静静地被一些压碎的橄榄的汁液染成棕色。遍地的番红花更是令人诧异不已。你不会相信这些花是静止不动的。它们如此欢快地绽放，雌蕊是那样鲜艳的橘红。不计其数的花朵，竞相开放，争奇斗艳，让人如痴如醉。花朵们翩翩起舞，那明亮的紫、橙色调，合着无形的美妙节奏欢快地摆动。你不得不相信它

---

1 everlasting [ˌevəˈlɑːstɪŋ] *adj.* 永恒的，持久的
2 spasmodic [spæzˈmɒdɪk] *adj.* 间歇的
3 in between 介于其间的地方
4 crocus [ˈkrəʊkəs] *n.* 番红花
5 pistil [ˈpɪstɪl] *n.* [植]雌蕊
6 reach out 此处意为"竞相开放"
7 violet [ˈvaɪələt] *n.* 紫罗兰，紫色
8 surging [ˈsɜːdʒɪŋ] *n.* 浪涌，冲击，此处引申为"摆动"
9 concerted [kənˈsɜːtɪd] *adj.* 商议好的，协定的

跋山涉水 叹壮丽神奇

move, and make some sort of crystalline sound of delight. If you sit still and watch, you begin to move with them, like moving with stars, and you feel the sound of their radiance. All the little cells of the flowers must be leaping with flowery life and utterance.

And now that[10] it is March, there is a rush of flowers. Down by the other stream, which turns sideways to the sun, and tangles the brier and bramble[11], down where the hellebore[12] has stood so wan[13] and dignified all winter, there are now white tufts[14] of primroses[15], suddenly come. Among the tangle and near the water-lip, tufts and bunches of primroses, in abundance. Yet they look more wan, more pallid[16], more flimsy[17] than English primroses. They lack some of the full wonder of the northern flowers. One tends to overlook them, to turn to the great, solemn-faced purple violets that rear up from the bank, and above all, to the wonderful little towers of the grape hyacinth[18].

This is the time, in March, when the sloe[19] is white and misty in the hedge-tangle by the stream, and on the slope of land the peach tree stands pink and alone. The

们在动而且发出了清脆的、水晶般欢快的声音。如果你静静地坐着欣赏花朵,你就会不由自主地随着它们舞动,那样的情形就好像跟着天上的星星在走动一样。当然,你还会听到花朵们的欢快声。花的每一个小细胞都跳跃着绚丽的生命和思想。

现在正是三月,也是花儿竞相开放的时节。在其他一些流向太阳的溪流边,荆棘灌木交错,菟葵无助而不屈地对抗冬天,一丛丛白色的樱草花出乎意料地生长着。丛丛的樱草花占满了杂乱的灌木丛和溪水的拐角处。可它们比菟葵更柔弱,更苍白,比英格兰的樱草花单薄许多。樱草花不像北方的花朵那样让人惊奇。人们往往不会注意到它,而是会被长在河岸边庄严而美丽的紫罗兰所吸引,会更愿意欣赏那些深紫色的风信子小花塔。

三月,刚好是溪边灌木丛中白色的野李花朦朦胧胧开放、粉色的桃树独自屹立在山

---

10 now that   既然,"now" 是连词
11 bramble ['bræmbl]   n.   荆棘
12 hellebore ['helɪbɔ:]   n.   [植]菟葵, 藜芦
13 wan [wɒn]   adj.   柔弱的, 无力的
14 tuft [tʌft]   n.   (头发、羽毛、草等的)一簇, 一束, 一丛
15 primrose['prɪmrəʊz]   n.   樱草类, 樱草花
16 pallid ['pælɪd]   adj.   苍白的, 暗淡的
17 flimsy ['flɪmzɪ]   adj.   浅薄的, 单薄的
18 hyacinth ['hæɪəsɪnθ]   n.   [植]风信子
19 sloe [sləʊ]   n.   野生的李树之类

almond[20] blossom, silvery pink, is passing, but the peach, deep-toned, bluey, not at all ethereal[21], this reveals itself like fresh, and the trees are like isolated individuals, the peach and the apricot[22]. It is so conspicuous[23] and so individual, that pink among the coming green of spring, because the first flowers that emerge from winter seem always white or yellow or purple. Now the celandines[24] are out, and along the edges of the podere, the big, sturdy, black-purple anemones[25], with black hearts.

The daisies[26] are out too, in sheets[27], and they too red-mouthed. The first ones are big and handsome. But as March goes on, they dwindle to bright little things, like tiny buttons, clouds of them together. That means summer is nearly there.

And when the tulips are gone[28], there is a moment's pause, before summer. Summer is the next move.

In the pause towards the end of April, when the flowers seem to hesitate, the leaves make up their minds to come out. For sometime, at the very ends of the bare boughs of fig trees, spurts[29] of pure green have been burning like little cloven

坡的时节。银粉色的杏花已渐渐谢去，桃树裹着深深的蓝，一点也不飘逸，这却是它的本来面目，而桃树与杏树，看起来就毫不相干。绿意盎然的春天里，桃树的粉色是如此别致而抢眼。在初春开的花，通常看起来都是白色、黄色或紫色的。白屈菜也绽出了苞蕾。在湖边高大强壮的深紫色银链花中，你可以发现黑色的花蕊。

雏菊穿着红色的衣服成群地跑出来。起初，开得饱满鲜艳，可是进入三月中下旬时，花就变成了光鲜的蕊，像小小的纽扣聚在一起。这预示着夏天的来临。

郁金香凋谢了，花儿们都短暂地歇息了一下。夏天即将来临。

寂静的四月底，在花儿们踌躇不定的时候，叶子们一股脑地长出来。一时间，纯净的绿色在无花果的光秃秃的树尖冒出，好像烛台顶那生动的

---

20 almond ['a:mənd] n. 杏仁
21 ethereal [ɪ'θɪərɪəl] adj. 轻的，轻飘的
22 apricot ['eɪprɪkɒt] n. 杏
23 conspicuous [kən'spɪkjuəs] adj. = obvious，显而易见的
24 celandine['seləndaɪn] n. [植]白屈菜
25 anemone [ə'nemənɪ] n. [植]银链花
26 daisy ['deɪzɪ] n. 雏菊
27 in sheets 大量地，大片地，这里引申为"成群地"
28 be gone 此处意为"凋谢"
29 spurt [spɜːt] n. 喷出（短促突然的爆发）

tongues of green fire vivid on the tips of the candelabrum[30]. Now these spurts of green spread out[31], and begin to take the shape of hands, feeling for the air of summer. And tiny green figs are below them, like glands on the throat of a goat...

By May, the nightingale will sing an unbroken song, and the discreet, barely audible Tuscan cuckoo will be a little more audible. Then the lovely pale-lilac irises[32] will come out in all their showering abundance of tender, proud, spiky[33] bloom, till the air will gleam[34] with mauve[35], and a new crystalline[36] lightness will be everywhere.

There will be tufts of iris everywhere, arising up proud and tender. The rose-coloured wild gladiolus[37] is mingled in the corn, and the love-in-the-mist opens blue, in May and June, before the corn is cut.

But as yet is neither May nor June, but the end of April, the pause between spring and summer, the nightingale singing uninterrupted, the bean-flowers dying in the bean-fields, the bean-perfume passing with spring, the little birds hatching in the nests, the olives pruned[38], and the vines, the last bit of late ploughing finished, and

绿色小火舌一样在燃烧。现在，这团绿焰伸展开来，变成小手的样子，触摸着夏天的气息。小小的绿色无花果在它们下面，像一只只山羊颈部的垂体……

五月一到，夜莺便不间断地唱着歌。这时候，小心翼翼的托斯卡纳杜鹃也会唱出平日里听不到的歌。接着，淡紫色的蝴蝶花大量地出现，展示着它们柔嫩、穗状的花，直到空气中露出紫红，四处飘着水晶般的透明、轻柔气息。

世界将变成一丛丛蝴蝶花的天下，它们得意而柔嫩地昂着头。五、六月，谷物还没收割的时候，在野外，玫瑰色的唐菖蒲生长在谷物中，其中还有开着蓝色花朵的黑种草。

但现在还没到五月或六月——只是四月末，春夏季之间的间歇。在这个时节里：夜莺不停地歌唱；豆地里的豆花正在凋谢；豆的芳香随着春天一起逝去；小鸟在巢里成长；橄榄

---

30 candelabrum [ˌkændɪˈlɑːbrəm] *n.* 烛台
31 spread out 这里指"伸长"
32 iris [ˈaɪərɪs] *n.* 蝴蝶花
33 spiky [ˈspaɪkɪ] *adj.* （植物）穗状的，有穗的
34 gleam [gliːm] *v.* 闪烁，隐约地闪现
35 mauve [məʊv] *n.* 淡紫色
36 crystalline [ˈkrɪstəlaɪn] *adj.* 水晶（般）的，透明的
37 gladiolus [ˌglædɪˈəʊləs] *n.* 剑兰，唐菖蒲
38 prune [pruːn] *v.* 修剪（树枝等）

not much work to hand, now, not until the peas are ready to pick, in another two weeks or so.

So the change, the endless and rapid change. In the sunny countries, the change seems more vivid, and more complete than in the grey countries. In the grey countries, there is a grey or dark permanency, over whose surface passes change ephemeral[39], leaving no real mark.

But in the sunny countries, change is the reality and permanence is artificial and a condition of imprisonment. Hence, to the northerner, the phenomenal[40] world is essentially tragical, because it is temporal and must cease to exist. Its very existence implies ceasing to exist, and this is the root of the feeling of tragedy.

But to the southerner, the sun is dominant that shadow, or dark, is only merely relative: merely the result of something getting between one and the sun.

In the human race, the one thing that is always there is the shining sun, and dark shadow is an accident of intervention[41].

For my part[42], if the sun always shine, and always will shine, in spite of millions of clouds of words. In the sunshine, even death is sunny. And there is no end to the sunshine.

That is why the rapid change of the Tuscan

---

39 ephemeral [ɪ'femərəl] adj. 短暂的
40 phenomenal [fɪ'nɒmɪnl] adj. 现象的，能知觉的，这里引申为"变化中的"
41 intervention [ˌɪntə'venʃn] n. 插入，介入
42 for my part = in my view 在我看来

已被修剪；葡萄已经过了最后的耕种；豌豆在两个星期后才会成熟，现在没有多少活要做。

这样才是变化，永不停息的快速变化。在阳光照耀的地方，变化似乎更显著，比在昏暗地带更彻底。而在没有阳光的地方，是一成不变的灰暗和阴暗。变化是短暂的，不会留下任何记号。

然而，对于生活在阳光地带的人，却有着不同的概念，变化对他们来说就是现实，永久是人创造的，是一种囚禁。因此，生活在北面的人认为，变化中的世界实际上是悲惨的，因为世界只是短暂的，是注定要消逝的。世界的存在本身就意味着结束，这就是伤感的根源。

而对于生活在南面的人们来说，阳光具有决定性的作用，阴影或黑暗不过是相关联的事物——只是在人和太阳之间才会出现的东西。

对于人类来说，在这个世界上，发光的太阳是永远在那里的，黑色的影子不过是一个干扰的意外罢了。

而在我看来，尽管争议纷纷，但太阳一直光芒四射，也将永远光芒四射。在阳光下，

spring is utterly free, for me, of any senses of tragedy. The sun always shines. It is our fault if we don't think like that.

From *Phoenix 1: The Posthumous Papers of D. H. Lawrence* (1972)

即便死亡也是充满阳光的。阳光没有终点。

托斯卡纳的春天飞快地流逝，而我没有感到一丝的悲伤，这就是原因所在。太阳永远在照耀，如果不这样想，那就是我们的错了。

含英咀华

在欧洲，意大利托斯卡纳早已享有盛誉。从古到今，这里都是名人造访度假的地方。19世纪英国诗人勃朗宁夫妇传奇般的爱情以私奔告终，他们逃离英国移居意大利，他们没有错过托斯卡纳。勃朗宁夫人写道："这里的空气似乎能穿透你的心扉。" 英国作家艾•摩•福斯特的多部作品也都以托斯卡纳地区为背景。这里的草地和葡萄园正是《看得见风景的房间》中男主人公向女主人公表白的地方。而本文是劳伦斯笔下描写托斯卡纳的一篇特别优美的散文，正如题目"如花的托斯卡纳"一样，作者带我们领略了这里花的世界：三月，有白色的野李花、粉色的桃树，还有雏菊穿着红色的衣服成群地跑出来；寂静的四月底，可以看到纯净的绿色在无花果的树尖冒出，而五月淡紫色的丁香花、六月玫瑰色的唐菖蒲也别有一番风情……

Anthony Trollope
安东尼·特罗洛普

安东尼·特罗洛普（1815~1882），出生于伦敦的一个律师家庭，是英国19世纪中下叶最重要的小说家之一。他是一位多产作家，发表的小说达47部之多，最著名的作品是"巴塞特郡系列小说"（Chronicles of Barsetshire, 1855~1867）。

Niagara

Of all the sights on this earth of ours which tourists travel to see — at least of all those which I have seen — I am inclined to[1] give the palm to the Falls of Niagara. I know no other one thing so beautiful, so glorious, and so powerful. At Niagara there is that fall of waters alone. But that fall is more graceful than Giotto's tower, more noble than the Apollo. The peaks of the Alps are not so astounding[2] in their solitude. The valleys of the Blue Mountains in Jamaica[3] are less green. The finished glaze of life in Paris is less invariable; and the full tide of trade round the Bank of England is not so inexorably[4] powerful.

That the waters of Lake Erie have come down in their courses[5] from the broad basins of Lake Michigan, Lake Superior, and Lake Huron; that these waters fall into Lake Ontario by the short and rapid river of Niagara; and that the falls of Niagara are made by a sudden break in the level of this rapid river, is probably known to all who will read this book. All the waters of these huge northern inland seas run over[6] that breach[7] in the rocky bottom of the stream; and

尼亚加拉瀑布

世界上游客观光的所有景致中，至少我曾游览过的美景中，我愿意把掌声献给尼亚加拉瀑布。我不知道还有什么能这么旖旎、这么壮丽、这么气势磅礴。尽管尼亚加拉只有瀑布，但它比乔托塔更优雅别致，比太阳神更宏伟壮丽。阿尔卑斯孤独的山峰不会那样令人震撼；牙买加蓝山的峡谷又少了几分绿意；呆滞无望的巴黎生活逊于恒定；英格兰中央银行周边的贸易潮流不会这么势不可挡。

来自密歇根湖、苏必利尔湖、休伦湖宽大盆地的伊利湖水顺势倾泻而下，流经短而湍急的尼亚加拉河注入安大略湖。这条急流水面上一个突兀的缺口形成了尼亚加拉瀑布，这可能是即将阅读这本书的人都知道的。北部巨大内陆海中的水在底

---

1 **be inclined to do**   (通常用被动语态) 倾向于
2 **astounding** [ə'saʊndɪŋ]   *adj.*   令人震惊的
3 **Jamaica** [dʒə'meɪkə]   *n.*   牙买加
4 **inexorably** [ɪn'eksərəbli]   *adv.*   无情地, 冷酷地
5 **course**   这里指 "路线"
6 **run over**   = overflow, 流出
7 **breach**   *n.*   缺口, 裂口

thence[8] it comes that the flow is unceasing[9] in its grandeur[10], and that no eye can perceive a difference in the weight, or sound, or violence of the fall whether it be visited in the drought of autumn, amid the storms of winter, or after the melting of the upper worlds of ice in the days of the early summer. How many cataracts[11] does the habitual tourist visit at which the waters fail him! But at Niagara the waters never fail. There it thunders over its ledge[12] in a volume that never ceases and is never diminished[13] — as it has done from times previous to the life of man, and as it will do till tens of thousands of years shall see the rocky bed of the river worn away[14] back to the upper lake.

It has been said that it matters much from what point the falls are first seen, but to this I demur[15]. It matters, I think, very little, or not at all. Let the visitor first see it all, and learn the whereabouts[16] of every point, so as to understand his own position and that of the waters; and then, having done that in the way of business, let him proceed to[17] enjoyment. I doubt whether it is the best to do this with all sight-seeing. But I am quite sure that it is the way in which

部岩石杂多的河流中溢出那个缺口，流水因此而流淌不息。不论是在干旱的秋季，在暴风雪肆虐的严冬，还是在地表积雪融化后的初夏，没有人能察觉出瀑布在态势、声势抑或气势上的丝毫变化。有多少瀑布曾辜负了经常来访的游人！但尼亚加拉的瀑布不会这样。流水冲击礁石发出的轰响永不断绝，永不衰减——正像它在人类出现之前那样，它也会一如既往地奔流下去，直到千万年后人们看到河床岩石被侵蚀溯至湖的上游。

有人说第一次欣赏瀑布时选择观景点很重要，对此我不敢苟同。我想这不太重要或者根本不重要。让游客先观赏瀑布的全景，然后观察每个落点，以便体会身处的位置和瀑布的方位，接着开始享受美景。我不知道这是不是最好的方法，但我深信这是一个愉悦

---

8 thence *adv.* 因此，由此
9 unceasing [ʌn'siːsɪŋ] *adj.* 不停的
10 grandeur ['grændʒə] *n.* 庄严，伟大
11 cataract ['kætərækt] *n.* 大瀑布
12 ledge [ledʒ] *n.* 暗礁
13 diminish [dɪ'mɪnɪʃ] *v.* 减少，变小
14 wear away 侵蚀，磨损
15 demur [dɪ'mɜː] *v.* 提出异议，反对
16 whereabouts ['(h)weərəbauts] *n.* 下落，所在之处
17 proceed to = go on，着手，继续进行

acquaintance may be best and most pleasantly made with a new picture.

The falls, as I have said[18], are made by a sudden breach in the level of the river. All cataracts are, I presume, made by such breaches; but generally the waters do not fall precipitously[19] as they do at Niagara, and never elsewhere, as far as the world yet knows, has a breach so sudden been made in a river carrying in its channel such or any approach to such a body of water. Up above the falls for more than a mile the waters leap and burst over rapids, as though conscious of the destiny that awaits them. Here the river is very broad and comparatively shallow; but from shore to shore it frets[20] itself into little torrents, and begins to assume the majesty[21] of its power. Looking at it even here, in the expanse which forms itself over the greater fall, one feels sure that no strongest swimmer could have a chance of saving himself if fate had cast him in even among those petty whirlpools[22]. The waters though so broken in their descent[23], are deliciously green. This color, as seen early in the morning or just as the sun has set, is so bright as to give to the place one of its chiefest charms.

This will be best seen from the farther end of the island — Goat Island as it is called —

地领略一个新的美景的方法。

如前所述，这个瀑布是由水面一个突兀的缺口形成的。我想，所有的瀑布都是如此，只不过其他瀑布一般不会像尼亚加拉瀑布这样骤然陡落；并且在世界已知的范围内，其他地方不会在河水流淌中或接近如此大的水体中出现这么突兀的一个缺口。溯流而上，距瀑布一英里多处，水流翻滚腾跃突成急流，好像意识到命运之神在此等待它们的到来。这儿的河流又宽又浅，但是从这一岸到下一岸它被削成小的湍流，开始呈现出巨大力量。即使是从这儿看，在那壮阔的水面形成了更大的瀑布，任何人都会确信即使是最强壮的游泳者，当被命运投入到即便很小的漩涡中，他也不可能生还。虽然水倾泻而下时破碎飞溅，却呈现着诱人的绿色。在清晨或日落时，这颜色是如此明媚，为瀑布增色不少。

这景象从一座小岛——所谓的山羊岛——的边缘看得最

跋山涉水 叹壮丽神奇

---

18 as I have said 作插入语，表示"如前所述"
19 precipitously [prɪ'sɪpɪtəslɪ] *adv.* 险峻地
20 fret [fret] *v.* 使（水面）起波浪
21 majesty ['mædʒəstɪ] *n.* 雄伟，庄严
22 whirlpool ['(h)wɜ:lpu:l] *n.* 漩涡，涡流
23 descent [dɪ'sent] *n.* 下降，降落

which, as the reader will understand, divides the river immediately above the falls. Indeed, the island is a part of that precipitously-broken ledge over which the river tumbles[24], and no doubt in process of[25] time will be worn away and covered with water. The time, however, will be very long. In the mean while, it is perhaps a mile round, and is covered thickly with timber[26]. At the upper end of the island the waters are divided, and, coming down in two courses each over its own rapids, form two separate falls. The bridge by which the island is entered is a hundred yards or more above the smaller fall. The waters here have been turned by the island, and make their leap into the body of the river below at a right angle with it — about two hundred yards below the greater fall. Taken alone, this smaller cataract would, I imagine, be the heaviest fall of water known; but taken in conjunction[27] with the other, it is terribly shorn[28] of its majesty. The waters here are not so green as they are at the larger cataract; and, though the ledge has been hollowed and bowed[29] by them so as to form a curve, that curve does not deepen itself into a vast abyss[30] as it does at the horseshoe[31] up above. This smaller fall is again divided; and the

清楚。正如读者所理解的那样，在瀑布的正上方小岛把水流分隔开来。实际上，这座岛是被河流侵蚀着的陡峭的大礁石的一部分。毋庸置疑，随着时间的推移，它将会被侵蚀消损并被水淹没，但这时间会很漫长。同时，它可能会是一英里见方，被浓荫覆盖。在山羊岛上缘，河水被分隔成两支急流，顺势跌落形成两个独立的瀑布。在离小瀑布一百码或更高的地方有座小桥通往山羊岛。这里的水被小岛改向，以一个合适的角度奔淌入大瀑布下方两百码处的河流中。单独来讲，我想这个小瀑布是最汹涌澎湃的，但连同大瀑布来讲，它的雄伟壮丽就会大大被削减。这儿的水不如大瀑布的绿，虽然礁石已经中空并被水流侵削出一个凹陷，但这个弯曲处不会跌落成像上面的马蹄瀑布那样巨大的深渊。这个小瀑布再次被分隔。紧走几步，当游客

24 tumble ['tʌmbl]　v.　滚动，跌落
25 in process of　= during，在……期间
26 timber ['tɪmbə]　n.　人树木，树林
27 conjunction [kən'dʒʌŋkʃn]　n.　连合，连同
28 shorn　shear 的过去分词，削减
29 bow [bəʊ]　v.　使……弯曲
30 abyss [ə'bɪs]　n.　深渊，无底洞
31 horseshoe ['hɔːsʃuː]　n.　马蹄铁形之物，这里指上面的大瀑布

visitor, passing down[32] a flight of steps and over a frail wooden bridge, finds himself on a smaller island in the midst of[33] it.

穿过一座松动的木桥时，会发现他已置身于另一个小岛中心了。

From *North America* (1862)

32 pass down　此处意为"通过"
33 in the midst of　＝ in the middle of，"midst"（古）在……中间，在……之间

含英咀华

　　全长58公里的尼亚加拉河在美国境内平静而温顺、毫无声息地流经平原之地，但流至美国与加拿大边境时，由于地貌的变化，河面由宽变窄，瀑布水流垂直而下，水声震耳欲聋，形成了湍急的水流。在一个90度急转弯处，河道上横亘着的一道石灰岩断崖，形成50米以上的落差，使水量丰富的尼亚加拉河水在经过这里时骤然陡落，就形成了举世闻名的尼亚加拉大瀑布。在这篇选文中，作者用形象的语言把被称为世界著名七大奇景之一的尼亚加拉大瀑布描写得惟妙惟肖，描绘出了丰沛而浩瀚的水汽和磅礴的气势，令读者感受到了它的震撼之美。

Ralph Waldo Emerson

拉尔夫·瓦尔多·爱默生

拉尔夫·瓦尔多·爱默生（1803~1882），美国散文作家、思想家、诗人。曾就读于哈佛大学，在校期间，他阅读了大量英国浪漫主义作家的作品，丰富了思想，开阔了视野。1832年以后，爱默生到欧洲各国游历，结识了浪漫主义先驱华兹华斯和柯尔律治，接受了他们的先验论思想，这对他思想体系的形成具有很大影响。1840年爱默生任超验主义刊物《日晷》（*The Dial*）的主编，进一步宣扬超验主义思想。后来他把自己的演讲汇编成书，这就是著名的《论文集》（*Collected Essays, 1841*）。爱默生的诗歌、散文独具特色，注重思想内容而没有过分华丽的辞藻，行文犹如格言，深入浅出，说服力强，具有典型的"爱默生风格"。

Stonehenge[1]

We left the train at Salisbury[2], and took a carriage to Amesbury[3], passing by old Sarum[4], a bare, treeless hill[5], once containing the town which sent two members to Parliament — now, not a hut — and, arriving at Amesbury, we stopped at the George Inn. After dinner we walked to Salisbury Plain. On the broad downs[6], under the gray sky, not a house was visible, nothing but Stonehenge, which[7] looked like a group of brown dwarfs in the wide expanse — Stonehenge and the barrows[8], which rose like green bosses about the plain, and a few hay ricks. On the top of a mountain the old temple would not be more impressive. Far and wide a few shepherds with their flocks sprinkled the plain, and a bagman drove along the road. It looked as if the wide margin given in this crowded isle to this primeval temple were accorded by the veneration[9] of the British race to the old egg out of which all their ecclesiastical[10] structures and

巨石阵

我们在索尔兹伯里下了火车，乘一辆马车前往阿姆斯伯利，沿途经过旧塞勒姆。这是一座光秃秃的小山，曾有两位英国国会成员诞生于此处的一个小镇，而现在这里却连一座茅屋也没有了。到达阿姆斯伯利后，我们住进了乔治客栈。晚饭后，我们步行去了索尔兹伯里平原。在灰蒙蒙的天空下，广阔的丘陵上看不见一座房屋，能看见的只有巨石阵，它们就像广袤大地上一群褐色的小矮人——石头阵和史前古墓，像大草原上绿色的岩丘一样毅然挺立，此外还有几堆干草。在一座山顶上，可以看见令人叹为观止的古庙。放眼望去，广阔无边的草原上只有几位牧羊人和散布在草地上

---

1 stonehenge ['stəʊnhendʒ] *n.* 圆形石林（英国威尔特郡的一处史前巨石柱群）
2 Salisbury ['sɔ:lzbərɪ] *n.* 索尔兹伯里(津巴布韦[原罗得西亚]首都)
3 Amesbury ['sɔ:lzbərɪ] *n.* 阿姆斯伯利，位于伦敦西南75英里的地方
4 old Sarum 旧塞勒姆，位于索尔兹伯里以北3公里的山丘，发展于青铜器时代（约公元前3000年），为盖尔特人的要塞
5 a bare, treeless hill 是old Sarum的同位语
6 downs *n.* 英国英格兰南部和西南部有草的丘陵地，这里指索尔兹伯里平原
7 which 引导非限制性定语从句，先行词为Stonehenge
8 barrow ['bærəʊ] *n.* mound built over a burial place in prehistoric times，古墓
9 veneration [ˌvenə'reɪʃn] *n.* 崇敬
10 ecclesiastical [ɪˌkli:zɪ'æstɪkl] *adj.* of clergymen，基督教会的

history had proceeded.

Stonehenge is a circular colonnade[11] with a diameter of a hundred feet, and enclosing a second and third colonnade within. We walked round the stones, and clambered over[12] them, to wont[13] ourselves with their strange aspect and groupings, and found a nook[14] sheltered from the wind among them, where C. (Thomas Carlyle[15], the author of "Sartor Resartus," etc.) lighted his cigar. It was pleasant to see that just this simplest of all simple structures—two upright stones and a lintel laid across—had long outstood all later churches, and all history, and were like what is most permanent on the face of the planet: these, and the barrows — mere mounds[16] of which there are a hundred and sixty within a circle of three miles about Stonehenge like the same mound on the plain of Troy[17], which still makes good to the passing mariner[18] on Hellespont[19], the vaunt[20] of Homer[21] and the

低头吃草的羊群，星星点点，一位旅行推销员在沿路前行。英国这如此拥挤不堪的小岛，能给予这样一个远古时代的庙宇如此宽广辽阔的空间，是跟英国民族对于"老朋友"的崇敬不谋而合的，而英国所有的教会结构及历史则恰恰是发源于它。

巨石阵由石柱围成一圈，直径可达百余英尺，内有两三层石柱。我们绕着这些巨石边走边看，攀爬上去，逐渐习惯了它们的奇特外表和构成，还找到一个隐蔽而安静的地方避风，托马斯·卡莱尔（《衣裳哲学》等书的作者）曾在这儿点着了他的烟。我们很高兴看到了所有简单的结构中最简单的一种——两根石柱竖直站

11 colonnade [ˌkɒləˈneɪd] n. 柱廊，此处指"石柱"
12 clamber over = climb with difficulty or effort, using the hands and feet，攀爬
13 wont [wəunt] = accustomed to doing something，适应做某事
14 nook [nuk] n. 隐蔽处，幽静处
15 Thomas Carlyle 托马斯·卡莱尔（1795~1881）系英国作家、评论家、历史学家，其以唯心主义批判资本主义，反对贫富不均，著作丰富，他的著作对英国社会表现出敏锐的洞察力
16 mound [maund] n. 土墩
17 Troy [trɔɪ] n. 特洛伊。特洛伊也称"伊利昂"，是古希腊殖民城市。公元前16世纪前后由古希腊人所建。位于小亚细亚半岛西端赫勒斯滂海峡（即达达尼尔海峡）的东南部，即今土耳其的希萨利克。公元前13至前12世纪时，这里颇为繁荣。公元前12世纪初，迈锡尼联合希腊各城邦组成联军，渡海远征特洛伊，战争延续了十年之久，史称"特洛伊战争"，特洛伊也因此闻名。城市在战争中变为了废墟。荷马史诗《伊利亚特》叙述了此次战争的经过。据传说，特洛伊城最后由希腊人用"木马计"攻破。19世纪，在特洛伊城发掘出了大批古物珍品
18 mariner [ˈmærɪnə] n. 海员
19 Hellespont [ˈheləspɒnt] n. 达达尼尔海峡（在土耳其欧亚两部分之间，连接马尔马拉海与爱琴海）
20 vaunt [vɔːnt] n. 夸张
21 Homer [ˈhəumə] n. 荷马，大约生活在公元前9世纪到公元前8世纪的希腊，是一个双目失明、到处行吟的诗人。主要著作有《伊利亚特》和《奥德赛》

跋山涉水 叹壮丽神奇

fame of Achilles[22]. Within the enclosure grow buttercups[23], nettles[24], and, all around, wild thyme, daisy, meadow-sweet, goldenrod, thistle, and the carpeting grass. Over us, larks were soaring and singing — as my friend said: "the larks which were hatched last year, and the wind which was hatched many thousand years ago." We counted and measured by paces the biggest stones, and soon knew as much as any man can suddenly know of the inscrutable[25] temple. There are ninety-four stones, and there were once probably one hundred and sixty. The temple is circular and uncovered, and the situation fixt astronomically[26] — the grand entrances here, and at Abury, being placed exactly northeast, "as all the gates of the old cavern temples are." How came the stones here[27], for these sarsens[28] or Druidical[29] sand-stones are not found in this neighborhood? The sacrificial[30] stone, as it is called, is the only one in all these blocks that can resist the action of fire, and, as I read in the books, must have been[31] brought one hundred

22 Achilles [ə'kɪliːz] n. 希腊神话人物。荷马史诗中的英雄。特萨利亚地区密尔弥冬人的王佩琉斯和海中神女忒提斯之子，俊美、敏捷，有捷足之称
23 buttercup ['bʌtəˌkʌp] n. 毛茛，金凤花
24 nettle ['netl] n. 荨麻
25 inscrutable [ɪn'skruːtəbl] adj. mysterious，神秘的
26 astronomically [ˌæstrə'nɒmɪkɪ] adv. 天文学地
27 How came the stones here ＝ how did the stones come here
28 sarsen ['saːsən] n. 砂岩漂砾
29 Druidical [druːˈɪdɪkl] adj. 德鲁伊教的
30 sacrificial [sækrɪ'fɪʃl] adj. 献祭的
31 must have been 情态动词对过去的推测，一定已经

立，一根石柱从上端横跨而过这种结构——在后来所有的教堂、所有的历史中脱颖而出，就像是这个星球表面最永恒的东西。这一切，还有那些古墓——在巨石阵周边方圆3英里的范围内一共有160个——就像特洛伊平原要上的土墩，那土墩至今仍可以取悦路过黑峡（即当今的达达尼尔海峡）的水手们，像荷马的夸张和阿喀琉斯的传说一样迷人。在巨石圈的周围生长着毛茛、荨麻和大量野生的百里香，遍地都是雏菊、白花绒线菊、黄花、蓟和茵茵绿草。在我们上方的天空，百灵鸟正在翱翔、歌唱，就如我的朋友所说的："我们上方飞着去年孵出的百灵鸟，周围吹着几千年前的风。"我们用步子计算和测量了那些最大的石头，很快便了解了那些关于这座神秘庙宇的一看便知的情况。共有94块巨石，但从前可能有160块呢。这环形的、露天的庙宇是按照天文学的要求布局的——这里以及阿布里的壮丽的大门，都和所有古老洞穴庙宇的大门一样，被精确地置于东北方。这些巨石是如何被搬运至此的呢？因为附近并未发现类似的砂石和德鲁伊

45

and fifty miles.

On almost every stone we found the marks of the mineralogist's[32] hammer and chisel[33]. The nineteen smaller stones of the inner circle are of granite[34]. I, who had just come from Professor Sedgwick's Cambridge Museum of metatheria[35] and mastodons[36], was ready to maintain that some cleverer elephants or mylodonta[37] had borne off[38] and laid these rocks one on another. Only the good beasts must have known how to cut a well-wrought tenon[39] and mortise[40], and to smooth the surface of some of the stones. The chief mystery is that[41] any mystery should have been allowed to settle on[42] so remarkable a monument[43], in a country on which all the Muses[44] have kept their eyes now for eighteen hundred years. We are not yet too late to learn much more than is known of this structure. Some diligent Fellowes or Layard will arrive, stone by stone, at the whole history, by that exhaustive British sense and perseverance, so whimsical[45] in its choice of objects, which leaves

教石头。祭坛的石头，正如我在书里读到的，是这些石头中唯一能抵抗大火的，它们一定是被搬运了150英里才到了此处。

几乎在每块石头上我们都能找到矿物学家锤锤凿凿过的痕迹。内圈的19块较小的石块是花岗石。我刚从塞奇威克教授主管的大懒兽和乳齿象的剑桥博物馆归来，这让我更坚信是一些更聪明的大象或磨齿兽把这些石头搬运至此并一块一块地叠积起来的。只有那些巨兽懂得如何去精确地切割凸榫和榫眼并将其中一些石头的表面打磨光滑。它的主要神秘之处在于，在这个1800年来一直受缪斯女神眷顾的国家，任何不可思议的事儿都有可能发生在如此非凡的遗迹上。了解更多有关这个建筑的知识对于我们来说还为时未晚。一些勤奋的费洛斯们或雷厄德们会纷至沓来，以彻底的英国精神及坚韧不拔的恒心研究每一块石头。而这种英国精神及恒心在选择研究对象时却总是让人费解，它不去探索自己的巨石阵的秘密，让它在荒野中与野兔为伴，却去揭开埃及金字塔和亚述故宫尼尼微的真

---

32 mineralogist [ˌmɪnəˈrælədʒɪst]　n.　矿物学者
33 chisel [ˈtʃɪzl]　n.　凿子
34 granite [ˈɡrænɪt]　n.　花岗岩
35 metatheria [ˌmetəˈθɪərɪə]　n.　后哺乳下纲，此处指"大懒兽"
36 mastodon [ˈmæstədɒn]　n.　乳齿象
37 mylodonta　n.　磨齿兽
38 borne off　= seize and carry away，bear off 的过去分词，搬走
39 tenon [ˈtenən]　n.　凸榫，榫舌
40 mortise [ˈmɔːtɪs]　n.　榫眼
41 that　在这里连接的是表语从句
42 settle on　= stay for some time
43 so remarkable a monument　= such a remarkable monument
44 Muse　n.　缪斯女神
45 whimsical [ˈwɪmzɪkl]　adj.　异想天开的，想入非非的

its own Stonehenge or Choir Gaur to the rabbits, while it opens pyramids, and uncovers Nineveh. Stonehenge, in virtue of[46] the simplicity of its plan, and its good preservation, is as if new and recent; and, a thousand years hence, men will thank this age for the accurate history it will yet eliminate[47].

From *English Traits* (1847)

相。由于布局简单，保存完好，巨石阵看上去仍崭新如初。千载之后，历史的流逝仍不会在巨石阵上留下任何痕迹，人们会为此而感激这个时代。

---

46 in virtue of = because of
47 eliminate = remove，消失，除去

含英咀华

英国的巨石阵一向被人们认为是世界之谜，它已经矗立了几千年之久，始终像幽灵一样留给每一个时代的人以猜疑和惶惑。本文中，作者对巨石阵的构成和外观作了细致的描写，也对巨石阵的形成作了分析和揣测。

Frederic Harrison

佛雷德里克·哈里森

佛雷德里克·哈里森（1831~1923），英国法学家、历史学家。他出生在伦敦，曾在伦敦大学国王学院和牛津大学学习。

跋山涉水 叹壮丽神奇

The Call of the Mountains

山谷的呼唤

Once more — perhaps for the last time — I listen to the unnumbered tinkling[1] of the cow-bells on the slopes — "the sweet bells of the sauntering[2] herd" — to the music of the cicadas[3] in the sunshine, and the shouts of the neat herd lads, echoing back from Alp[4] to Alp. I hear the bubbling of the mountain rill, I watch the emerald[5] moss[6] of the pastures gleaming in the light, and now and then the soft white mist creeping along the glen[7], as our poet says, "puts forth an arm and creeps from pine to pine." And see, the wild flowers, even in this waning[8] season of the year, the delicate lilac[9] of the dear autumn crocus, which seems to start up elf-like out of the lush grass, the coral beads of the rowan[10], and the beech-trees just begun to wear their autumn jewelry of old gold. As I stroll about these hills, more leisurely, more thoughtfully than I used to do of old in my hot mountaineering[11] days, I have tried to think out what it is that makes the Alpine

又一次——也可能是最后一次——我聆听着山坡上串串牛铃发出的叮当声——这是漫步山间的牛群发出的甜美的叮当声——聆听着阳光下蝉儿的歌唱，聆听着优雅的放牧小伙子的呼唤声——这些声音在阿尔卑斯山间回荡。我倾听着山间小溪潺潺的流水声，观赏着牧场上翠绿的苔藓在阳光下闪光，时而看到柔和的白雾沿着山谷慢慢散开，如诗人所述："伸出臂膀葡匐在松树间"。看，这些可爱的野花，即使在这一年中略显苍白的季节，也依然绽放。淡紫色的秋季番红花就像小精灵一样从嫩绿的草中浮现，花楸树长出珊瑚色的珠子，山毛榉树开始披上古金色的秋日珠宝。我在群山中漫

1 tinkling ['tɪŋklɪŋ]　n.　叮当作响声
2 sauntering ['sɔːntərɪŋ]　adj.　=wandering，闲逛的，漫步的
3 cicada [sɪ'kɑːdə]　n.　蝉。
4 Alps [ælps]　n.　[the-]阿尔卑斯山脉
5 emerald ['emərəld]　adj.　翠绿色的
6 moss [mɒs]　n.　苔藓
7 glen [glen]　n.　溪谷，幽谷
8 waning ['weɪnɪŋ]　adj.　逐渐减弱或变小的，这里引申为"略显苍白的"
9 lilac ['laɪlək]　n.　淡紫色
10 rowan ['rəʊən]　n.　花楸树
11 mountaineering [ˌmaʊntə'nɪərɪŋ]　n.　登山运动，爬山

landscape so marvelous a tonic[12] to the spirit — what is the special charm of it to those who have once felt all its inexhaustible[13] magic. Other lands have rare beauties, wonders of their own, sights to live in the memory for ever.

In France, in Italy, in Spain, in Greece and in Turkey, I hold in memory many a superb[14] landscape. From boyhood upward I thirsted for all kinds of Nature's gifts, whether by sea, or by river, lake, mountain, or forest. For sixty years at least I have roved about[15] the white cliffs, the moors[16], the riversides, lakes, and pastures of our own islands from Penzance to Cape Wrath, from Beachy Head to the Shetlands. I love them all. But they can not touch me, as do the Alps, with the sense at once of inexhaustible loveliness and of a sort of conscious sympathy with every fiber of man's heart and brain. Why then is this so?

I find it in the immense range of the moods in which nature is seen in the Alps, as least by those who have fully absorbed all the forms, sights, sounds, wonders, and adventures they offer. An hour's walk will show them all in profound[17] contrast and yet in exquisite[18] harmony. The Alps form a book of Nature as wide and as mysterious as Life.

步，比以往那些登山的日子里更加悠闲自在，更加思绪万千，努力在想是什么使得阿尔卑斯山的风景如此奇妙，如此让人精神振奋——是什么特殊魅力让人一次就感觉到它的无尽神奇。其他的地方不会有如此美丽、让人终生难忘的奇观和风景。

我记得在法国、意大利、西班牙、希腊和土耳其，也有很多绝美的风景。从孩童时起，我就渴望大自然的各种美景——无论是在海边、河边、湖边、山中，抑或在林间。60年来，从彭冉到好望角，从壁池滩头到谢德兰群岛，我漫游过白色峭壁、漠泽荒野、河边湖畔、田园牧场。我爱这所有的美景，但是它们不像阿尔卑斯山脉那样令我如此感动，无限的喜爱之情油然而生，我的心、我的思绪都与这山形成共鸣。原因何在？

我发现那些完全理解体会到阿尔卑斯山景色、声音、奇观和惊险的人才可以欣赏到它

---

12 tonic ['tɒnɪk] *n.* 补药，补剂
13 inexhaustible [ˌɪnɪgˈzɔːstəbl] *adj.* = endless，用不完的，无尽的
14 superb [suːˈpɜːb] *adj.* 极好的
15 rove about = wander / roam，漫游
16 moor [mɔː(r)] *n.* 荒野，旷野
17 profound [prəˈfaʊnd] *adj.* 极深的，深奥的，这里引申为"鲜明的"
18 exquisite [ɪkˈskwɪzɪt] *adj.* 精致的，细腻的

跋山涉水 叹壮丽神奇

Earth has no scenes of placid[19] fruitfulness more balmy[20] than the banks of one of the larger lakes, crowded with vineyards, orchards[21], groves and pastures, down to the edge of its watery mirror, wherein[22], beside a semi-tropical vegetation, we see the image of some medieval castle, of some historic tower, and thence the eye strays up[23] to sunless gorges, swept with avalanches, and steaming with feathery cascades[24]; and higher yet one sees against the skyline ranges of terrific crags[25], girt[26] with glaciers[27], and so often wreathed[28] in storm clouds.

All that Earth has of most sweet, softest, easiest, most suggestive of langor and love, of fertility and abundahce — here is seen in one vision beside all that Nature has most hard, most cruel, most unkind to Man — where life is one long weary battle with a frost bitten soil, and every peasant's hut has been built up stone by stone, and log by log, with sweat and groans, and wrecked hopes. In a few hours one may pass from an enchanted garden, where every sense is satiated[29], and every flower and leaf and gleam

---

19 placid ['plæsɪd] adj. = peaceful，安静的，平和的
20 balmy ['bɑːmɪ] adj. 芳香的
21 orchard ['ɔːtʃəd] n. 果园
22 wherein [(h)weər'ɪn] int. 在那里，在其中
23 stray up = wander，游离，这里指目光转到别处
24 cascade [kæs'keɪd] n. 小瀑布
25 crag [kræg] n. 峭壁，危岩
26 girt [gɜːt] gird 的过去分词，围绕，环绕。这里是过去分词结构 修饰前面的名词短语
27 glacier ['glæsɪə] n. 冰河，冰川
28 wreath [riːθ] v. 遮覆，覆盖，包围
29 satiated ['seɪʃɪeɪtɪd] adj. = satisfied，满足的，满意的

的自然，自然存在于深远的心境中。在山中漫步一小时就足以体会到这些鲜明的对比和优雅的和谐。阿尔卑斯山脉本身就是一本自然的书，如生命般宽广神秘。

阿尔卑斯山脉中最大的湖岸边芳香宜人，地球上再也找不到静谧的、硕果累累的景色了。这里满山遍布了葡萄园、果园、小树林、草原，一直延伸到如镜的水边，在一处亚热带森林旁，我们看到了中世纪城堡和闻名遐迩的塔，然后眼神又游移到阴暗的峡谷，那里会发生雪崩，轻柔的瀑布散发出阵阵水气；再高一些就可以看见被冰层覆盖的峭壁的壮美轮廓，其间时常缭绕着冰雪云层。

地球上最甜美、最温柔、最简单、最显而易见的爱恋之情，最丰盛和富饶的拥有——在这里一览无余，尽管大自然对人类苛刻、冷酷、无情——生命是与被风霜侵袭的土壤长期艰苦卓绝斗争的过程，每个农民的小屋都是用一块块石头、一根根木头夹带着汗水、呻吟、破碎的梦想垒起的。在几个小时的时间内，你可能会经过迷人的花园，敞开心扉，

of light is intoxication[30], up into a wilderness of difficult crags and yawning[31] glaciers, which men can reach only by hard-earned skill, tough muscle and iron nerves…

The Alps are international, European, Humanitarian. Four written languages are spoken in their valleys, and ten times as[32] many local dialects. The Alps are not especially Swiss — I used to think they were English — they belong equally to four nations of Europe; they are the sanatorium[33] and the diversory[34] of the civilized world, the refuge, the asylum[35], the second home of men and women famous throughout the centuries for arts, literature, thought, religion. The poet, the philosopher, the dreamer, the patriot[36], the exile, the bereaved[37], the reformer, the prophet[38], the hero have all found in the Alps a haven of rest, a new home where the wicked cease from troubling, where men need neither fear nor suffer. The happy and the thoughtless, the thinker and the sick — are alike at home here. The patriot exile inscribed on his house on Lake Leman — "Every land is fatherland to the brave man." What he might have written is — "This land is fatherland to all men." To young and

尽情享受，每一朵花、每一片叶、每一缕阳光都会让你如痴如醉，向上走你就可能进入到危险的峭壁、裂开的冰川中，只有经过艰苦训练、技巧纯熟、肌肉结实、意志坚强的人才能到达那里。

阿尔卑斯山脉是国际化、欧洲化的，有着博爱的人道主义精神。这里语言多样，有四种官方语言，更有十倍之多的当地方言。阿尔卑斯山脉并非瑞士独有——我过去认为它们是英国的——它们属于欧洲的四个国家；它们是文明世界的疗养院、遮阴处，是几世纪以来那些在艺术、文学、思想、宗教文明等领域声名卓著的人们的避难所、救济院、第二家园。诗人、哲学家、梦想家、爱国者、放逐者、失去亲人的人、改革家、预言家、英雄，所有这些人都认为阿尔卑斯山脉是休养的天堂、没有邪恶烦扰的新家园，在这里人们没有恐惧和痛苦。快乐的人，粗心的人，有思想的人，生病的人——都在这里找到了家的感觉。被放逐的爱国者在乐曼湖的房子上刻着——"每一寸土地都是勇敢者的家园。"他可能已经写下的是——"这片土地是人类的家园。"无论是对于年

30 intoxication [ɪn,tɒksɪ'keɪʃn] n. 此处意为"陶醉"
31 yawning [jɔ:nɪŋ] adj. 裂开大口的，豁开的
32 ten times as = ten times the amount of, 十倍多
33 sanatorium [,sænə'tɔ:rɪəm] n. 疗养院，休养所
34 diversory [daɪ'və:sərɪ] n. 路边隐蔽处
35 asylum [ə'saɪləm] n. 庇护所，收容所
36 patriot ['peɪtrɪət] n. 爱国者
37 bereaved [bɪ'ri:vd] n. 丧失亲人的人
38 prophet ['prɒfɪt] n. 预言者，预言家

old, to strong and weak, to wise and foolish alike, the Alps are a second fatherland.

From *My Alpine Jubilee* (1908)

轻人、年老的人、强壮的人、虚弱的人、聪明的人、愚蠢的人，阿尔卑斯山脉都是他们的第二家园。

跋山涉水 叹壮丽神奇

含英咀华

在文中作者细致地描写了阿尔卑斯山脉的美丽景色，表达了自己面对美丽的大自然时的激动心情。本文句式整齐，用词优美，描写出阿尔卑斯山脉的雄伟、壮观，充分抒发出作者面对美丽的山峰时所感受到的视野辽阔、风景宜人、山清水秀和环境幽雅。读者阅读时仿佛置身于伟岸的山峰之间，呼吸着新鲜的空气，感受着山谷间回荡的声音，从字里行间可以体会到山间独特的美。

Robert Smythe Hichens

罗伯特·S·希琴斯

罗伯特·S·希琴斯（1864～1950），英国小说家，出生于肯特郡，曾就读于皇家音乐学院以及一所新闻学校。他创作了多部小说，其代表作包括《绿色康乃馨》（*The Green Carnation, 1894*），《贝拉夫人》（*Bella Donn, 1909*），《凄艳断肠花》（*The Paradine Case, 1933*）等。希琴斯还创作了很多短篇故事以及歌词。他曾为伦敦《世界》杂志做了3年的音乐评论家。

The Nile

I do not find in Egypt any more the strangeness that once amazed, and at first almost bewildered[1] me. Stranger by far[2] is Morocco[3], stranger the country beyond Biskra, near Mogar, round Touggourt, even about El Kantara. There I feel very far away, as a child feels distance from dear, familiar things. I look to the horizon expectant[4] of I know not what magical occurrences, what mysteries. I am aware of the summons[5] to advance to marvelous lands, where marvelous things must happen. I am taken by that sensation of almost trembling[6] magic which came to me when first I saw a mirage[7] far out in the Sahara. But Egypt, though it contains so many marvels, has no longer for me the marvelous atmosphere. Its keynote is seductiveness[8].

In Egypt one feels very safe. Smiling policemen in clothes of spotless[9] white — emblematic[10], surely, of their innocence! —

1 bewilder [bɪ'wɪldə] v. 使……不知所措
2 by far （与比较级或最高级连用）大量，甚多
3 Morocco [mə'rɒkəʊ] n. 摩洛哥
4 expectant [ɪks'pektənt] adj. 期待的，期望的
5 summons ['sʌmənz] n. 召唤
6 trembling ['tremblɪŋ] adj. 发抖的，哆嗦的
7 mirage ['mɪrɑːʒ] n. 海市蜃楼，幻想
8 seductiveness [sɪ'dʌktɪvnəs] n. 诱惑，引申为"令人神往的魅力"
9 spotless ['spɒtləs] adj. 无脏污的
10 emblematic [ˌemblə'mætɪk] adj. 作为象征的

尼罗河

我在埃及再也无法找到那种一度令我十分迷惑，曾经让我颇感惊奇的奇异之处。摩洛哥才更让人惊叹！这个神奇的国家远到比斯克拉，近到摩格尔，周围有图古尔特甚至有坎塔拉。那些地方让我感到很遥远，就像一个孩子远离他所亲近、熟悉的事物一样。我望向天际，满怀希望地憧憬未来时，我不知道会有什么奇异的事情发生。我感觉到了这块神奇土地的召唤，在这里一定会发生不可思议的事情。当我在撒哈拉沙漠中第一次看到海市蜃楼时，我感受到了那种神奇得让你发抖的感觉。但是埃及，尽管有许多奇迹，对于我来说再也不是那种非凡奇异的氛围了。它的基调定格为一种令人神往的魅力。

在埃及很有安全感。微笑的警察身着象征着他们的纯洁无私的一尘不染的白制服，他们似乎无处不在，平静地站在阳光下。非常绅士、非常温和、虽然有些不真实，他们就是金字塔中的都因人。尼罗

seem to be everywhere, standing calmly in the sun. Very gentle, very tender, although perhaps not very true, they are the Bedouins[11] at the Pyramids[12]. Up the Nile the fellaheen[13] smile as kindly as the policemen, smile protectingly upon you, as if they would say, "Allah[14] has placed us here to take care of the confiding stranger." No ferocious[15] demands for money fall upon my ears; only an occasional suggestion is subtly[16] conveyed to[17] me that even the poor must live and that I am immensely rich. An amiable, an almost enticing[18] seductiveness[19] seems emanating[20] from the fertile soil, shining in the golden air, gleaming softly in the amber[21] sands, dimpling[22] in the brown, the mauve, the silver eddies of the Nile. It steals upon one. It ripples over one. It laps one as if with warm and scented waves. A sort of lustrous[23] languor[24] overtakes one. In physical well-being one sinks down, and with wide eyes one gazes and listens and enjoys, and thinks not of the morrow[25].

The dahabiyeh — her very name, the /

河上游的劳动者笑得像警察一样，那么仁慈和蔼，这种微笑保护着你，好像在说："真神阿拉让我们驻守在这里保护那些虔诚的外来者。"此处听不到索要钱财的声音，只是我偶然才会意识到：即使穷人也必须生活，而我则很富足。亲切迷人的诱惑似乎正从肥沃的土壤中散发，在金色的空气中闪光，在琥珀色的沙砾中温柔地闪烁，在褐色且泛着淡紫、闪着银光的尼罗河漩涡中泛起涟漪；波光粼粼，涟漪起伏，层层叠叠，仿佛伴随着温暖而馨香的波浪向前延伸。这时候，人会突然感到一种明亮的倦怠，突然就沉浸到了一种身体上的安宁当中，睁开双眼，凝视远方，聆听潺潺流水，享受自然美景，把明天的一切抛在了脑后。

11 Bedouin ['beduɪn] *n.* 都因人(沙漠地带从事游牧的阿拉伯人)
12 Pyramid ['pɪrəmɪd] *n.* (古埃及的)金字塔
13 fellaheen [feləhi:n] *n.* fellah的复数形式，指阿拉伯国家的农夫，转译为"劳动者"
14 Allah ['ælə] *n.* (伊斯兰教的) 阿拉，真主
15 ferocious [fə'rəuʃəs] *adj.* 残忍的，凶猛的
16 subtly ['sʌtlɪ] *adv.* 敏锐地，巧妙地，精细地
17 convey to 传达（意思、见解、感情等）
18 enticing [ɪn'taɪsɪŋ] *adj.* 引诱的，迷人的
19 seductiveness [sɪ'dʌktɪvnɪs] *n.* 诱惑力
20 emanate ['eməneɪt] *v.* 散发，发出
21 amber ['æmbə] *adj.* 琥珀色的
22 dimple ['dɪmpl] *v.* 使起涟漪
23 lustrous ['lʌstrəs] *adj.* 光亮的，有光泽的
24 languor ['læŋgə] *n.* 怠惰，疲倦
25 morrow ['mɒrəu] *n.* [the -] 翌日

啵山涉水 叹壮丽神奇

Loulia, has a gentle, seductive, cooing[26] sound — drifts broadside to the current with furled[27] sails, or glides smoothly on before an amiable north wind with sails unfurled. Upon the bloomy banks, rich brown in color, the brown men stoop[28] and straighten themselves, and stoop again, and sing. The sun gleams on their copper skins, which look polished[29] and metallic. Crouched[30] in his net behind the drowsy[31] oxen, the little boy circles the livelong day with the sakieh. And the sakieh raises its wailing[32], wayward voice and sings to the shadoof[33]; and the shadoof sings to the sakieh; and the lifted water falls and flows away into the green wilderness of doura[34] that, like a miniature forest, spreads on every hand to the low mountains, which do not perturb[35] the spirit, as do the iron mountains of Algeria.

And always the sun is shining, and the body is drinking in[36] its warmth, and the soul is drinking in its gold. And always the ears are full of warm and drowsy and monotonous[37] music. And always the eyes see the lines of brown bodies, on

26 cooing ['ku:lɪŋ] *adj.* 喔啊声
27 furled [fɜ:ld] *adj.* 卷起的
28 stoop [stu:p] *v.* 俯身
29 polished ['pɒlɪʃt] *adj.* 擦亮的，闪亮的
30 crouch ['krautʃ] *v.* 蹲下
31 drowsy ['drauzɪ] *adj.* 昏昏欲睡的，此处意为"慵懒的"
32 wailing [weɪlɪŋ] *n.* 悲叹声，哭泣声
33 shadoof [ʃa:'du:f] *n.* （埃及等地汲水用的）桔槔
34 doura ['duərə] *n.* [植] 蜀黍，高粱
35 perturb [pə'tɜ:b] *v.* 扰乱，使混乱
36 drink in = take in 吸收，此处意为"沐浴在……"
37 monotonous [mə'nɒtənəs] *adj.* 单调的。它的名词形式是"monotony"，意为"单调，无味"

哒哈彼耶——她真正的名字，读作"鲁利亚"，富有魅力、温和轻柔的声音——风帆卷起时，它便顺着水流漫无目标地漂游，而风帆扬起时，它又会乘着柔和的北风轻柔地滑行。而在那开满花的、深褐色的河岸上，皮肤黝黑的男人俯身，站起，再俯身，唱着嘹亮的歌。阳光洒在他们古铜色的皮肤上，看起来闪着金属的光泽。小男孩蹲在慵懒的牛群后的网中，与水车共度着漫长的一天。水车发出响亮的声音，周而复始，似在对桔槔歌唱；桔槔也回应着；被提起的水散落并流向茫茫一片绿色的蜀黍地中，蜀黍就像一片微小的森林，从四面八方延伸到小山脚下，就像阿尔及利亚的铁山一样并不会扰乱这奇妙的境界。

太阳总是光辉耀眼，身体沐浴在温暖的阳光下，灵魂沉浸在金色之中。耳中萦绕着温暖平静而又单一的乐曲。在棕色的水面上和河岸边尽收眼底的是皮肤黝黑的身影，伴随着精确的单音俯身、站直、再俯身、再站直。鲁利亚似乎总是在静悄

the brown river-banks above the brown waters, bending[38], straightening, bending, straightening, with an exquisitely[39] precise monotony. And always the /Loulia/ seems to be drifting, so quietly she slips up, or down, the level waterway.

And one drifts, too; one can but drift, happily, sleepily, forgetting every care. From Abydos to Denderah one drifts, and from Denderah to Karnak, to Luxor, to all the marvels on the western shore; and on to Edfu, to Kom Ombos, to Assuan, and perhaps even into Nubia, to Abu — Simbel, and to WadiHalfa. Life on the Nile is a long dream, golden and sweet as honey of Hymettus. For I let the "divine serpent," who at Philae may be seen issuing[40] from her charmed cavern, take me very quietly to see the abodes[41] of the dead, the halls of the vanished, upon her green and sterile[42] shores. I know nothing of the bustling[43], shrieking steamer that defies her, churning into angry waves her waters for the edification[44] of those who would "do" Egypt and be gone before they know her[45].

If you are in a hurry, do not come to Egypt. To hurry in Egypt is as wrong as to fall asleep in Wall street, or to sit in the Greek Theatre at

悄地流淌，水流时而弯曲，时而笔直。

游人的脚步也随着流水前行；也只能是随波前行，愉快地，困倦地，忘却了所有忧虑。从阿拜多斯到丹德拉赫，从丹德拉赫到凯尔耐克，再到卢克索古城，到达西部海岸所有神奇之处，继而到埃德福，到欧普斯港口，到阿斯旺大坝，或者到努比亚，到阿布·辛拜勒神庙，再到湾迪·哈沃夫。尼罗河的生活就像一场绵长的梦，像伊米托斯山上的蜂蜜，甜美诱人。我让"圣蛇"——在菲莱被认为是从埃及颇具魅力的洞穴中爬出来的——静静地带着我沿着荫绿、瘦瘠的海岸奔赴那些亡灵的住所，那些消逝的殿堂。而一些欲受尼罗河水洗礼的埃及"浏览者"，坐在尖叫忙乱的汽艇之上，无视尼罗河温柔敦厚的性情，将河水搅动得怒涛翻涌，往往还未识得尼罗河的真面，便又匆匆而去。对于此番行为，我无语可置。

如果你只是想匆忙赶路，就不要去埃及。在埃及来去匆匆就如在华尔街睡大觉，抑或

38 bending   现在分词，作状语，表伴随
39 exquisitely ['ekskwɪzɪtlɪ] adv. 精巧地
40 issue ['ɪsju:] v. 出来，出现
41 abode [ə'bəud] n. 住所，住处
42 sterile ['steraɪl] adj. 不毛的，贫瘠的
43 bustling ['bʌslɪŋ] adj. = busy, 熙熙攘攘的，忙乱的
44 edification [,edɪfɪ'keɪʃn] n. 陶冶，教诲
45 churning into...before they know her   从句中的现在分词作伴随状语，之中还包含一个由who引导的定语从句，修饰前面的"those"

Taormina, reading "How to Make a Fortune with a Capital of Fifty Pounds."

From *The Spell of Egypt* (2004)

是在陶欧米纳的希腊大剧院品读《五十英镑的资本如何致富》，这就大错特错了。

含英咀华

　　本文摘自《埃及的魔力》(*The Spell of Egypt, 1911*)，在这本书中作者按照旅行的行程描写了埃及的风景民俗。在选文中作者怀着好奇的心情来到埃及的尼罗河探索，细致描绘了尼罗河的风景，这里的一草一木都充满了无限的魅力和神秘色彩。同时作者也用相当多的笔墨描写了居住在这里的人们所具有的同样让人难以抗拒的吸引力，让读者感受到埃及作为人类古文明的发源地是值得去游历的，值得去细心慢慢寻味她的神奇所在的。正如文中所说，来埃及旅游不能着急，如果匆匆而过，那就如在华尔街上睡一觉一样，大错特错了。

Bradford Torrey
布莱福特·托雷

布莱福特·托雷（1843～1912），出生于马萨诸塞州，主要作品有《丛林中的鸟》(Birds in the Bush, 1885),《佛罗里达素描》(A Florida Sketch-Book, 1894)。托雷在作品中塑造并反映了中产阶级试图在利用城市之便的同时又享受乡村生活的观点，这并不像早期的浪漫主义观点，他的这一观点不排斥都市生活，相反通过倡导绿色空间减轻城市生活的不利。他认为人们即使在城市中也可以成为自然世界的观察者，这种观点受到了读者的普遍青睐。他把在大自然的闲庭漫步与游记写作融为一体，使读者沉醉于度假胜地的美景之中，正是他的真实而又优雅的文笔以及对大自然细微的描写在19世纪80年代吸引了众多的读者。

蹈山涉水 叹壮丽神奇

On the Beach at Daytona

代托纳海滩

The first eight days of my stay in Daytona were so delightful that I felt as if I had never before seen such fine weather, even in my dreams. My east window looked across the Halifax River to the peninsula[1] woods. Beyond them was the ocean. Immediately after breakfast, therefore, I made toward the north bridge, and in half an hour or less was on the beach. Beaches are much the same the world over, and there is no need to describe this one — Silver Beach, I think I heard it called — except to say that it is broad, hard, and, for a pleasure-seeker's purpose, endless. It is backed by low sand-hills covered with impenetrable[2] scrub, — oak and palmetto[3], — beyond which is a dense growth of short-leaved pines. Perfect weather, a perfect beach, and no throng[4] of people: here were the conditions of happiness; and here for eight days I found it. The ocean itself was solitude. Day after day not a sail was in sight[5]. Looking up and down[6] the beach, I could usually see somewhere in the distance a carriage or two, and as many

待在代托纳的最初八天里，我感觉非常的愉快以至于我感觉好像从未见过这样的好天气，即便是在梦里。透过东面的窗户能看见哈利法克斯河，再往远处就是丛林遍布的半岛景色，再往前看就是大海。于是一吃完早餐，我就动身向北桥走去，不到半个小时就到了海滩。世界上的海滩在极大程度上都是相似的，因此也没有必要来描述这个早有耳闻的所谓的"银色海岸"——我想我听说过它被称为广博的、浩瀚的，对于寻求惬意的人来说，它是无边无际的。它的后面是一些小沙丘，上面覆盖着难以穿透的木丛——橡树和美洲蒲葵——另一边是一片密集的针叶林。晴朗的天气，美妙的沙滩，稀少的游人：这就是幸福快乐的所在；这就是我这八天里所寻找到的。只有海洋自己是孤独的，日复一日没有一只船帆映入眼帘。环顾这海滩，我经常能看到不远处有一两驾马车或是几个徒步的游客；但我通常只是走一小段

---

1 peninsula [pə'nɪnsjələ] n. 半岛
2 impenetrable [ɪm'penɪtrəbl] adj. 不能穿过的
3 palmetto [pæl'metəu] n. 美洲蒲葵，棕榈科之一种
4 throng [θrɒŋ] n. = crowd，人群；大群
5 in sight 此处意为"映入眼帘"
6 look up and down 原意指"上下打量"，这里引申为"环顾海滩"

61

foot passengers[7]; but I often walked a mile, or sat for half an hour, without being within hail[8] of any one. Never were airs more gentle or colors more exquisite[9].

As for birds, they were surprisingly scarce[10], but never wanting altogether. If everything else failed, a few fish-hawks[11] were sure to be in sight. I watched them at first with eager interest. Up and down the beach they went, each by himself, with heads pointed downward, scanning the shallow water. Often they stopped in their course, and by means of laborious flapping[12] held themselves poised over a certain spot. Then, perhaps, they set their wings and shot downward clean[13] under water. If the plunge was unsuccessful, they shook their feathers dry and were ready to begin again. They had the fisherman's gift. The second and even the third attempt might fail, but no matter; it was simply a question of time and patience. If the fish was caught, their first concern seemed to be to shift their hold upon it, till its head pointed to the front. That done, they shook themselves vigorously and started landward, the shining white victim wriggling[14] vainly in the clutch[15] of

路或是坐下休憩半个小时，不跟任何人打招呼。心境从未如此平静过，色彩从未如此绚烂过。

至于鸟儿，它们惊人地稀少，且从不愿意集群，如果看不到其他鸟类，一些鱼鹰定会映入你的眼帘。起初我抱着极大的兴趣看着它们，它们独自在海滩上下盘旋，头朝下，扫视着浅浅的海水。在这个过程中它们经常会突然停下来，不断地挥动着翅膀使得它们能够在某一点保持平衡。然后，它们或许会收起翅膀干净利落地扎进水中，如果这个猛冲不成功，它们就会抖干羽毛准备再次出击。它们拥有渔民捕鱼的本领。第二次甚至于第三次尝试都可能失败，但这没关系；这只是时间与耐心的问题。如果抓到了鱼，鱼鹰似乎先调整叼的位置，直到鱼头朝向前方。然后，它们就会用力地抖动着身体飞向陆地，而那闪闪发光的白色的受害者在猛禽的利爪下徒劳地扭动着。我一直以为它们会带着它们的猎物飞到半岛上一些隐蔽的地方，直到有一天我站在一个小沙丘上碰巧看到一只鱼鹰飞过我的头顶我才发现不是这样的。

7 foot passengers 这里指"徒步旅行的游客"
8 hail [heɪl] n. 招呼
9 exquisite ['ekskwɪzɪt] adj. 精致的，细腻的，此处意为"绚烂的"
10 scarce [skeəs] adj. 缺乏的，稀少的
11 fish-hawk [fɪʃ-hɔːk] n. 鱼鹰
12 flap [flæp] v. （鸟）扇动翅膀
13 clean [kliːn] adv. 熟练地，干净利落地
14 wriggle ['rɪgl] v. 扭动
15 clutch [klʌtʃ] n. 抓紧，掌握

the talons[16]. I took it for granted that they retired with their quarry[17] to some secluded[18] spot on the peninsula, till one day I happened to be standing upon a sand-hill as one passed overhead. Then I perceived that he kept on straight across the peninsula and the river. More than once, however, I saw one of them in no haste[19] to go inland. On my second visit, a hawk[20] came circling about my head, carrying a fish. I was surprised at the action, but gave it no second thought, nor once imagined that he was making me his protector, till suddenly a large bird dropped rather awkwardly[21] upon the sand, not far before me. He stood for an instant on his long, ungainly[22] legs, and then, showing a white head and a white tail, rose with a fish in his talons, and swept away landward out of sight[23]. Here was the osprey's[24] parasite[25], the bald eagle, for which I had seen on the watch. Meantime, the hawk too had disappeared. Whether it was his fish which the eagle had picked up (having missed it in the air) I cannot say. I did not see it fall, and knew nothing of the eagle's presence until he fluttered[26] to the beach.

Some days later, I saw the big thief —

---

16 talon ['tælən]   n.   爪
17 quarry ['kwɒrɪ]   n.   猎物
18 seclude [sɪ'klu:d]   vt.   隔离（隔绝），"secluded spot"这里引申为"隐蔽的地方"
19 in no haste   = in no hurry 不匆忙，不急
20 hawk [hɔ:k]   n.   鹰
21 awkwardly ['ɔ:kwədlɪ]   adv.   笨拙地
22 ungainly [ʌn'ɡeɪnlɪ]   adj.   笨拙的
23 out of sight   看不见
24 osprey ['ɒspreɪ]   n.   鹗（一种食鱼的大鹰）
25 parasite ['pærəsaɪt]   n.   寄生虫
26 flutter ['flʌtə]   v.   （鸟）鼓翼，振翅

我察觉到它径直飞过了半岛和河流。然而我不只一次地看到其中一只并不急着飞向内陆。再一次望去时，一只鱼鹰正抓着一条鱼在我头上盘旋。我对这种举动很惊奇，但并没有多想，更没想到它把我当成保护者了，直到一只大鸟突然笨拙地降落在离我不远处的沙滩上。它靠着那两条长而笨拙的双腿在瞬间站了起来，露出了白色的头和尾巴，爪子里抓着一条鱼，然后很快掠过陆地，飞出我的视野。刚才映入我眼帘的就是鱼鹰的寄生虫——秃鹰：我在电视里看到过它。与此同时，鱼鹰也消失了。至于刚才那条被秃鹰捡着的鱼（在天上丢失的）是不是它的战利品我也不得而知，我没看到鱼落下来，也没意识到鹰的存在，直到它鼓翼飞向沙滩。

几天后，我看到了大强盗——美国自由的象征——运用它的聪明伎俩的始末。我正在过桥，不经意转身向上看（说是碰巧，其实我经常这么干）。在高空中有两只鸟——一只鱼鹰和一只黑头黑尾的鹰，其中一只鸟在追逐着另外一只。这只鱼鹰想尽力保

跋山涉水 叹壮丽神奇

63

emblem[27] of American liberty — play his sharp game to the finish. I was crossing the bridge, and by accident turned and looked upward. (By accident, I say, but I was always doing it.) High in the air were two birds, one chasing the other, — a fish-hawk and a young eagle with dark head and tail. The hawk meant to save[28] his dinner if he could. Round and round he went, ascending at every turn, his pursuer after him hotly. For aught[29] I could see, he stood a good chance of escape, till all at once another pair of wings swept into the field of my glass.

"A third is in the race! Who is the third?

Speeding away swift as the eagle bird?"

It was an eagle, an adult, with head and tail white. Only once more the osprey circled. The odds were against him, and he let go[30] the fish. As it fell, the old eagle swooped[31] after it, missed it, swooped again, and this time, long before it could reach the water, had it fast in his claws. Then off he went, the younger one in pursuit. They passed out of sight behind the trees of an island, one close upon the other, and I do not know how the controversy ended; but I would have wagered[32] a trifle on the old white-head, the bird of Washington.

The scene reminded me of one I had

护它的美餐。它一圈又一圈的盘旋，每次转弯时都尽力地盘旋上升，而它的追随者穷追不舍。它很有机会逃脱，此时另一双翅膀进入了我的视野。

"第三只进入了角逐！谁是那第三只？

拥有鹰一样速度的鸟正飞离而去？"

这是一只白头白尾的成年鹰。鱼鹰又盘旋了一圈。优势顿失的鱼鹰只好放弃了鱼。鱼一掉下来，老鹰就猝然扑过去，第一次扑空了，接着又来了一次，远在鱼儿落入水面之前就已经把它牢牢地抓住了。然后它飞走了，那只幼小的鹰则在后面紧追不舍。它们很快就一前一后地消失在了一个岛中的森林里，我不知道这场争夺是如何终止的，但我可以打个小赌，赌那只白头老鹰赢，它可是华盛顿的市鸟。

这画面让我想起了两周前去南部的路上在佐治亚看到的场景。火车停在了一个偏远的车站；一些乘客聚集在一辆车后，

---

27 emblem ['embləm] n. 象征，徽章，此处意为"象征"
28 mean to do sth. 意欲做某事
29 aught [ɔːt] n. =anything，任何事物
30 let go = release one's hold of，放手，松开
31 swoop [swuːp] v. 抓取，突然袭击
32 wager ['weɪdʒə] v. 打赌，赌博

witnessed in Georgia a fortnight before, on my way south. The train stopped at a backwoods station; some of the passengers gathered upon the steps of the car, and the usual bevy[33] of young Negroes came alongside. "Stand on my head for a nickel?" said one. A passenger put his hand into his pocket; boy did as he had promised, — in no very professional style, be it said, — and with a grin stretched out his hand[34]. The nickel glistened[35] in the sun, and on the instant a second boy sprang forward, snatched it out of the sand, and made off in triumph amid the hilarious[36] applause of his fellows. "Where is our boasted honor among thieves?" I imagined him asking. The bird of freedom is a great bird, and the land of the free is a great country. Here, let us hope, the parallel ends. Whether on the banks of Newfoundland or elsewhere, it cannot be that the great republic would ever snatch a fish that did not belong to it.

From *A Florida Sketch-Book* (1894)

旁边经常跟着一群年轻的黑人孩子。"做个倒立就能给我一个硬币吗?"其中一个男孩说。一个乘客把手伸进了他的口袋,这个男孩履行了他的诺言——并不如他所说的一样专业——然后露齿一笑伸出了他的双手。硬币在阳光下闪闪发光,一瞬间另一个男孩突然跳了出来,把硬币从沙子中拿了出来,然后在胜利的喝彩声中匆匆离开了。"在这些小偷身上哪里能看到我们所称赞的荣耀呢?"我猜想他会这么问。自由的鸟才是伟大的鸟,自由的国度才是伟大的国家。在这里,让我们祈祷相同的结局。不管在纽芬兰岛的岸边或者是其他地方,再也不会有一个大国去夺取本来不属于它的东西。

33 bevy ['bevi] *n.* = group,群
34 with a grin stretched out his hand with +名词／名词短语＋分词,表示独立主格
35 glisten [glɪsn] *v.* 闪亮,闪闪发光
36 hilarious [hɪ'leərɪəs] *adj.* 喜不自禁的,欢闹的,愉快的

含英咀华

在选文中作者通过自己敏锐的观察力和优美的语言描写了代托纳海滨波澜壮阔的景象。晴朗的天气，美妙的沙滩，稀少的游人，一丝幸福快乐感油然而生。不经意间，一些鱼鹰定会映入你的眼帘，它们时而独自在海滩上下盘旋，扫视着浅浅的海水，时而突然停下来，不断地挥动着翅膀干净利落地扎进水中捕捉"战利品"，既而很快掠过陆地，飞出你的视野，让人不禁感叹："自由的鸟才是伟大的鸟，自由的国度才是伟大的国家。"

悠悠泛舟
品岸边风光

Rafting Down the Neckar
内卡河上木筏行

The Flowing Canal
奔腾的运河

To Rome by Pisa and Siena
经比萨和锡耶纳到罗马

Kayaking the Fjords of New Zealand
泛舟新西兰峡湾

Mark Twain

马克·吐温

马克·吐温（1835~1910），原名塞姆·朗赫恩·克列门斯（*Samuel Langhorne Clemens*），是美国的幽默大师、小说家、作家，亦是著名的演说家。马克·吐温于1835年11月30日出生在美国密苏里州佛罗里达的乡村的一个贫穷律师家庭，于1910年去世，享年七十五岁，安葬于纽约州的艾玛拉。代表作有《卡拉维拉斯郡著名的跳蛙》（*The Celebrated Jumping Frog of Calaveras County, 1867*）、《汤姆·索亚历险纪》（*The Adventures of Tom Sawyer, 1876*）、《哈克贝里·费恩历险记》（*Adventures of Huckleberry Finn, 1884*）。他的写作融幽默与讽刺于一体，既富有独特的个人机智与妙语，又不乏深刻的社会洞察与剖析，曾被誉为是文学史上的林肯。

Rafting down the Neckar[1]

We discharged[2] the carriage at the bridge. The river was full of logs — long, slender, barkless pine logs — and we leaned on the rails of the bridge, and watched the men put them together into rafts[3]. These rafts were of a shape and construction to suit the crookedness[4] and extreme narrowness of the Neckar. They were from fifty to one hundred yards long, and they gradually tapered[5] from a nine-log breadth at their sterns[6], to a three-log breadth at their bow[7]-ends. The main part of the steering[8] is done at the bow, with a pole; the three-log breadth there furnishes room for only the steersman, for these little logs are not larger around than an average young lady's waist. The connections of the several sections of the raft are slack and pliant[9], so that the raft may be readily bent into any sort of curve required[10] by the shape of the river.

The Neckar is in many places so narrow that a person can throw a dog across it, if he

内卡河上木筏行

车到桥头的时候，我们付了钱打发马车回去了。河面上漂满了原木——细长的、没有树皮的松树圆木——我们倚靠在桥栏上，看着人们用这些木头做成木筏。这些木筏的形状和结构都适用于内卡河河道弯曲和极窄的特点。它们的长度从50码到100码不等，由尾部9根原木的宽度逐渐缩小到船头3根原木的宽度。大部分的掌舵工作都是由舵手在船头用篙来完成的——船头3根原木的宽度只能容纳一个舵手，因为这些小木材的粗细也不过一名普通妇女的腰围大小。木筏几部分的连接是松散的，灵活性也较强，以便随时变向来适应河流水流的形式。

内卡河的很多地方都非常狭窄，以至于你可以把一只小狗扔到对面。当一些地方水流陡变时，撑筏者就不得不使出几招绝技，引航变向。河流并不总是淹没整个河床的——河床的宽度达到30码，有些地方

---

1 Neckar ['nekə] *n.* 内卡河（德国西南部河流）
2 discharge [dɪs'tʃɑːdʒ] *v.* 解雇，解除，这里引申为"打发走"
3 raft [rɑːft] *n.* 筏
4 crookedness ['krukɪdnəs] *n.* 弯曲，歪斜
5 taper ['teɪpə] *v.* 逐渐变小
6 stern [stɜːn] *n.* 船尾
7 bow [baʊ] *n.* 船头
8 steering ['stɪ(ə)rɪŋ] *n.* 掌舵，操舵
9 pliant ['plaɪənt] *adj.* 易受影响的，易弯的
10 required 过去分词短语作后置定语，修饰前面的"curve"

has one; when it is also sharply curved in such places, the raftsman has to do some pretty nice snug piloting to make the turns[11]. The river is not always allowed to spread over its whole bed — which is as much as thirty, and sometimes forty yards wide — but is split into[12] three equal bodies of water, by stone dikes which throw the main volume, depth, and current into the central one. In low water these neat narrow-edged dikes project four or five inches above the surface, like the comb of a submerged roof, but in high water they are overflowed. A hatful of rain makes high water in the Neckar, and a basketful produces an overflow.

There are dikes abreast[13] the Schloss Hotel, and the current is violently swift at that point. I used to sit for hours in my glass cage, watching the long, narrow rafts slip along through the central channel, grazing[14] the right-bank dike and aiming carefully for the middle arch of the stone bridge below; I watched them in this way, and lost all this time hoping to see one of them hit the bridge-pier[15] and wreck itself sometime or other, but was always disappointed. One was smashed there one morning, but I had just stepped into my room a moment to light a pipe, so I lost it.

While I was looking down upon[16] the rafts

甚至达到40码——但是石堤将水流三等分，并把主要的水流汇集到中心水道中去。在浅水期，这些整齐的、狭窄的石堤会露出水面四五英寸，就像被淹没的房屋的屋顶。但在深水期，它们就都会被河水淹没。在内卡河，一帽子的雨水就能使水位上涨，一满筐的雨水就会使水决堤！

舒劳斯旅馆与几条堤坝走向相同，在它附近的那段河流，水流湍急。我时常坐在自己的房间，透过玻璃看那长而狭窄的木筏沿着中心水道顺流而下，擦过堤岸的右侧边缘，小心地对准下游石桥的中下孔滑。我就这样望着它们，在对什么时候能看到它们撞在桥墩，成为残骸的憧憬中迷失了自我。然而，我总是失望。一天早晨，有一条木筏粉碎在那里，不过在我刚刚踏进房间去点烟的时候撞击发生，因此我还是错过了。

在海尔布隆的那个早晨，

---

11 make the turns　这里指"引航变向"
12 be split into　被分割成
13 abreast [ə'brest]　*adv.*　并肩地，相并地
14 graze [greɪz]　*v.*　轻轻擦过，掠过
15 bridge-pier　*n.*　桥墩
16 look down upon　此处意为"俯瞰"

that morning in Heilbronn, the daredevil[17] spirit of adventure came suddenly upon[18] me, and I said to my comrades:

"I am going to Heidelberg on a raft. Will you venture[19] with me?"

Their faces paled a little, but they assented with as good a grace as they could. Harris wanted to cable his mother — thought it his duty to do that, as he was all she had in this world — so, while he attended to this, I went down to the longest and finest raft and hailed the captain with a hearty "Ahoy, shipmate[20]!" which put us upon pleasant terms at once, and we entered upon business[21]. I said we were on a pedestrian tour to Heidelberg, and would like to take passage with him. I said this partly through young Z, who spoke German very well, and partly through Mr. X, who spoke it peculiarly. I can UNDERSTAND German as well as the maniac that invented it, but I TALK it best through an Interpreter.

The captain hitched up[22] his trousers, then shifted his quid[23] thoughtfully. Presently he said just what I was expecting he would say — that he had no license to carry passengers, and therefore was afraid the law would be after him in case the matter got noised about[24] or any accident

---

17 daredevil ['deədevl] *adj.* 胆大的，冒失的
18 come on/upon sb. 突临
19 venture ['ventʃə] *v.* 敢尝试，冒险一试
20 shipmate ['ʃɪpmeɪt] *n.* 同船水手，此处意为"伙计"
21 enter upon business 这里引申为"进入正题"
22 hitch up 此处指"提上"
23 quid [kwɪd] *n.* 咀嚼物，烟草块
24 get noise about 此处意为"宣扬"

当我俯瞰木筏时，勇敢的冒险精神突然产生了，我对我的同伴们说：

"我准备乘木筏去海德堡。你们和我一起去冒险吗？"

他们脸色吓得苍白，不过还是尽量优雅地表示了赞同。哈里想给他的母亲发一封电报——认为这是他的职责，因为他是母亲在这个世界上唯一的亲人——因此，他去发电报了。与此同时，我跑上那条最长、最好的木筏，热情地向船长打招呼道："嗨，伙计，你好啊！"这一问候使气氛立刻活跃起来，接着我们便进入了正题。我说，我们原本是要徒步旅行到海德堡去的，但现在打算乘坐他的木筏去那里。我的这些话有一部分是通过蔡德先生翻译的，他的德语说得很好；另一部分则是通过爱克司先生翻译的，他的德语说得尤其好。我能听懂德语，在这方面我的水平可跟德语的创造者相比，不过我要通过翻译才能把它说好。

木筏上的老大提提裤子，思虑地动动嘴里嚼着的烟草块，说出了我预料中的话——他没有运送旅客的执照，担心万一这件事宣扬出去或者万一出了事故，他

happened. So I CHARTERED the raft and the crew and took all the responsibilities[25] on myself.

With a rattling song[26] the starboard watch[27] bent to their work and hove the cable short, then got the anchor home, and our bark moved off with a stately stride, and soon was bowling[28] along at about two knots[29] an hour.

Our party was grouped amidships[30]. At first the talk was a little gloomy, and ran mainly upon the shortness of life, the uncertainty of it, the perils[31] which beset[32] it, and the need and wisdom of being always prepared for the worst; this shaded[33] off into low-voiced references to the dangers of the deep, and kindred[34] matters; but as the gray east began to redden and the mysterious solemnity and silence of the dawn to give place to[35] the joy-songs of the birds, the talk took a cheerier tone, and our spirits began to rise steadily…

From *A Tramp Abroad* (1880)

会惹上官司。于是，我租下了这条木筏，雇了他的舵手，一切责任由我承担。

伴着一阵激昂的号子声，右弦的舵手们弯腰开始了自己的活计，收起缆索，升起筏锚，我们的木筏便飞速地向前驶去。很快，它的时速就达到了约2海里/小时。

我们一行人聚集在木筏的中央。起初，大家的交谈有些低沉，主要是围绕着生命短暂、难测、危机重重、时刻做好最坏的准备是必需和明智的这些内容。这种交谈渐渐变成低语，内容都是些海洋的危险之类的东西。然而，当灰色的东方出现红霞，在黎明那神秘的庄严和静寂中响起小鸟欢快的歌声时，大家的谈话也欢快了许多，我们的情绪也逐渐高涨起来……

25 take the responsibilities 承担责任
26 rattling song 号子声
27 starboard watch *n.* （船员轮流当值的）右舷班
28 bowl [bəul] *v.* 迅速而平稳地行驶
29 knot [nɒt] *n.* 海里
30 amidship [ə'mɪdʃɪp] *n.* 在船中部
31 peril ['perəl] *n.* = venture危险，冒险
32 beset [bɪ'set] *v.* 烦扰，困扰
33 shade [ʃeɪd] *v.* 渐变
34 kindred ['kɪndrəd] *adj.* 同类的
35 give place to 让位于

悠悠泛舟 品岸边风光

含英咀华

　　内卡河是德国西南部莱茵河右岸的支流，源出黑森林，靠近多瑙河河源，穿过覆盖着藤本植物、峰顶有封建时代城堡的群山，美丽的河谷幽深开阔。内卡河的老桥是海德堡最著名的标识，桥墩似乎烙上了历史的印迹，一节节的桥拱也诉说着岁月的悠然。老桥的桥头，有两座稳重地耸立着的双塔，更是在为海德堡依旧辉煌闪耀着做最大的诠释。乘着狭窄的木筏沿着中心水道，顺流而下，美景尽收眼底，别有一番风情。

Henry David Thoreau

亨利·戴维·梭罗

亨利·戴维·梭罗（1817~1862），美国作家、自然主义者，出生于马萨诸塞州的康科德，1837年毕业于哈佛大学，是个品学兼优的学生。1845年7月4日，28岁的梭罗独自一人来到距离康科德两英里的瓦尔登湖畔，建造了一个小木屋住了下来。此后他根据自己对生活的观察与思考，整理并发表了两本著作《康科德和梅里马克河上的一周》(*A Week on the Concord and Merrimack Rivers, 1839*)和《瓦尔登湖》(*Walden, 1854*)。1862年5月6日，梭罗因病去世，年仅45岁。梭罗才华横溢，勤奋著书，一生共创作了20多部一流的散文集。他被称为自然随笔的创始者，其文简练有力，朴实自然，富有思想性，在美国19世纪散文作家中独树一帜。

悠悠泛舟 品岸边风光

The Flowing Canal

The canal runs, or rather is conducted, six miles through the woods to the Merrimack[1], at Middlesex[2].

And as we did not care to loiter[3] in this part of our voyage, while one ran along the tow-path[4] drawing the boat by a cord, the other kept it off[5] the shore with a pole, so that we accomplished the whole distance in little more than an hour.

This canal, which is the oldest in the country, and has even an antique[6] look beside the more modern railroads, is fed by the Concord[7], so that we were still floating on its familiar water. It is so much water which the river lets for the advantage of commerce. There appeared some want of harmony in its scenery, since it was not of equal date with the woods and meadows[8] through which it is led, and we missed the conciliatory[9] influence of time on land and water; but in the lapse[10] of ages, Nature will recover and

奔腾的运河

运河向前奔流，或者更确切地说，是被引导着流向前方，流过了6英里的森林，流到了位于米德尔塞克斯的梅里马克河。

在这段航程中，你若不喜欢闲荡，可以任由一个人在岸边用纤绳拉船，另一个人撑着长篙防止船撞上河岸，短短的一个多小时的时间足够完成整个航程。

这是美国最古老的运河，它倚靠在现代化的铁路边，愈显悠久。它源于康科德河，因此我们一直是漂流在这熟悉的水域上。它水流丰沛，你丝毫感觉不到它是为商业利益而开凿的分流。运河穿越的森林和草地在年代上与它不可同日而

---

1 Merrimack ['merɪ'mæk] n. 梅里马克河，美国东北部河流，源出新罕布什尔州中部的怀特山脉，向南流入马萨诸塞州，折向东北注巴顿大西洋

2 Middlesex ['mɪdlseks] n. 米德尔塞克斯郡[英国英格兰原郡名]

3 loiter ['lɔɪtə] v. = hang around, 闲荡，徘徊

4 tow-path n. （河或运河沿岸的）曳船道，纤路

5 keep off 阻止，防止，此处译为"防止船撞上河岸"

6 antique [æn'ti:k] adj. 古代的

7 Concord ['kɔŋkɔ:d] n. 康科德（美国马萨诸塞州东部一镇）

8 meadow ['medəu] n. 草地，牧场

9 conciliatory [kən'sɪlɪətərɪ] adj. = harmonious, 调和的

10 lapse [læps] n. （时间的）流逝

indemnify[11] herself, and gradually plant fit shrubs[12] and flowers along its borders. Already the kingfisher sat upon a pine over the water, and the bream and pickerel[13] swam below. Thus all works pass directly out of the hands of the architect into the hands of Nature, to be perfected.

It was a retired and pleasant route, without houses or travelers, except some young men who were lounging[14] upon a bridge in Chelmsford[15], who leaned impudently[16] over the rails to pry[17] into our concerns, but we caught the eye of the most forward, and looked at him till he was visibly discomfited[18]. Not that there was any peculiar efficacy[19] in our look, but rather a sense of shame left in him which disarmed him.

As we passed under the last bridge over the canal, just before reaching the Merrimack the people coming out of church paused to look at us from above, and apparently, so strong is custom, indulged[20] in some heathenish[21] comparisons; but we were the truest observers of this sunny day.

By noon we were let down into the

语，在景色上似乎缺少某种和谐时间对陆地和水的影响是不协、调的。但是，随着时光的流逝，大自然的自我修复和调整尽显其能，渐有一些适宜的灌木花卉在它的岸边滋长出来。翠鸟在河边的松枝上栖息，淡水太阳鱼、美洲狗鱼在水中畅游。建筑师手上所有的工作径直转到大自然的手中，任其完善。

这是一个偏远而愉快的航线，没有房屋，没有游人。只是在切姆斯德福的一座桥上，有几个年轻人在闲逛，他们冒冒失失侧身靠在桥上，上下打量我们，但我们也紧盯他们中最前面那个人的眼睛不放，最后他们很明显地显得有些窘迫，并不是因为我们的目光有什么特异功能，而是他心中余存的羞耻感使自己缴械投降了。

通过运河上最后一座桥后我们便抵达了梅里马克河。人们从教堂鱼贯而出，从桥上向下打量着我们，议论纷纷，显然，强大的世俗力量又在发威了，沉醉于某种异教徒式的比较之中；在这阳光明媚的日子里，我们才是实实在在的观察者。

11 indemnify [ɪn'demnɪfaɪ] v. 补偿，保护，此处指 "自我修复"
12 shrub [ʃrʌb] n. 灌木
13 pickerel ['pɪkərəl] n. 美洲狗鱼
14 lounge [laʊndʒ] v. = hang around，闲荡，闲逛
15 Chelmsford 切姆斯德福，美国马萨诸塞州东北部城镇
16 impudently ['ɪmpjudəntli] adv. 冒失地
17 pry [praɪ] v. 窥探，盯着看
18 discomfited [dɪs'kʌmfɪtɪd] adj. 窘迫的，不安的
19 efficacy ['efɪkəsɪ] n. 功效，效力
20 indulge [ɪn'dʌldʒ] v. 纵情于，放任，此处 "indulge in" 表示 "沉醉于"
21 heathenish ['hi:ðənɪʃ] adj. 异教的，异教徒的，非基督教的

悠悠泛舟 品岸边风光

Merrimack through the locks[22] at Middlesex, just above Pawtucket Falls, by a serene[23] and liberal-minded man, who came quietly from his book, though his duties, we supposed, did not require him to open the locks on Sundays. With him we had a just and equal encounter of the eyes, as between two honest men.

The movements of the eyes express the perpetual and unconscious courtesy[24] of the parties. It is said that a rogue does not look you in the face, neither does an honest man look at you as if he had his reputation to establish. I have seen some who did not know when to turn aside their eyes in meeting yours. A truly confident and magnanimous[25] spirit is wiser than to contend for[26] the mastery in such encounters. Serpents[27] alone conquer by the steadiness of their gaze. My friend looks me in the face and sees me, that is all.

The best relations were at once established between us and this man, and though few words were spoken, he could not conceal a visible interest in us and our excursion. He was a lover of the higher mathematics, as we found, and in the midst of some vast sunny problem, when we overtook him and whispered our conjectures[28]. By this man we were presented with the freedom of

---

22 lock [lɒk]   n.   （运河、水坝等的）船闸，水闸
23 serene [sɪ'ri:n]   adj.   安详的，宁静的
24 courtesy ['kɜ:təsɪ]   n.   = politeness，礼貌
25 magnanimous [mæg'nænɪməs]   adj.   宽宏大量的，有雅量的
26 contend for   为……而争斗
27 serpent ['sɜ:pənt]   n.   阴险狠毒的人
28 conjecture [kən'dʒektʃə]   n.   推测，臆测

晌午了，我们穿过了位于庞塔凯特瀑布上方的米德尔塞克斯船闸，顺流而下进入梅里马克河。此前，一位恬静厚道的人轻轻放下书本，前来为我们开闸，尽管我们猜想，他并没有义务要在星期天开闸。我们平和的目光与他的目光不期而遇，这种对视只可能存在于两个诚恳的人之间。

这种眼神的移动表达出了一种出自我们内心的礼貌，据说，无赖不会正视你的脸，而一个正直的人看着你时，他也不会显得高人一等。我见过一些人，他们不知何时转移自己与他人相遇时目光。在这种目光交会时，真正的自信和儒雅比咄咄逼人更明智。只有奸诈之人为压制别人而瞪视，我的朋友看着我的脸，便了解了我，仅此而已。

尽管交谈不多，但我们和这个人立即建立起了美好的友情。显然，他无法掩饰对我们及我们这次旅行的兴趣。我们发现，他是一个高等数学爱好者，当我们遇见他，轻声说出自己的想法时，他正沉浸在一个有趣的问题中。他引领我们进入浩渺的梅里马克河，此时，我们感觉自己好像在无边

the Merrimack. We now felt as if we were fairly launched on the ocean-stream of our voyage, and were pleased to find that our boat would float on Merrimack water. We began again busily to put in practice those old arts of rowing, steering, and paddling. It seemed a strange phenomenon to us that the two rivers should mingle[29] their waters so readily, since we had never associated them in our thoughts.

We were thus entering the State of New Hampshire on the bosom of the flood formed by the tribute of its innumerable valleys. The river was the only key which could unlock its maze[30], presenting its hills and valleys, its lakes and streams, in their natural order and position. The MERRIMACK, or Sturgeon River, is formed by the confluence of the Pemigewasset, which rises near the Notch of the White Mountains, and the Winnipiseogee, which drains the lake of the same name, signifying "The Smile of the Great Spirit." From their junction it runs south seventy-eight miles to Massachusetts, and thence[31] east thirty-five miles to the sea. I have traced its stream from where it bubbles out of the rocks of the White Mountains above the clouds, to where it is lost amid the salt billows of the ocean on Plum Island beach. At first it comes on murmuring to itself by the base of stately and retired mountains, through moist primitive[32] woods whose juices

无际的海洋中漫游，发现自己漂浮在梅里马克河水面，这令我们欣喜不已。我们重温了古老的划船、掌舵、荡桨艺术，忙得不亦乐乎。两条河流如此亲密地融合在一起，对我们来说是一个奇观，因为，这是我们从来没有想到过的。

在无数支流汇集而成的洪流怀抱中，我们进入新罕布什尔州。开启这个迷宫唯一的钥匙就是梅里马克河，这个州的山峦、河谷、湖泊和溪流在自然法则和地势作用下呈现出来。梅里马克河，也称鲟河，由源于怀特峰峡谷附近的佩米杰瓦塞特河和温尼皮西欧吉河——从与该河同名的湖泊泄出——汇集而成，意为"巨灵的微笑"。从它们的交界处向南78英里可到达马萨诸塞州，再沿此向东35英里就到了大海边。我曾追随过它的全部流程，潺潺细流从高耸入云的怀特峰山岩中流出，一直流到普勒姆海滩，最后汇入到飘着咸味的海涛中。起初，它们喃喃自语在庄严古老的大山脚下流淌，穿越潮湿的原始森林，吮

---

29 mingle ['mɪŋgl] v. 混合，融合
30 unlock its maze 此处意为"开启迷宫"
31 thence [ðens] adv. 从那以后
32 primitive ['prɪmətɪv] adj. 原始的

it receives, where the bear still drinks it, and the cabins of settlers are far between, and there are few to cross its stream; enjoying in solitude[33] its cascades still unknown to fame; by long ranges of mountains of Sandwich and of Squam, slumbering[34] like tumuli[35] of Titans, with the peaks of Moosehillock, the Haystack, and Kearsarge reflected in its waters; where the maple and the raspberry[36], those lovers of the hills, flourish amid temperate dews; — flowing long and full of meaning, but untranslatable as its name Pemigewasset, by many a pastured[37] Pelion and Ossa, where unnamed muses haunt, tended by Oreads, Dryads, Naiads, and receiving the tribute of many an untasted Hippocrene[38]. There are earth, air, fire, and water, — very well, this is water, and down it comes.

Falling all the way, and yet not discouraged by the lowest fall. By the law of its birth[39] never to become stagnant[40], for it has come out of the clouds, and down the sides of precipices[41] worn in the flood, through beaver[42] dams broke loose, not splitting but splicing[43] and mending itself, until it found a breathing place[44] in this low land. There is

吸森林里熊所啜饮的浆液。拓荒者的小木屋遥不可及，潺潺溪流很少有人能横越；一些无名的瀑布独自享受孤寂；从桑威奇和斯夸姆的连绵山脉中蜿蜒流过，那些山脉犹如泰坦巨人的坟墓；水中倒映着穆斯希洛克山、黑斯塔克山和卡萨吉山。群峰的情人——枫树和山莓在娇弱的露珠里搔首弄姿；它源远流长、意蕴深远，但又像它的名字佩米杰瓦塞特一样令人难以理解。它那里的许多山峰有不知名的仙人看护，河水得到山岳女神俄瑞阿得斯、得律阿得斯和那伊阿得斯的抚育，接受了众多世间无人品味过的山之灵泉的馈赠。这里有大地、天空、雷火和净水——好极了，这是净水，它源源而来。

水一路奔腾，即使落差再小也不气馁。它与生俱来的原则就是永不停滞，因为，它来自云端，沿着峭壁一泻而下，穿过海狸筑成的水坝后分裂开来，但并不是四散而逃，而是不断黏结、修复自身，直到发现喘息之处——低洼之地。现在，在流入大海之前被太阳光蒸发掉的危险已经不复存在，它甚至可以重新收回自己每晚

---

33 solitude ['sɒlɪtjuːd] n. = loneliness，孤独，孤寂
34 slumber ['slʌmbə] v. 熟睡
35 tumuli ['tjuːmjulɪ] n. = tomb，坟墓
36 raspberry ['raːzbərɪ] n. 覆盆子
37 pasture ['paːstʃə] vt. 放牧
38 Hippocrene ['hɪpəuˈkriːnɪ] n. （希腊神话）灵泉之水
39 law of its birth 意为"与生俱来的原则"
40 stagnant ['stægnənt] adj. 不流动的
41 precipice ['presəpɪs] n. 断崖峭壁
42 beaver ['biːvə] n. 海狸
43 splice [splaɪs] v. 使结合，使连接
44 a breathing place 此处指"喘息之处"

no danger now that the sun will steal it back to heaven again before it reach the sea, for it has a warrant even to recover its own dews into its bosom again with interest at every eve.

It was already the water of Squam and Newfound Lake and Winnipiseogee, and White Mountain snow, dissolved, on which we were floating, and Smith's and Baker's and Mad Rivers, and Nashua and Souhegan and Piscataquoag, and Suncook and Soucook and Contoocook, mingled in incalculable proportions, still fluid, yellowish, restless all, with an ancient, ineradicable[45] inclination[46] to the sea.

From *Walden* (1864)

凝聚的露珠。

　　现在，我们所漂流的水域，已经属于斯夸姆河、纽芬得湖和温尼皮西欧吉河了，还有怀特峰的积雪融水。史密斯河、贝克河、梅得河、纳舒厄河、索希根河、皮斯卡塔康格河、森库克河、苏库克河和康托库克河，这些水流以不可计算的比例混合在一起，聚成淡黄色的河水，在其固有天性的促使下带着原始气息永不停歇地奔向大海。

---

45 ineradicable [ˌɪnɪ'rædɪkəbl]　*adj.*　不能根除的，根深蒂固的
46 inclination [ˌɪnklɪ'neɪʃn]　*n.*　倾向，趋向

含英咀华

　　在选文中作者用清新的文笔对奔腾的流水及河流四周的景色进行了优美细致的描绘，思想与景境融合在一起，像湖水的澄澈透明、山林的茂密苍翠，给人以美好的遐想和深刻的思考，使读者顿时感到全身心脱离了尘世的喧嚣和功利的羁绊，与自然融为一体，在自然中感悟人生，感悟哲理。

Charles Dickens

查尔斯·狄更斯

查尔斯·狄更斯,作者介绍见 "*In and about the City*"。

To Rome by Pisa and Siena

经比萨和锡耶纳到罗马

There is nothing in Italy, more beautiful to me, than the coast-road between Genoa[1] and Spezia[2]. On one side: sometimes far below, sometimes nearly on a level with the road, and often skirted[3] by broken rocks of many shapes: there is the free blue sea, with here and there a picturesque[4] felucca[5] gliding slowly on; on the other side[6] are lofty[7] hills, ravines besprinkled[8] with white cottages, patches of dark olive woods, country churches with their light open towers, and country houses gaily painted. On every bank and knoll[9] by the wayside, the wild cactus[10] and aloe[11] flourish in exuberant[12] profusion[13]; and the gardens of the bright villages along the road, are seen, all blushing in the summer-time with clusters of the Belladonna[14], and are fragrant in the autumn and winter with golden oranges and lemons.

在我看来，在意大利没有什么可以与位于热那亚和斯培西亚之间的那条滨海大道相媲美的了。一面是奔腾的蓝色海洋，它的水位时而很低，时而几乎与路面持平，海水的边缘是许多不同形状的石头，海面上随处都有别致的三桅小帆船慢慢飘过。另一面则是高高的山丘，峡谷周围布满了白色的村舍，还有黑色的橄榄树、乡村教堂和明亮敞开的城堡，以及色彩明快的庄园点缀。路旁的每处浅滩和小山上，都生长着茂盛的野生仙人掌和芦荟。夏日沿河明亮的庄园里，可以看到一簇簇盛开的红色颠茄花；而在秋冬季节，金橘和柠檬的芳香溢满庄园。

1 Genoa ['dʒenəuə] *n.* 热那亚（意大利城市）
2 Spezia ['spetsja:] *n.* 斯培西亚（意大利城市）
3 skirt [skɜ:t] *v.* 位于……边缘
4 picturesque [ˌpɪktʃə'resk] *adj.* 独特的，别致的
5 felucca [fe'lʌkə] *n.* 三桅小帆船
6 on one side…on the other side 此处为"一面……，另一面……"
7 lofty ['lɒftɪ] *adj.* 高耸的，巍峨的
8 besprinkle [bɪ'sprɪŋkl] *v.* 布满
9 knoll [nəul] *n.* 小山，圆丘
10 cactus ['kæktəs] *n.* 仙人掌
11 aloe ['æləu] *n.* 芦荟
12 exuberant [ɪg'zju:bərənt] *adj.* 繁茂的，丰富的
13 profusion [prə'fju:ʒn] *n.* 众多，大量
14 belladonna [ˌbelə'dɒnə] *n.* （植物）颠茄

Some of the villages are inhabited, almost exclusively, by fishermen; and it is pleasant to see their great boats hauled[15] up on the beach, making little patches[16] of shade, where they lie asleep, or where the women and children sit romping[17] and looking out to the sea, while they mend their nets upon the shore. There is one town, Camoglia, with its little harbour on the sea, hundreds of feet below the road; where families of mariners[18] live, who, time out of mind[19], have owned coasting-vessels in that place, and have traded to Spain and elsewhere. Seen from the road above, it is like a tiny model on the margin of[20] the dimpled[21] water, shining in the sun. Descended into, by the winding mule-tracks, it is a perfect miniature[22] of a primitive seafaring[23] town; the saltest, roughest, most piratical[24] little place that ever was seen. Great rusty iron rings and mooring-chains, capstans[25], and fragments of old masts and spars, choke up the way; hardy rough-weather boats, and seamen's clothing, flutter[26] in the little harbour or are drawn out[27] on the sunny stones to dry; on the parapet[28] of the

有些村庄，几乎所有的居民都是渔民。他们把巨大的船只拖上海滩，形成一些荫凉，渔民会躺在那里睡觉；妇女和孩子们坐在那里边织网，边嬉闹，远眺大海。看到这样的情景你会感觉很快乐。有一个叫卡莫格利亚的小镇，它的小海港在大路下面数百英尺的地方，水手们的家就在那里。很久以前，他们就有沿海贸易船只，与西班牙和其他地方进行贸易往来。从大路上看去，小海港就像是泛着涟漪的大海边缘上的一个小模型，在阳光的照射下闪着光芒。沿着蜿蜒的骡车道下去，你会发现它是一个原始航海小镇的完美缩影，那将是你生平所见的最有咸味、最粗野、最具海盗气息的小地方。大量锈蚀的铁环、锚索、绞盘和旧船桅的断片和碎屑塞满了道路。饱经风浪的船

悠悠泛舟 品岸边风光

---

15 haul [hɔːl] v. = pull 拖
16 patch [pætʃ] n. 片
17 romp [rɔmp] v. 嬉戏喧闹
18 mariner ['mærɪnə] n. 海员，水手
19 time out of mind 很久以前
20 on the margin of 在……边缘
21 dimpled ['dɪmpld] adj. 泛出涟漪的
22 miniature ['mɪnɪətʃə] n. 小画像，小模型
23 seafaring ['siːfeərɪŋ] adj. 航海的
24 piratical [paɪ'rætɪkl] adj. 海盗的
25 capstan ['kæpstən] n. 绞盘
26 flutter ['flʌtə] v. 摆动
27 be drawn out 此处意为"平铺"
28 parapet ['pærəpɪt] n. 栏杆，护墙

rude pier, a few amphibious-looking[29] fellows lie asleep, with their legs dangling[30] over the wall, as though earth or water were all one to them, and if they slipped in, they would float away, dozing comfortably among the fishes; the church is bright with trophies of the sea, and votive offerings[31], in commemoration of[32] escape from storm and shipwreck. The dwellings not immediately abutting[33] on the harbour are approached by blind low archways, and by crooked[34] steps, as if in darkness and in difficulty of access they should be like holds of ships, or inconvenient cabins under water; and everywhere, there is a smell of fish, and sea-weed, and old rope.

The coast-road whence Camoglia is descried so far below, is famous, in the warm season, especially in some parts near Genoa, for fire-flies. Walking there on a dark night, I have seen it made one sparkling firmament[35] by these beautiful insects: so that[36] the distant stars were pale against the flash and glitter that spangled[37] every olive wood and hill-side, and pervaded[38] the whole air.

It was not in such a season, however, that we traversed[39] this road on our way to Rome.

---

29 amphibious-looking　看起来像两栖动物的
30 dangle ['dæŋgl] v.　摇晃地悬挂着
31 votive offerings　祭祀的贡品
32 in commemoration of　= in honor of，纪念……
33 abutting [ə'bʌtɪŋ] adj.　相邻的
34 crooked ['krʊkɪd] adj.　弯曲的
35 firmament ['fɜːməmənt] n.　苍穹，天空
36 so that　= with the result that，因此；结果是
37 spangle ['spæŋgl] vt.　使……闪烁
38 pervade [pə'veɪd] v.　弥漫，遍及
39 traverse ['trəvɜːs] v.　越过，经过

只和水手的衣服，或是在小海港中迎风招展，或是铺在阳光下的石头上晾干。在粗糙的码头护墙上，一些酷似两栖动物的家伙正躺在那里睡觉。他们的腿悬挂在墙外，似乎对他们来说无所谓水与陆。如果掉入水中，他们就随波漂走，在鱼儿们之间舒服地打一会盹。从海上得来的战利品和祭祀的贡品醒目地摆在教堂里，这是为了纪念水手们从暴风雨和船难中能够逃生。水手们的房屋并不是直接与海港相接的，而是通过隐蔽而低矮的拱门和弯曲的台阶逐步靠近海港，如同在黑暗和艰难中，他们摸索着进入船舱或不便利的水下房仓的通道一样。到处是鱼腥味、海藻和破绳索。

从滨海大道可以远远地看到下面的卡莫格利亚。温暖的季节里，卡莫格利亚，尤其是热那亚附近的那些地方，以萤火虫而出名。漆黑的夜晚在那里漫步，我看到那些美丽的昆虫飞在天空中闪闪发光；那闪烁的光芒点缀了每片橄榄树林和每座小山丘，照亮了整个天空，连远处的星星也黯然失色。

然而，在我们前往罗马经

悠悠泛舟 品岸边风光

The middle of January was only just past, and it was very gloomy and dark weather; very wet besides. In crossing the fine pass of Bracco, we encountered such a storm of mist and rain, that we travelled in a cloud the whole way. There might have been[40] no Mediterranean[41] in the world, for anything that we saw of it there, except when a sudden gust of wind[42], clearing the mist before it, for a moment, showed the agitated[43] sea at a great depth below, lashing the distant rocks, and spouting up[44] its foam furiously. The rain was incessant; every brook and torrent was greatly swollen[45]; and such a deafening[46] leaping, and roaring, and thundering of water, I never heard the like of in my life.

Hence, when we came to Spezia, we found that the Magra, an unbridged river on the high-road to Pisa, was too high to be safely crossed in the Ferry Boat, and were fain[47] to wait until the afternoon of next day, when it had, in some degree, subsided. Spezia, however, is a good place to tarry at. by reason, firstly, of[48] its beautiful bay; secondly, of its ghostly Inn; thirdly, of the head-dress of the women, who wear, on one side of their head, a small doll's straw hat,

过这里时，却没赶上这样的季节。此时一月中旬刚过，天气阴郁，还很潮湿。在横越美丽的伯拉科关口时，我们遭遇了浓雾和暴风雨，以至于整个旅途都是阴郁的天气。我们根本看不到地中海的存在，除非突然来一阵狂风吹走眼前浓雾，这样才能看到下面澎湃的海水抽打着远处的岩石，猛烈地喷出它的泡沫。雨不停地下着，每一条小溪和急流都迅速地涨起来，这样震耳欲聋的撞击声、咆哮声和轰鸣声，是我从未听到过的。

当我们到达斯培西亚时，发现马格拉河水位太高，以至于乘渡船不能安全过河，而马格拉河上又没有通往比萨的桥梁。于是，我们欣然接受了事实，等第二天下午水势稍平时再过河。不过，斯培西亚却是个滞留的好地方。首先是因为它那美丽的海湾；其次是恐怖的客栈；最后则是那里女性的

---

40 might have been   might + 完成时，表示对过去的一种推测
41 Mediterranean [ˌmedɪtəˈreɪnɪən] n. 地中海
42 a gust of wind   一阵风
43 agitated [ˈædʒɪteɪtɪd] adj. = excited，激动不安的，这里指海水猛烈、咆哮的
44 spout up   此处意为"喷出"
45 swollen [ˈswəʊlən] adj. 涨水的，涨满的
46 deafening [ˈdefnɪŋ] adj. 震耳欲聋的
47 fain [feɪn] adj. 欣然的，乐意的
48 by reason of   = because of，因为，后面两个"of"之前都省略了"reason"

stuck on to the hair, which is certainly the oddest and most roguish[49] head-gear that ever was invented.

The Magra safely crossed in the Ferry Boat — the passage is not by any means agreeable, when the current is swollen and strong — we arrived at Carrara, within a few hours. In good time next morning, we got some ponies, and went out to see the marble quarries[50].

They are four or five great glens[51], running up into a range of lofty hills, until they can run no longer, and are stopped by being abruptly strangled by Nature. The quarries, 'or caves,' as they call them there, are so many openings, high up in the hills, on either side of these passes, where they blast and excavate[52] for marble: which may turn out[53] good or bad: may make a man's fortune very quickly, or ruin him by the great expense of[54] working what is worth nothing. Some of these caves were opened by the ancient Romans, and remain as they left them to this hour. Many others are being worked at this moment; others are to be begun tomorrow, next week, next month; others are unbought, unthought of; and marble enough for more ages than have passed since the place was resorted to, lies hidden everywhere: patiently

头饰。她们在头的一侧佩戴着玩偶草帽，这种草帽的设计应该是最怪异、最顽皮的了。

我们乘渡船安全地渡过了马格拉河——当水流湍急、河水上涨时，渡河一点也不令人惬意——数小时后，我们到达了卡拉拉。第二天早上，我们找来了几匹小马去参观采石场。

采石场从四五个巨大的峡谷，向上一直延伸到高山上，直到被大自然的鬼斧神工挡住去路，不能再延伸为止。采石场，或者当地人所谓的"窑洞"，其实就是很多山上的洞穴。人们可以在这些洞穴中的任何一个洞口引爆、开凿大理石。这种开采的结果可好可坏：它可以使一个人暴富，也可以使一个人倾其所有，却血本无归。这些山洞有些是罗马人开采的，至今仍保留着被遗弃时的样子；另外有许多山洞是新近开采的；有一些可能会在明天、下周、下个月开始开采；还有的尚未被人承包、未被考虑到。自被人们发现

---

49 roguish ['rəʊgɪʃ] adj. 捣蛋的，顽皮的
50 marble quarry 此处意为"采石场"
51 glen [glen] n. 溪谷，幽谷
52 excavate ['ekskəveɪt] v. 挖开，凿通
53 turn out 结果是，原来是，这里可不译出
54 by the great expense of 付出很大的代价

awaiting[55] its time of discovery.

以来，这里就有足够多的大理石隐藏在各处，供未来的人开采，耐心地等待被发现的时刻。

From *Pictures from Italy* (1844)

---

55 **await** [ə'weɪt] *v.* 等候，准备……以待

悠悠泛舟　品岸边风光

含英咀华

在选文中作者描写了位于热那亚和斯培西亚之间的滨海大道一带的美丽风光，在描写中，文笔细腻流畅，带有浓郁的海岸气息。从作者的描绘中，我们可以领略滨海大道波澜壮阔的景象，体会当地渔民的生活状态。

Janna Graber

杰娜·格雷博

杰娜·格雷博是美国自由记者，美国旅行作家协会的一员，曾为*Parade, Outside, Redbook, Reader's Digest, the Chicago Tribune*等多家国家报刊撰稿。目前她是《环游世界旅行》(*Go World Travel Magazine*)的责任编辑，这是一本展示全世界最精彩的人与地点的国际性杂志。杰娜在科罗拉多州获得国际关系社会学的学位，能讲一口流利的德语，擅长游记散文、随笔，作品富有现代气息。

Kayaking[1] the Fjords[2] of New Zealand

泛舟新西兰峡湾

I'm beginning to wonder if I've landed in a country of maniacs[3]. At least, that's the impression I get while walking through the narrow avenues of Queenstown, New Zealand.

The alpine[4] region looks tranquil[5] enough at first glance. Tiny Queens-town, population 17,000, sits nestled on the shores of beautiful Lake Wakatipu in the middle of a lush valley. The mighty[6] Remarkables Mountain Range surrounds the small community, rising[7] up like sharp-edged giants from the rich, dark earth. It's a stunning geography that any city would envy.

Queenstown itself has an Aspen-like feel, a fashionable community with a small-town heart. Chic[8] resorts sit among modest hillside homes with window box flowers and tidy yards, and the active city streets reveal orderly shops and outdoor cafés.

我开始怀疑我是否来到了一个疯狂的国度。至少，那是我漫步于狭长的新西兰皇后镇林荫大街时的印象。

第一眼望去，这片高山地区显得那么安宁。皇后镇是一个拥有17,000人的小镇，就像一位温柔美丽的少女，轻轻地依偎在美丽的瓦尔蒂普湖畔，坐落于绿树葱葱的山谷中。雄伟的卓越山脉环绕着整个小镇，似棱角锋利的巨人从富饶的黑色大地上缓缓站起来。小镇得天独厚的地理位置令任何城市都艳羡。

皇后镇本身有一种白杨的气质，它是个有一个小核心商业区的时尚社区。别致的度假胜地坐落在山腰，每个房子的窗台都摆满了美丽鲜艳的花开，且院落整洁。商店和户

---

1 kayak ['kaɪæk] n. 皮划艇，独木舟。这里做动词，表示"乘舟游览"
2 fjord [fjɔːd] n. 峡湾(峭壁间的狭长的海湾)
3 maniac ['meɪnɪæk] n. 疯子，此处意为"疯狂"
4 alpine ['ælpaɪn] adj. 高山的
5 tranquil ['træŋkwɪl] adj. = peaceful，安静的，宁静的
6 mighty ['maɪtɪ] adj. 强有力的
7 rising 现在分词作状语，表伴随
8 chic [ʃiːk] adj. 别致的

But a closer look uncovers a unique side of this mountain community, for tucked[9] in between small restaurants and tourist stores are dozens of "adventure companies" offering[10] everything from heli-hiking[11] and hang-gliding[12] to skydiving[13] and jet boating.

Although well-known for its peaceful sheep-ranching[14] and rural tradition, this island nation of 3.8 million has been called the "Adventure Destination" of the world. Thousands flock to the southwestern tip of the South Island each year, where tiny Queenstown (aka "Adventure Capitol") serves up experiences never to be forgotten.

Fiordland[15] (as the Kiwis spell it) National Park is an isolated area known for its awe-inspiring fjords, dramatic mountain peaks, tumbling[16] waterfalls and abundant wildlife. In this "Switzerland of the South Pacific," tall mountains drop dramatically into the dark seas in a stunning display of nature's majesty. No wonder so many movies, including "Lord of the Rings[17]", have chosen to film here.

外咖啡厅整齐地排列在热闹的城市街道上。

但是，仔细一看，就会发现这个山区小城独一无二的一面，在小饭馆和旅游商店中夹杂着几十个"冒险公司"，它们经营各种活动项目，包括滑雪运动、滑翔运动、高空跳伞运动以及喷气式汽艇活动等等。

虽然以宁静优雅的牧场和独特的乡村传统而闻名，但这个只有380万人口的岛国却被称为世界的"冒险之都"。每年都有成千上万的人来到南岛的西南部，在皇后镇体验令人终生难忘的冒险之旅。

峡湾国家公园是一个与世隔绝的地区，以其令人震撼的峡湾、雄伟壮丽的山峦、气势宏大的瀑布和丰富的野生生物而闻名遐迩。在这个素有"南太平洋瑞士"之称的地方，高山陡然跌入深海，这一震撼景象尽显自然的神奇。这也难怪

9 tuck [tʌk] v. 挤进
10 offering 现在分词作后置定语，修饰前面的 "adventure companies"
11 heli-hiking n. 滑雪的一种，是人乘直升飞机达到山顶，再从山上滑雪下来的运动
12 hang-gliding n. 悬挂式滑翔运动
13 skydiving n. 空中杂技跳伞，花样跳伞
14 sheep-ranching n. 养殖羊，此处引申为"牧场"
15 fiordland n. 峡湾，位于新西兰南岛
16 tumbling ['tʌmblɪŋ] adj. 歪斜状的，此处意为"滚滚而下"
17 Lord of the Rings 此处指电影《指环王》

The park is located in a remote region of the island, and we wonder how to get there. Should we drive? Take a bus tour? Eventually we decide on a two-night boat cruise[18] on Doubtful Sound, one of the less-traveled regions of the park. The cruise company will provide the transportation.

But Doubtful Sound is not easy to reach. It takes four hours and a well-orchestrated journey involving two buses, a boat and a van for us to reach the deep waters of the Sound. By the time[19] we reach our ship, the Fiordland Navigator, civilization is left far behind[20].

Within minutes we're tossed room keys, shown our simple but shipshape[21] cabins, and given safety instructions. Then it's time to head into the fjords. A light rain is falling, but the air is not cold as we stand on deck, watching nature's most incredible show pass by.

Lush green mountains rise majestically from the water. Dreamy white clouds drift along their massive midriffs[22], while the peaks reach above the cottony[23] mass toward the sky. It's like living in a beautiful postcard.

Occasionally, dolphins swim near, jumping and leaping, while tiny penguins float nearby.

包括《指环王》在内的许多电影都选择在此拍摄。

国家公园坐落在小岛的一个偏远的地区，我们在想如何才能到达那里。驾车前往？坐观光车？最终我们决定在神奇湾坐巡游船两日游，那里是公园里游人较少的地区。巡游公司提供交通。

然而神奇湾并不容易到达。我们精心策划的旅途中需要乘坐两辆巴士、一艘船、一辆篷车，共花了4个小时才到达峡湾的深水区。当我们上了峡湾领航员号时，喧闹的文明世界被远远地抛在了身后。

没过几分钟，我们就拿到了房门钥匙，看了我们的住所，那是简单而整洁的小木屋，还有人给我们做了安全说明。接着该是奔赴峡湾的时候了。天公不作美，下起了小雨，但天气并不冷，我们站在甲板上，观赏着沿途令人心旷神怡的风光。

郁郁葱葱的高山威严地屹立在水中，山峰直入云霄，梦幻般的白云缭绕在巨大的山腰。这风景就像一张美丽的明信片。

偶尔会有海豚游近，欢快地在水上跳跃，小企鹅

---

18 cruise [kru:z] n. 巡航，巡游
19 by the time ＝when，引导时间状语从句，表示"当……的时候"
20 leave behind 留于身后，走后留下
21 shipshape ['ʃɪpʃeɪp] adj. 整洁的，并然有序的
22 midriff ['mɪdrɪf] n. [解]膈，中腹部，此处意为"山腰"
23 cottony ['kɒtnɪ] adj. 棉花状的

The ship is in search of a calm inlet[24] so we can drop anchor[25] and go out in kayaks, allowing us more intimate contact with nature. It is almost dusk when we find a protected cove and the ship drops anchor. A warm rain falls with dreamlike stillness, while a thick haze[26] covers the sea, giving the water a heavenly quality.

The crew urges us on. They pull out dozens of kayaks as well as two tender boats. Those who want to explore on their own will[27] use kayaks; others will explore in the craft. My parents opt for the boats; I head toward the kayaks.

Immediately, I feel overwhelmed[28] by the stunning scene surrounding me. I stop paddling and coast[29], delighting in[30] what I see. All is silent except for the in-and-out swoosh[31] of kayak paddles.

Then it dawns on[32] me: this is what brings people to this island nation — the chance to throw away cares and rediscover the thrill[33] of nature, beauty and even life itself.

I hug the shoreline, awed[34] by the vast numbers of green ferns[35] and leafy trees.

24 inlet ['ɪnlet] n. 水湾，小港
25 drop anchor 船停锚，抛锚
26 haze [heɪz] n. 薄雾
27 on one's own will 愿意地，此处的"will"是名词，表"意愿"
28 overwhelmed ['əʊvə'welmd] adj. 被淹没的，被压倒的，此处引申为"为……所倾倒的"
29 coast [kəʊst] v. 靠惯性滑行
30 delight in 以……为乐
31 swoosh [swuːʃ] n. 哗哗声，嗖嗖声
32 dawn on/upon sb. 变得（为人所）明白
33 thrill [θrɪl] n. 激动，狂喜
34 awed [ɔːd] adj. =surprised，此处意为"惊叹的"
35 fern [fɜːn] n. 羊齿植物，蕨类植物

也在周围游来游去。我们希望能找到一个平静的水湾，这样我们就可以停船换乘独木舟出游，更亲密地接触自然。大约黄昏时分，我们的船停在了一个安全的港湾里，船就抛锚了。此时天空飘着毛毛细雨，更添梦幻色彩，浓雾笼罩着海面，令这片水域如天堂一般。

船员们鼓励我们继续前行。他们驶出几十只独木舟，两艘巡检船。愿意自己去探险游玩的可以使用独木舟，不愿意的可以坐在船上游览。我的父母选择了坐船，我则踏上了独木舟。

刹那间，我就为周围令人叹为观止的景色倾倒了，我停下桨任舟漂行，愉悦地欣赏着风景，除了独木舟撞击水声外，四处一片静悄悄。

我逐渐领悟到：抛开忧虑，重拾自然带给人们的震撼，重新认识美丽，重新领悟生命本身的意义——这些才是吸引人们来到这个岛国的原因。

我于湖滨停舟，为大片绿色蕨类植物和郁郁葱葱的树林惊叹。这些生长在陡峭的山坡上的植被是如此茂密以至于我

悠悠泛舟 品岸边风光

The vegetation[36] is so thick on the steep mountainsides that I can't even see the earth below it. A bird flits[37] from the shelter of one dripping tree to another, then disappears in the foliage[38].

Huge drops of water fall on my face as I paddle[39] underneath tree limbs[40] sticking out over the water. Moss covers the thick limbs. I can see the rocks below in the crystal clear[41] water, and pull in closer for a look at the plant life that has grown together, giving the illusion[42] of a thick green carpet covering the mountainside.

Eventually, I pull back out into the open Sound. I can see my parents in the boat, listening intently as their guide describes the local fauna[43]. Even through the drizzle[44], I can see the smiles on their faces. My mom waves to me, nudging[45] my dad and pointing me out. I laugh and signal back, content in my kayak. It is a shared experience that we will always remember.

I stare up[46] into the torrential[47] skies and watch huge drops pouring, one by one, into the sea. I feel tiny in this land of natural wonders.

36 vegetation [ˌvedʒɪˈteɪʃn] n. 植物，草木
37 flit [flɪt] vt. 掠过，轻快地飞过
38 foliage [ˈfəʊlɪɪdʒ] n. 叶子(总称)，这里指丛林
39 paddle [ˈpædl] v. 划桨，此处为"停靠"
40 limb [lɪm] n. 树枝
41 crystal clear = entirely clear，完全透明的
42 illusion [ɪˈluːʒn] n. 幻觉，错觉
43 fauna [ˈfɔːnə] n. 动物群
44 drizzle [ˈdrɪzl] n. 细雨
45 nudge [nʌdʒ] v. (用肘)轻推；轻撞
46 stare up = stare at and look up 仰头凝视
47 torrential [təˈrenʃl] adj. 猛烈的

都看不见下面的泥土。一只小鸟掠过沾满露水的树梢，继而消失在丛林中。

雨下大了，雨点落在脸上，我停靠到一棵树下，这棵树的树枝伸到了水面上，粗枝上覆盖着苔藓。透过清澈如晶的水面水下的岩石清晰可见，再靠近一点可以看见簇生在一起的植被，这会令人产生错觉，就像大山的身上披了一条墨绿的毯子。

最终，我返回到了广阔的峡湾中，看见父母正在船上专心致志地听导游描述当地的动物群。尽管下着毛毛细雨，我依然能看清他们脸上绽放的笑容。母亲向我挥挥手，并用肘轻推父亲，指给他看，我笑着作了回应，在独木舟中一种满足感油然而生。这次与家人共同度过的美好时光我们将会永远铭刻在心。

我仰头凝望着滚滚乌云，看着大雨倾盆而下，一滴一滴地落入海洋中。在充满自然奇观的土地上，我觉得自己是如此渺小。这种感觉是如此震撼以至于我忘记了打在脸上的雨水，此刻一切都不重要了。因为现在，我正在我黄色独木舟上，划

The experience is so powerful that I ignore the streams of water running down my face. Right now, it's unimportant. For now, I am in a yellow kayak, paddling through the protective cove[48] of Doubtful Sound. I am in awe of[49] the world and the gift that New Zealand has given me.

And for once in my life, words seem woefully[50] inadequate.

From *EnCompass AAA Magazine* (2003)

桨穿过神奇湾的安全港湾。我为这个世界，为新西兰给我的礼物而惊叹。

这还是我生命里第一次觉得，语言是如此的苍白无力。

---

48 protective cove   安全港湾
49 in awe of   原意指"对……存敬畏之心"，此处引申为"为……而惊叹"
50 woefully ['wəʊfəlɪ]   *adv.*   悲伤地，不幸地，这里指"语言是如此苍白无力"

含英咀华

杰娜·格雷博的足迹遍布世界各地，她以特殊的视角描写自己游历各地的所见所闻，并将自己的亲身感受融入作品当中，阅读她的作品犹如亲眼看见这些美丽的景色，感受到投入大自然中的激情和快乐。

异域情怀
国各有别

A Glance at the Country
匈牙利一瞥

Rural Life in England
英国的乡村生活

Spain
西班牙之旅

Kenya: Patchwork of Experiences
肯尼亚——缤纷印象

H. Tornai De Kover

H.托奈・德・考文

H.托奈・德・考文，他留给这个世界的信息太少，我们甚至不知道他的出生地，不知道他的生卒年代，也不知道他经历过怎样的生活。他唯一留下的就是在1911年出版的著作《一窥匈牙利众地》（*Peeps at Many Lands: Hungary, 1911*）。

A Glance at the Country

Hungary consists of Hungary proper, with Transylvania[1] (which had independent rule at one time), Croatia[2] and Slavonia[3] (which have been added), and the town of Fiume[4] on the shores of the Adriatic Sea[5].

The lowlands are exceedingly beautiful in the northeast and west, where the great mountain peaks rise into the clear blue sky or are hidden by big white clouds, but no beauty can be compared to the young green waving corn or the ripe ears when swaying[6] gently in the breeze. One sees miles and miles of corn, with only a tree here and there to mark the distances, and one cannot help[7] comparing the landscape to a green sea, for the wind makes long silky waves, which make the field appear to rise and fall like the ocean. In the heat of midday the mirage[8], or, as the Hungarians call

匈牙利一瞥

匈牙利是由特兰西瓦尼亚（曾经独立）、克罗地亚和斯拉沃尼亚（后加入的）以及亚得里来海岸城市阜姆组成的。

匈牙利东北部和西部的低地格外迷人，那里有壮观的山脉。山峰或直耸入明朗蔚蓝的天空，或躲入无际的白云之中，但没有什么能媲美随风舞动的生机勃勃的玉米或那微风中轻轻摇曳的成熟了的玉米穗。一眼望去，尽是绵延数公里的玉米地，只有标识距离的几棵树散布其间，让人不禁觉得这景色就像一片绿色的海洋，因为风吹过便形成了一股股如丝般柔长的碧波，看上去像极了大海中高低起伏的波

---

1 Transylvania [,trænsɪl'veɪnɪə] *n.* 特兰西瓦尼亚。特兰西瓦尼亚原为匈牙利王国之领土，在土耳其攻占布达佩斯后，成为匈牙利贵族的避难所，居民们抗拒土耳其文化的入侵，在一战后，1919年举行全民公投，正式成为罗马尼亚的一部分

2 Croatia [krəʊ'eɪʃɪə] *n.* 克罗地亚，南斯拉夫成员共和国名，于1991年6月25日宣布脱离原南斯拉夫独立

3 Slavonia [slə'vəʊnɪə] *n.* 斯拉沃尼亚（南斯拉夫北部一地区）

4 Fiume ['fju:meɪ] *n.* 阜姆（原南斯拉夫西北部港市里耶卡）

5 the Adriatic Sea: *n.* 亚得里亚海，位于意大利、斯洛文尼亚、克罗地亚、波斯尼亚和黑塞哥维那、黑山和阿尔巴尼亚之间，是地中海的一个属海，南部通过奥特朗托海峡与伊奥尼亚海相连

6 sway [sweɪ] *v.* 使摇动，此处译为"摇曳"

7 cannot help = cannot prevent or avoid，不禁

8 mirage ['mɪrɑ:ʒ] *n.* 海市蜃楼

it, "Délibáb," appears and shows wonderful rivers, villages, cool green woods — all floating in the air. Sometimes one sees hundreds of white oxen and church towers, and, to make the picture still more confusing and wonderful, it is all seen upside down[9]. This, the richest part of the country, is situated between the rivers Danube[10] and Theiss[11], and runs right down to the borders of Servia[12]. Two thirds of Hungary consists of mountainous districts, but one third has the richest soil in Europe.

Great rivers run through the heart of the country, giving it the fertility which is its great source of wealth. The great lowlands, or "Alfold," as the Magyars[13] call them, are surrounded by a chain of mountains whose heights are nearly equal to some Alpine[14] districts. There are three principal mountain ranges— the Tátra, Mátra, and Fátra — and four principal rivers-the Danube, Theiss, Drave, and Save. Hungary is called the land of the three mountains and four rivers, and the emblem[15] of these form the chief feature in the coat-of-arms[16] of the country.

浪。正午时分还会出现海市蜃楼，天空中浮现出奇异的溪流、村庄和清爽的绿树，匈牙利人称之为"Délibáb"。有时也会出现成千上万的白色牛群和教堂，更加神奇和美妙的是，整个画面是颠倒的。这片匈牙利最富庶的土地位于多瑙河与蒂萨河之间，靠近塞尔维亚边境。匈牙利境内三分之二的面积是山地，但另外的三分之一却拥有着欧洲最肥沃的土地。

几条主要河流流经这个国家中心地带，是该地区富庶的源泉。被马扎尔人称为"大平原"的低地，四面环山，其山脉几乎达到一些阿尔卑斯山区的高度。共有三大主要山脉：塔特拉山、马特拉山、法特拉山；四大主要河流：多瑙河、蒂萨河、德拉瓦河和萨瓦河。匈牙利被称为"三山四河大地"，这些山脉河流的图案也构成了这个国家国徽的主要特征。

---

9 upside down　= with the upper part underneath instead of on top, 颠倒
10 Danube ['dænju:b]　n.　多瑙河。多瑙河在欧洲仅次于伏尔加河，是第二长河，它发源于德国西南部的黑林山的东坡，自西向东流经奥地利、捷克、斯洛伐克、匈牙利、塞尔维亚、保加利亚、罗马尼亚，在罗马尼亚的苏利纳附近注入黑海。它流经9个国家，是世界上干流流经国家最多的河流。支流延伸至瑞士、波兰、意大利、波斯尼亚—黑塞哥维那、捷克以及斯洛文尼亚、摩尔多瓦等7国，最后在罗马尼亚东部的苏利纳注入黑海
11 Theiss [taɪs]　n.　<德>=Tisza, 蒂萨河[东欧]（多瑙河支流）
12 Servia ['sə:vjə]　n.　Serbia（塞尔维亚）的旧称
13 Magyar ['mægɪɑ:]　n.　马扎尔人（匈牙利的基本居民）
14 Alpine ['ælpaɪn]　adj.　阿尔卑斯山的
15 emblem ['embləm]　n.　象征，符号，图案
16 coat-of-arms　n.　（用做家族、城镇、大学等的标志）盾形纹章，盾徽

异域情怀 国各有别

The Carpathian[17] range of mountains stretches from the northwest along the north and down the east, encircling the lowlands and sending forth[18] rivers and streams to water the plains. These mountains are of a gigantic bulk and breadth; they are covered with fir and pine trees, and in the lower regions with oaks and many other kinds. The peaks of the high Tátra are about 9,000 feet high, and, of course, are bare of[19] any vegetation, being snow-covered even in summer-time. On the well-sheltered sides of these mountains numerous baths is to be found, and they abound inmineral waters. Another curious feature is the deep lakes called "Tengerszem" (Eyes of the Sea). According to folklore they are connected with the sea, and wonderful beings live in them. However, it is so far true that they are really of astonishing depth. The summer up in the Northern Carpathians is very short, the nights always cold, and there is plenty of rain to water the rich vegetation of the forests. Often even in the summer there are snowstorms and a very low temperature.

The Northeastern Carpathians include a range of lower hill running down to the so-called Hegyalja, where the wonderful vine which produces the vine of Tokay[20] is grown. The south-eastern range of the Carpathians divides the

喀尔巴阡山脉从西北部经过整个北部一直延伸到东部地区，环绕整个低地地区，送来清流溪水灌溉土地。这些山脉山体巨大，山上一般生有冷杉和松树，地势低的地方还会有橡树及其他种类的树木。塔特拉山脉海拔约9000英尺，当然这么高的山顶上是没有植被的，即使在夏季也被积雪覆盖着。而在遮蔽良好的山上面可以找到无数富含矿物质的温泉。这些山脉的另一显著特征是山上有被称为"海洋之眼"的深湖。相传这些湖都连通着大海，里面有奇异的生物。然而，目前为止我们所能肯定的只是这些湖泊的确深得惊人。喀尔巴阡山脉北部地区的夏季非常短，夜晚总是清冷的，那里雨量充沛，足够浇灌丰富的森林植被。即使在夏天也经常会出现暴风雪及低温天气。

喀尔巴阡山脉的东北部地区有一片较低的山脉一直延伸到一个我们叫做里亚拉加的地方，用来酿制托卡伊葡萄酒的葡萄就产自这里。其东南部山

---

17 Carpathian [kɑ:'peɪθɪən] *adj.* 喀尔巴阡山脉的
18 send forth = send forward，送来
19 be bare of = without
20 Tokay [təʊ'keɪ] *n.* （匈牙利产的）葡萄酒

county of Máramaros from Erdély (Transylvania). The main part of this country is mountainous and rugged, but here also there is wonderful scenery. Everything is still very wild in these parts of the land, and the mineral waters abound everywhere, the bathing places are very primitive.

The only seaport the country possesses is Fiume, which was given to Hungary by Maria Theresa, who wanted to give Hungary the chance of developing into a commercial nation. Besides the deep but small mountain lakes, there are several large ones; among these the most important is the Balaton[21], which, although narrow, is about fifty miles long. Along its borders there are summer bathing places, considered very healthy for children. Very good wine is produced here, as in most parts of Hungary which are hilly, but not situated too high up among the mountains. The lake of Balaton is renowned for[22] a splendid kind of fresh-water fish, the Fogas[23]. It is considered the best fish after trout — some even prefer it and it grows to a good size.

The chief river of Hungary is the Danube, and the whole of Hungary is included in its basin. It runs through the heart of the country, forming many islands; the greatest is called the Csallóköz, and has over a hundred villages on it. One of

脉把马拉马勒什郡从特兰西瓦尼隔开。匈牙利大部分地区都多山，崎岖不平，但这里也有美妙的风光。这片土地上的一切都还处于原生态，温泉水资源丰富，海滨浴场尚未开发。

匈牙利唯一的港口是阜姆，当年玛利亚·特丽萨把它送给了匈牙利，她想给匈牙利一个成为商业国家的机会。除了山上那些极深的小湖泊外，匈牙利还有几个大的湖泊，其中最重要的是巴拉顿湖，虽然它很窄，却有50英里长，沿湖边有许多夏日海滨浴场，据说在这里洗浴对儿童的健康很有好处。就像匈牙利大多数多山而山势不太高的地区一样，这里也盛产美酒。巴拉顿湖以盛产淡水梭鲈鱼而闻名，鲈鱼是除鲑鱼外最好的鱼——有些人甚至更喜欢鲈鱼，而且这种鱼能长到很大的个头。

匈牙利的主要河流是多瑙河，整个匈牙利都在它的流域内，该河流经匈牙利的心脏地区，形成了许多岛屿，其中

---

21 Balaton ['bælətən]   n.   巴拉顿湖，位于匈牙利首都布达佩斯西南约90千米处，外多瑙山地包科尼山东南侧，是东北—西南走向断层形成的湖泊，是匈牙利和中欧最大的湖泊。巴拉顿湖又名匈牙利海。湖形狭长，长78千米，宽1.5～15千米，面积600平方千米

22 be renowned for   = be famous for

23 Fogas ['fɔgəs]   n.   匈牙利梭鲈

the prettiest and most cultivated of the islands is St. Margaret's Isle, near Budapest[24], which has latterly been joined to the mainland by a bridge. Some years ago only steamers conveyed the visitors to it; these still exist, but now carriages can drive on to the island too. It is a beautiful park, where the people of Budapest seek the shade of the splendid old trees. Hot sulfur[25] springs are to be found on the island, and there is a bath for the use of visitors.

The Danube leaves Hungary at Orsova, and passes through the so-called Iron Gates[26]. The scenery is very beautiful and wild in that part, and there are many points where it is exceedingly picturesque[27], especially between Vienna and Budapest. It is navigable[28] for steamships, and so is the next largest river[29], the Theiss. This river begins its course in the Southeastern Carpathians, right up among the snow-peaks, amid wild and beautiful scenery, and it eventually empties its waters into the Danube at Titel. The three largest rivers of Hungary feed the Danube, and by that means[30] reach the Black Sea[31].

最大的岛叫卡萨克罗，岛上有一百多个村庄。最漂亮且最肥沃的岛是圣玛格丽特岛，该岛靠近布达佩斯，最近刚建了连通小岛与大陆的跨河大桥。多年前只有蒸汽船载客入岛，现在马车也可通往岛上。小岛就像一个漂亮的公园，布达佩斯市民可以在那里享受古树的荫凉。岛上还有硫磺泉，游客可以享受一下硫磺浴。

多瑙河在奥索瓦河流出匈牙利境内，流经铁门。那里非常美而且充满原始的味道，很多河段都风景如画，尤其是维也纳和布达佩斯之间的河段。多瑙河上可以行驶轮船，第二大河蒂萨河上也可以。该河发源于喀尔巴阡山脉东南部，然后北上跨越雪山，流经粗犷原始的美景，最后在小城提特里流入多瑙河。匈牙利的三大河流都注入多瑙河，最后通过多瑙河注入黑海。

24 Budapest [ˌb(j)uːdəˈpest] 布达佩斯（匈牙利首都）
25 sulfur [ˈsʌlfə] n. 硫，硫磺
26 Iron Gates n. 铁门（位于原南斯拉夫与罗马尼亚两国间多瑙河上的一峡谷）
27 picturesque [ˌpɪktʃəˈresk] adj. 风景如画的
28 navigable [ˈnævɪɡəbl] adj. 可通船的
29 so+助动词+主语结构 表示前一肯定事实也适用于后者，这里指 the next largest river is also navigable for steamships
30 by that means = in that way
31 the Black Sea n. 黑海，欧洲东南部和亚洲小亚细亚半岛之间的内海。因水色深暗、多风暴而得名。黑海向西通过博斯普鲁斯海峡、马尔马拉海、达达尼尔海峡与地中海相通，向北经刻赤海峡与亚速海相连。黑海形似椭圆形。东西最长1150千米，南北最宽611千米，中部最窄263千米，面积42.2万平方千米，海岸线长约3400千米。平均水深1315米，最大水深2210米

Hungary lies under the so-called temperate zone, but there does not seem much temperance[32] in the climate when we think of the terrible, almost Siberian winters that come often enough and the heat waves occasioning[33] frequent droughts in the lowlands. The summer is short in the Carpathians; usually in the months of August and September the weather is the most settled. June and July are often rainy — sometimes snowstorms cause the barometer[34] to fall tremendously. In the mountain districts there is a great difference between the temperature of the daytime and that of the night. All those who go to the Carpathians do well to take winter and Alpine clothing with them.

From *Hungary* (1911)

匈牙利地处温带地区，但气候并不怎么温和，因为这里的冬天经常是西伯利亚式的严酷，而在夏季热干风经常袭击这里的低地。喀尔巴阡山区的夏季很短暂，基本就是八、九两个月，六月、七月是雨季，有时暴风雨会导致气压急速下降。山区里白天跟夜晚的温差很大。想去喀尔巴阡山地区的人最好穿带上冬装和爬山服。

32 temperance ['tempərəns] *n.* （气温、气候的）温和
33 occasion [ə'keɪʒən] *v.* 致使，引起
34 barometer [bə'rɒmɪtə] *n.* 气压表

含英咀华

匈牙利国家起源于东方游牧民族——马扎尔游牧部落，"匈牙利"是"十个部落"的意思。它位于欧洲中部喀尔巴阡山盆地。北面与斯洛伐克交界，东北面和东面与乌克兰和罗马尼亚毗邻，南面与原南斯拉夫和克罗地亚接壤，西南面和西面与斯洛文尼亚和奥地利相连，是一个内陆国家。选文中作者从整体着眼，淡化细节的描写，向读者介绍了匈牙利的概况，包括流经匈牙利的主要河流、主要山脉、主要港口以及那里的气候特点。

Washington Irving

华盛顿·欧文

华盛顿·欧文，作者介绍见 "*Alhambra*"。

Rural Life in England

英国的乡村生活

In some countries the large cities absorb the wealth and fashion of the nation; they are the only fixed abodes of elegant and intelligent society, and the country is inhabited almost entirely by boorish[1] peasantry[2]. In England, on the contrary, the metropolis[3] is mere gathering place, or general rendezvous[4], of the polite classes, where they devote a small portion of the year to[5] a hurry of gayety[6] and dissipation[7], and, having indulged[8] this kind of carnival, return again to the apparently more congenial[9] habits of rural life. The various orders of society are therefore diffused[10] over the whole surface of the kingdom, and the most retired[11] neighborhoods afford specimens of the different ranks.

The English, in fact, are strongly gifted with[12] the rural feeling. They possess a quick sensibility to the beauties of nature, and a keen relish[13] for the pleasures and employments of the

在一些国家，大城市是国家财富的集散地，是时尚中心，是众多文人雅士唯一的固定居所，而乡下居住的全是乡野村夫。在英国，情况却恰恰相反，大都市仅仅是文雅阶层聚集或聚会的场所。每年只有一小段时间，人们在那里匆匆寻求快乐和消遣，并沉迷在这种狂欢的气氛当中，之后，便又回到乡村，去享受那悠然自得的乡间生活。因而各种社会阶层的人遍布全国，最僻静的居住区为我们提供了各个阶层生活的真实写照。

事实上，英国人天生就有很浓的乡村情节。他们能快速感知自然之美，沉浸于乡间的情趣之中，热爱乡村的工作。这

---

1 boorish ['buərɪʃ] *adj.* = vulgar，粗野的，粗俗的
2 peasantry ['pezntrɪ] *n.* 农民（总称）
3 metropolis [mə'trɒpəlɪs] *n.* 大都市
4 rendezvous ['rɒndɪvu:] *n.* 约会，约会地点，此处意为"聚集或聚会的场所"
5 devote sth. to 把（时间、精力等）专用于（某项目、活动等）
6 gayety ['geɪətɪ] *n.* 愉快，轻快
7 dissipation [,dɪsɪ'peɪʃn] *n.* = pleasure，娱乐，消遣
8 indulge [ɪn'dʌldʒ] *v.* 纵情于，放任
9 congenial [kən'dʒi:nɪəl] *adj.* 同性质的，适意的
10 diffuse [dɪ'fju:s] *v.* 散播，此处意为"遍布"
11 retired [rɪ'taɪəd] *adj.* 幽静的，僻静的
12 be gifted with 天生具有
13 relish ['relɪʃ] *n.* 兴趣，爱好

country. This passion seems inherent in them. Even the inhabitants of cities, born and brought up among brick walls and bustling[14] streets, enter with facility[15] into rural habits, and evince[16] tact[17] for rural occupation. The merchant has his snug[18] retreat in the vicinity of[19] the metropolis, where he often displays as much pride and zeal in the cultivation of his flower-garden, and the maturing of his fruits, as he does in the conduct of his business, and the success of a commercial enterprise. Even those less fortunate individuals who are doomed to pass their lives in the midst of din and traffic, contrive to[20] have something that shall remind them of the green aspect of nature. In the most dark and dingy[21] quarters of the city, the drawing-room[22] window resembles frequently a bank of flowers; every spot capable of vegetation has its grass-plot and flower-bed; and every square its mimic[23] park, laid out with picturesque taste, and gleaming with refreshing verdure[24].

Those who see the Englishman only in town are apt to[25] form an unfavorable opinion

种感情是英国人与生俱来的。即使是从小在城市高墙间和熙熙攘攘的街道上长大的城里人，也能迅速融入乡村的生活，对乡村的风俗习惯应对自如。多数商人在乡村都有一处静谧舒适的小屋，在那里他们养花种草，收获丰硕的果实，并对此表现出就像他们在商海中取得成功时所表现出来的那种骄傲和热情。即使那些注定在喧嚣的城市中央度过一生的不幸之人，也竭尽全力弄一些东西让自己永远铭记大自然的那一抹绿。在大城市黑暗肮脏的角落里，客厅里时常摆满了鲜花，千姿百态，姹紫嫣红；每一片空地，只要土壤不太贫瘠，就会绿草茵茵，鲜花满地；每一个广场，都伴有微型公园，郁郁葱葱，如诗如画，清新怡然。

有些人只看到了生活在城市里的英国人，往往会对英国人的社会性格形成不好的

---

14 bustling ['bʌslɪŋ] adj. = busy，熙熙攘攘的，忙乱的
15 with facility 容易地
16 evince [ɪ'vɪns] v. 表明具有，显示出（品质、才能、特色等）
17 tact [tækt] n. 机智，手法。evince tact: 此处引申为 "对乡村的风俗习惯应对自如"
18 snug [snʌg] adj. = comfortable，舒适的
19 in the vicinity of 邻近，附近
20 contrive to = manage to，设法办到
21 dingy ['dɪn(d)ʒɪ] adj. 肮脏的，不干净的
22 drawing-room [drɔɪŋruːm] n. 客厅
23 mimic ['mɪmɪk] adj. 小型的
24 verdure ['vɜːdʒə, -djə] n. 翠绿
25 be apt to do sth. = be likely to do sth.，易于……，有……的倾向

of his social character. He is either absorbed in[26] business or distracted by[27] the thousand engagements that dissipate[28] time, thought, and feeling in this huge metropolis. He has, therefore, too commonly a look of hurry and abstraction. Wherever he happens to be, he is on the point of going somewhere else; at the moment he is talking on one subject, his mind is wandering to another; and while paying a friendly visit[29], he is calculating how he shall economize time so as to pay the other visits allotted[30] in the morning. An immense metropolis, like London, is calculated to make men selfish and uninteresting. In their casual and transient[31] meetings they can but deal briefly in commonplaces. They present but the cold superficies[32] of character — its rich and genial[33] qualities have no time to be warmed into a flow.

It is in the country that the Englishman gives scope to his natural feelings. He breaks loose gladly from the cold formalities[34] and negative civilities of town, throws off his habits of shy reserve, and becomes joyous and free-hearted. He manages to collect round him all the conveniences and elegancies of polite

印象。在大都市里，要么忙于工作，要么为耗时、费神、浪费情感的数以千计的事务而分神。因此，他经常神色匆匆，心不在焉。无论在哪儿，他都急着赶往下一个目的地；无论谈论什么话题，他的思绪都会飘落到另一个话题上；即使在拜访好友时，他也在计算着如何安排时间才能赶得上去看另一个人。诸如伦敦之类的大都市，会使人变得斤斤计较，自私无趣。在短暂而随便的聚会上，他们也只简单处理一些平常事。他们所展现的只是人性冷酷的一面——他们内心的热情和友善的本质没有机会展现。

只有在乡村，英国人才能释放出他们自然的感情。他打破那些繁文缛节，扔掉那份拘谨和保守，真正变得愉快而轻松。他设法保留礼貌社会的所有便利与高雅，同时驱走它所带来的种种限制。在他乡村

26 be absorbed in 专心于
27 be distracted by 分心，分神
28 dissipate ['dɪsɪpeɪt] vt. 使……浪费
29 pay a friendly visit 拜访好友
30 allot [ə'lɒt] v. 分配，分摊，在这里指事先约好的
31 transient ['trænzɪənt] adj. 短暂的
32 superficies [ˌsjuːpəfɪʃiːz] n. 表面（外表）
33 genial [dʒɪ'nɪəl] adj. 亲切的，友善的
34 formality [fɔː'mælətɪ] n. 礼节，仪式，繁文缛节

life, and to banish[35] its restraints. His country-seat abounds with[36] every requisite[37], either for studious[38] retirement, tasteful gratification[39], or rural exercise. Books, paintings, music, horses, dogs, and sporting implements[40] of all kinds, are at hand[41]. He puts no constraint either upon his guests or himself, but in the true spirit of hospitality provides the means of enjoyment, and leaves every one to partake according to his inclination.

The taste of the English in the cultivation of land, and in what is called landscape-gardening, is unrivalled[42]. They have studied nature intently, and discovered an exquisite sense of her beautiful forms and harmonious combinations. Those charms which in other countries she lavishes[43] in wild solitudes, are here assembled round the haunts[44] of domestic life. They seem to have caught her coy[45] and furtive[46] graces, and spread them, like witchery[47], about their rural abodes.

Nothing can be more imposing than the magnificence of English park scenery. Vast lawns that extend like sheets of vivid green, with here

的陋室里必需品应有尽有，用于幽居读书、娱情自乐或乡间运动。书籍、油画、音乐、骏马、狗以及各种运动设备都可信手拈来。无论是对客人还是对他自己，他都不会强加限制，尽量为客人提供各种娱乐设施，然后根据各人的喜好去参与，尽显好客之情。

英国人在土地耕种及所谓的风景园林艺术上的品位可谓无人能及，他们仔细研究自然，对自然美景和万物和谐的组合有独到的感受。这种种自然之美，如若换成其他国家，必然会在荒凉与孤独之中自生自灭，可在英国却会被人搜集起来，放置在日常生活的方方面面。英国人似乎捕捉到了自然界娇羞、隐秘的美，并像巫师散播咒语一样把这些美丽的东西留在乡间居室的周围。

没有什么能比英国公园

异域情怀 国客有别

---

35 banish ['bænɪʃ]   v.   驱逐
36 abound with   = fill with, 充满，富于
37 requisite ['rekwɪzɪt]   n.   必需品
38 studious ['stju:dɪəs]   adj.   勤奋的，努力于……的
39 gratification [ˌɡrætɪfɪ'keɪʃən]   n.   满足，喜悦。此处意为"享受"
40 sporting implements   运动设备
41 at hand   = within reach 在手边，在近处
42 unrivalled [ʌn'raɪvld]   adj.   无对手的，无匹敌的
43 lavish ['lævɪʃ]   v.   浪费
44 haunt [hɔ:nt]   n.   常去的地方
45 coy [kɔɪ]   adj.   羞怯的，腼腆的
46 furtive ['fɜ:tɪv]   adj.   秘密的，隐秘的
47 witchery ['wɪtʃ(ə)rɪ]   n.   巫术，魔法

and there clumps of gigantic trees, heaping up[48] rich piles of foliage[49]; the solemn pomp of groves and woodland glades[50], with the deer trooping in silent herds across them; the hare, bounding away to the covert; or the pheasant, suddenly bursting upon the wing; the brook, taught to wind in natural meanderings or expand into a glassy lake; the sequestered[51] pool, reflecting the quivering trees, with the yellow leaf sleeping on its bosom, and the trout roaming fearlessly about its limpid waters; while some rustic[52] temple or sylvan[53] statue, grown green and dank with age, gives an air of classic sanctity to the seclusion.

These are but a few of the features of park scenery; but what most delight me, is the creative talent with which the English decorate[54] the unostentatious abodes of middle life. The rudest habitation, the most unpromising and scanty[55] portion of land, in the hands of an Englishman of taste, becomes a little paradise. With a nicely discriminating[56] eye, he seizes at once upon its capabilities and pictures in his mind the future landscape. The sterile spot grows into loveliness under his hands, and yet the operations of art which produce the effect are scarcely to be perceived. The cherishing and training of some

的秀美景色更加壮观的了。广袤的草坪延伸开来，像鲜亮的绿毯，到处是参天的大树，枝繁叶茂，郁郁葱葱。成群的鹿儿静悄悄地穿梭在林间的空地上；野兔突然钻入草丛；野鸡振翅而飞；小溪蜿蜒曲折，一直延伸汇入清澈如镜的湖泊里；小潭静幽，映着随风摇摆的枝叶，拥着睡梦中的黄叶，鲑鱼也在这清澈的水中徜徉；一些乡村的教堂和林间古老的雕像，虽因时间久远而布满青苔，也为这远离尘嚣的地方披上神圣的气息。

这只是公园美景的一角；但真正令我兴奋的还是英国人把中等人家的房屋装饰得朴实无华的天赋。一座陋宅，哪怕是一处最贫瘠、最毫无生机的土地，到了有品位的英国人手里，都变成了小小的天堂。他别具慧眼，一眼就能看出这块土地有无美化的可能，能立刻在心中勾勒出它装扮后的样子。经过他们巧夺天工的雕

48 heap up 堆积起来
49 foliage ['fəulɪdʒ] n. 叶子（总称）
50 glade [gleɪd] n. 林间空地
51 sequestered [sɪ'kwestəd] adj. 幽静的
52 rustic ['rʌstɪk] adj. 乡村的
53 sylvan ['sɪlvən] adj. 多林木的，森林的
54 decorate with 装饰。句中"with"提前，"with which"引导非限制定语从句
55 scanty ['skæntɪ] adj. 少量的，不多的
56 discriminating [dɪs'krɪmɪneɪtɪŋ] adj. 有辨别能力的

trees; the cautious pruning[57] of others; the nice distribution of flowers and plants of tender and graceful foliage; the introduction of a green slope of velvet turf; the partial opening to a peep of blue distance, or silver gleam of water: all these are managed with a delicate tact, a pervading yet quiet assiduity[58], like the magic touchings with which a painter finishes up a favorite picture.

The residence of people of fortune and refinement in the country has diffused a degree of taste and elegance in rural economy that descends to the lowest class. The very laborer, with his thatched cottage[59] and narrow slip of ground, attends to[60] their embellishment[61]. The trim hedge, the grass-plot before the door, the woodbine[62] trained up against the wall, and hanging its blossoms about the lattice[63], the pot of flowers in the window, the holly, providently[64] planted about the house, to chat winter of its dreariness, and to throw in a semblance[65] of green summer to cheer the fireside: all these bespeak[66] the influence of taste, flowing down from high sources, and pervading the lowest levels of the public mind. If ever Love,

琢，贫瘠的地方可以变成一道美丽的风景，且看不出任何雕琢的迹象。对某些树要精心栽培；对另一些要精心修剪；布局巧妙的花草、天鹅绒般柔软的一坡草坪、映入眼帘的一抹蓝天或一湾波光粼粼的清水，都经过巧妙的设计，处处充溢着他的心血，却不露任何痕迹，就好似画家成功完成了一幅美丽的画作。

在乡村，生活殷实并有教养的人家，即使在其种种农活中也体现着高雅的情趣。即使小农之家也不例外。一名小小的劳工，住的是一间茅草屋，屋前只有一块狭长的空地，但他也懂得如何装扮自己的住所。修剪得整整齐齐的篱笆，门前弄得平平整整的草坪，爬满墙壁并在格架上静静盛开的忍冬花，摆在窗台上的盆栽，房屋四周的冬青，即使到了寒冷的冬天仍满目青翠，为炉火旁的人带来夏意——所有这一

---

57 pruning ['pru:nɪŋ] n. 修剪
58 assiduity [ˌæsɪ'dju:ɪtɪ] n. 勤勉，刻苦
59 thatched cottages 茅草屋
60 attend to 此处意为"用心"
61 embellishment [ɪm'belɪʃmənt] n. 装饰，布置
62 woodbine ['wʊdbaɪn] n. 忍冬属植物
63 lattice ['lætɪs] n. 格栅式百叶窗（门、棚架等）
64 providently ['prɒvɪdəntlɪ] adv. 有远虑地
65 semblance ['sembləns] n. 类似（外观，假装）
66 bespeak [bɪ'spiːk] v. 显示

as poets sing, delights to visit a cottage, it must be the cottage of an English peasant.

From *The Sketch Book of Geoffrey Crayon* (1819~1820)

切都说明了自上而下英国乡村人的高雅情趣。如果历代诗人所吟诵的爱神真的喜欢降临陋室茅舍，那么他所光顾的肯定是英国乡村人的茅舍。

含英咀华

选文中作者描绘了英国农村的恬静、壮丽、广阔和淡雅之美。品读远离城市喧嚣的乡村风情，享受微风拂面、溪水潺潺、林鸟啾啾、淡淡花香的古典淡雅的气氛，体会英国人朴实无华的生活，别有一番滋味。

Richard Ford

理查德·福特

理查德·福特(1796~1858)，英国作家，1817年毕业于牛津大学。他花了四年时间在西班牙游历，并于1845年出版了他的得意之作《西班牙旅游者手册》（*Handbook for Travelers in Spain, 1845*）。这本书共分两卷，1847年再版时只有一卷，其余的材料收录在《西班牙采集》（*Gatherings from Spain, 1846*）。福特还为《每季评论》（*Quarterly Review*）及其他刊物供稿。

Spain

Various as are the objects worth observing in Spain[1], many of which are to be seen there only, it may be as well[2] to mention what is not to be seen, for there is no such loss of time as finding this out oneself, after weary chase and wasted hour. Those who expect to meet with well-garnished arsenals[3], libraries, restaurants, charitable[4] or literary institutions, canals, railroads, tunnels, suspension-bridges, steam-engines, omnibuses, manufactories, polytechnic[5] galleries, pale-ale breweries, and similar appliances and appurtenances[6] of a high state of political, social, and commercial civilization, had better stay at home. In Spain there are no turnpike-trust meetings, no quarter-sessions, no courts of justice, according to the real meaning of that word, no treadmills, no boards of guardians, no chairmen, directors, masters-extraordinary of the court of chancery[7], no assistant poor-law commissioners[8]. There are no anti-tobacco-teetotal-temperance-meetings, no auxiliary—missionary-propagating societies,

西班牙之旅

尽管在西班牙有各种各样值得观赏的景观，并且很多只能在这里看到，我们最好还是提及一下那些没有看到的，因为在疲惫的奔波及消耗了大量的时间之后，一个人不能立即把这些都一一搜寻出来。那些来到西班牙期望见到外观装饰上乘的兵工厂、图书馆、餐馆、慈善文化机构、运河、铁路、隧道、吊桥、蒸汽机、公交车、制造厂、各类美术馆、低度啤酒厂以及其他类似的具有高度政治、社会和商业文明特征的装置设备之类的东西的人最好待在家里。在西班牙没有收税卡信托集会，没有地方法庭，没有法院，不言而喻，也就没有单调的工作，没有保护所委员会，没有主席、主管和掌管大法庭的特别官员，也没有民法法官助理。这里没有

1 various as are the objects worth observing in Spain　= though various objects are worth observing in Spain
2 may be as well　= no harm will come from doing something，做某事也无妨
3 arsenal ['ɑːsənəl]　n.　兵工厂
4 charitable ['tʃærətəbl]　adj.　（为）慈善事业的
5 polytechnic [,pɒlɪ'teknɪk]　adj.　有关多种工艺的
6 appurtenance [ə'pɜːtɪnəns]　n.　装置，设备
7 chancery ['tʃɑːnsərɪ]　n.　大法官法庭
8 assistant poor-law commissioners　民法法官助理

nothing in the blanket and lying-in asylum line, nothing, in short, worth a revising-barrister of three years' standing's notice, unless he is partial to[9] the study of the laws of bankruptcy. Spain is no[10] country for the political economist, beyond affording an example of the decline of the wealth of nations, and offering a wide topic on errors to be avoided, as well as for experimental theories, plans of reform and amelioration[11]. In Spain, Nature reigns; she has there lavished her utmost prodigality[12] of soil and climate, which Spaniards[13] have for the last four centuries been endeavoring to[14] counteract by a culpable[15] neglect of agricultural speeches and dinners, and a non-distribution of prizes for the biggest boars, asses, and laborers with largest families.

Those who aspire to[16] the romantic, the poetical, the sentimental, the artistic, the antiquarian[17], the classical, in short, to any of the sublime[18] and beautiful lines, will find both in the past and present state of Spain, subjects enough in wandering with lead-pencil and notebook through this singular country, which hovers[19] between Europe and Africa, between civilization

反烟酒集会，没有辅助传教士传教的协会，什么都没有，总而言之，没有什么能引起一个具有三年资历的律师的关注，除非他偏爱研究有关破产的法律。西班牙不是一个政治经济学家施展才能的地方，也不是一个为实验性理论、改革计划和改良方案提供空间的理想之地，它所能提供的只是一个国家财富衰败的例子，一个关于如何避免错误的广泛话题。在西班牙，自然主宰一切；她有着极其丰富的土壤和气候资源，之前的四个世纪里西班牙人致力于用一种被后世责备的忽略农业对话和饮食的方式对抗这多变的土壤和气候；她还以出产体形硕大的猪、驴以及丰富的劳动力而闻名。

那些渴望浪漫、富有诗意、多愁善感、具有艺术天赋、有历史感、古典的人，简言之，渴望壮丽和美好事

---

9 be partial to = having a strong liking for someone or something，偏爱某人或某事
10 no = not a
11 amelioration [əˌmiːliəˈreɪʃn] n. 改良
12 prodigality [ˌprɒdɪˈɡæləti] n. 丰富
13 Spaniard [ˈspænjəd] n. 西班牙人
14 endeavor to = attempt to，致力于
15 culpable [ˈkʌlpəbl] adj. deserving blame，该责备的
16 aspire to = desire strongly to achieve something，渴望
17 antiquarian [ˌæntɪˈkweəriən] n. 古文物的，古迹的
18 sublime [səˈblaɪm] n. 壮丽的，卓越的
19 hover = remain near something，在某地旁

and barbarism[20]; this land of the green valley and barren mountain, of the boundless plain and the broken sierra[21]; those Elysian gardens of the vie, the olive, the orange, and the aloe; those trackless, vast, silent, uncultivated wastes, the heritage of the wild bee; in flying from the dull uniformity, the polished monotony of Europe, to the racy[22] freshness of that original, unchanged country, where antiquity treads on the heels[23] of today, where Paganism[24] disputes the very altar with Christianity[25], where indulgence[26] and luxury contend with[27] privation and poverty, where a want of all that is generous or merciful is blended with the most devoted heroic virtues, where the most cold-blooded cruelty is linked with the fiery[28] passions of Africa, where ignorance and erudition[29] stand in violent and striking contrast.

There let the antiquarian pore[30] over the stirring memorials of many thousand years, the vestiges of Moorish elegance, in that storehouse of ancient customs, that repository of all elsewhere long forgotten and passed by; there let him gaze upon those classical monuments, unequalled almost in Greece and Italy, and

物的人，将会发现从古至今都可以带着铅笔和笔记本在这个毗邻欧洲和非洲，夹在文明和原始风尚之间的非凡的国家中漫游；这片土地充满了绿色的山谷和贫瘠的山丘，充满了无尽的平原和断裂的山脊；这片乐土上充满了竞争、橄榄、柑橘和芦荟；那些无迹的、巨大的、安静的、未经耕作的荒地是野蜂的遗产；冲出枯燥的平淡，冲出欧洲优雅的单调，来到这活泼清新的、新颖的、未曾改变的国家；这里历史紧跟着现代，这里异教与基督教争论祭坛的归属，这里放纵和奢华与贫困和贫穷相竞争，这里慷慨和仁慈的需求混杂着奉献和英勇的美德，这里最冷血的残忍与非洲的热情相关联，这里无知和博学代表着强烈和鲜明的对比。

让那些文物研究者在古代风俗的宝库中，在被别处长久

---

20 barbarism ['bɑ:bərɪzəm] n. 暴行，此处引申为"原始风尚"
21 sierra [sɪ'erə] n. （锯齿状）山脊；（山势陡峭的）群峰，峰峦
22 racy [reɪsl] = vivid，生动的
23 tread on the heels = follow someone closely，紧跟
24 Paganism ['peɪgənɪzəm] n. 异教（信仰）
25 Christianity [,krɪstɪ'ænəti] n. 基督教
26 indulgence [ɪn'dʌldʒəns] n. 纵容
27 contend with = struggle in order to overcome a rival, competitor or difficulty，竞争
28 fiery ['faɪərɪ] adj. 热情的，热烈的
29 erudition [,eru:'dɪʃən] n. 博学
30 pore [pɔ:] v. 注视，凝视；沉思，默想

on those fairy Aladdin palaces, the creatures of Oriental gorgeousness and imagination, with which Spain alone can enchant[31] the dull European; there let the man of feeling dwell on[32] the poetry of her envy-disarming decay, fallen from her high estate, the dignity of a dethroned[33] monarch, borne with unrepining self respect, the last consolation of the innately[34] noble, which no adversity can take away; let the lover of art feed his eyes with the mighty masterpieces of ideal Italian art, when Raphael and Titian strove to decorate the palaces of Charles, the great emperor of the age of Leo X[35].

Let him gaze on the living nature of Velazquez and Murillo, whose paintings are truly to be seen in Spain alone; let the artist sketch frowning forms of the castle, the pomp and splendor of the cathedral, where God is worshiped in a manner as nearly befitting his glory as the arts and wealth of finite man can reach. Let him dwell on the Gothic gloom of the cloister[36], the feudal turret[37], the vast Escurial[38], the rock-built alcazar of imperial[39] Toledo[40], the sunny

遗忘的仓库中，沉思令人激动的千年墓碑，沉思摩尔人高雅的遗迹；让他凝望那些即使在希腊和意大利都无双的名胜古迹，让他凝视那些阿拉丁宫殿般的建筑，那些有着东方华美和想象力的生物。这些足以让西班牙使整个枯燥乏味的欧洲陶醉；让内心敏感的人思考她腐败的诗意，她从她高高的地位上滑落，带着被废黜君主的尊严，带着生来没有苦恼的自我欣赏，没有逆境可以剥夺的天生贵族气质是她最后的安慰；让艺术爱好者紧盯着完美的意大利艺术的杰作，回想拉斐尔和提香努力装饰着伟大的与利奥十世同龄的查理五世的宫殿。

让他凝视委拉斯奎兹与穆列罗的性格，只有在西班牙才能看到这些画作；让艺术家描绘城堡的结构、大教堂的光辉

---

31 enchant [ɪn'tʃɑːnt] v. fill somebody with great delight, 使某人陶醉
32 dwell on = think at length about something, 细想某事
33 dethrone [diː'θrəʊn] v. 废黜，废立，(国王)废位
34 innately [ɪ'neɪtlɪ] adv. 天生就有地，此处引申为"天赋地"
35 Leo X 利奥十世。利奥十世的名字是 Giovanni di Lorenzo de' Medici。他是洛伦佐·德·美第奇的儿子，并于1513年作为新教皇继位
36 cloister ['klɔɪstə] n. 修道院，寺庙
37 turret ['tʌrət] n. 塔楼
38 Escurial [es'kjuərɪəl] n. （西班牙马德里附近的）（埃尔）埃斯科里亚尔建筑群（包括西班牙国王陵墓、宫殿、教堂、修道院和庙宇等，建于1563~1584年）
39 imperial [ɪm'pɪərɪəl] adj. 帝国的
40 Toledo [tə'liːdəu] n. 托莱多（美国港市）

towers of stately Seville[41], the eternal snows and lovely Vega of Granada; let the geologist clamber over mountains of marble, and metal-pregnant sierras; let the botanist cull[42] from the wild hothouse of nature plants unknown, unnumbered, matchless in color and breathing the aroma[43] of the sweet south; let all, learned and unlearned, listen to the song, the guitar, the castanet[44]; or join in the light fandango[45] and spirit-stir-ring bull-fight; let all mingle with[46] the gay, good-humored, temperate peasantry, free, manly, and independent, yet courteous and respectful; let all live with the noble, dignified, high-bred, self-respecting Spaniard; let all share in their easy, courteous society; let all admire their dark-eyed women, so frank and natural, to whom the voice of all ages and nations has conceded the palm of attraction, to whom Venus has bequeathed[47] her magic girdle

41 Seville *n.* 塞维利亚。塞维利亚（西班牙语：Sevilla），是西班牙安达鲁西亚自治区和塞维利亚省的首府，城市人口约一百三十万，是西班牙第四大城市，也是西班牙唯一有内河港口的城市。全市人口65万。瓜达尔基维尔河从市中穿流而过，古市区的建筑仍然保留着几个世纪前摩尔人统治过的痕迹。塞维利亚曾是一个重要的港口，西班牙的船队从新大陆运来大批黄金、白银，经过塞维利亚转运往欧洲各地

42 cull [kʌl] *v.* 收集，采摘

43 aroma [ə'rəumə] *n.* 香气，此处译为"香甜的"

44 castanet [kæstə'net] *n.* 响板

45 fandango [fæn'dæŋgəu] *n.* 一种西班牙舞，范丹戈舞

46 mingle with = combine with，与某物混合

47 bequeath [bɪ'kwi:ð] *v.* arrange, by making a will, to give (property) to someone when one dies，将（财物）等遗赠给（某人），此处引申为"赋予"

和壮丽，在那里有限的人类用配得上其光辉的艺术和财富来尊崇上帝。让他详述修道院的哥特式阴暗、封建的塔楼、巨大的埃斯科里亚尔建筑群、岩石建造的托莱多帝国城堡、高贵塞维利亚的阳光明媚的塔、格兰纳达薄呢永恒的雪和美丽的织女星；让地质学家攀登遍布大理石的高山和蕴藏着金属的山脊；让植物学家收集野外自然温室中未知的、数不清的、多彩并且呼吸着甜美南方香气的植物；让所有无论是否学习过音乐的人，倾听这歌曲、这吉他、这响板；或者加入轻快的范丹戈舞的行列和令人兴奋的斗牛活动；让所有人融入这快乐的、心情好的、温和的农民中，他们自由、刚强、独立并且客气、有礼貌；让所有人和高尚的、尊贵的、优良的、有自尊心的西班牙人民同住；让所有人分享他们舒适、有序的社会；让所有人赞美他们坦率自然的黑眼睛女人，无论老少、无论哪个民族都承认她们的吸引力，维纳斯将她有魔力的优雅腰带和独特魅力赋予了她们；让所有人开始

of grace and fascination; let all-but enough on starting on this expedition[48], "where," as Don Quixote said, "there are opportunities, brother Sancho, of putting our hands into what are called adventures up to our elbows."

From *Gatherings from Spain* (1846)

这次远征吧，正如堂吉河德所言："桑丘，我们的双手能否触到奇遇由我们的双肘决定吧。"

---

48 expedition [ˌekspə'dɪʃən] *n.* 远征

含英咀华

　　西班牙这个名字来自于腓尼基语，意为"野兔"，是因古迦太基人在伊比利亚半岛海岸一带发现了很多野兔而得名。它位于欧洲西南伊比利亚半岛上，南隔直布罗陀海峡与非洲相望，东临地中海，是一个充满热情、富于活力的国家。它素以斗牛、舞蹈、吉他闻名天下。斗牛是西班牙的"国粹"，是那里传统的民族文化。在这篇文章中作者并没有像其他游记一样去介绍西班牙的风景名胜，而是从西班牙的政治、文化、宗教等细微方面入手，让读者从不同的侧面了解了西班牙。

Bob Riel
鲍勃·里利

鲍勃·里利是一位作家、顾问，目前居住在亚利桑那州。在波士顿大学获得政治学硕士学位后，他作为一名报社记者开始了自己的写作生涯。他的作品很富有现代气息。他发表在"里利世界中的旅游"博客中的作品主要以跨文化和旅行为主题。他的作品有《环游世界的两段旅程：旅行生活的故事和感受》（*Two Laps Around the World: Tales and Insights from a Life Sabbatical, 2007*），在书中以时间顺序记述了他和他的妻子环球旅行的经历。

Kenya: Patchwork of Experiences

肯尼亚——缤纷印象

Any trip to Kenya is going to result in[1] an intense patchwork[2] of experiences — from the dreadfully frustrating to the sublimely[3] beautiful. This, at least, is the conclusion I reached after a visit to Kenya with my wife, Lisa, for a wildlife safari[4]. We encountered a crumbling[5] infrastructure[6], inefficient airlines and a constant pleading for money, but also incredibly friendly people, astounding landscapes, and rich cultural encounters. In the end, we wouldn't have traded any part of the experience. We returned home with a collage of lasting memories.

The safari began early on a Sunday morning when our guide, Ben, picked us up in Nairobi. We had a six-hour drive ahead of[7] us on this day and we would be in the vehicle every day for the next week, crossing the equator[8] twice and bouncing along more than one thousand miles of Kenyan roads.

"So, we will be together for six days," I said

每次去肯尼亚，感受都是丰富多彩的——从颠沛流离、历尽坎坷到震撼人心、恢宏壮丽的美景。而这，至少是我和妻子丽莎在肯尼亚野外旅行后得出的结论。我们遇到了破败的基础设施，效率低下的航空公司，乞求施舍的乞丐，但也有热情好客的肯尼亚人民，令人惊叹的美景和丰富的文化底蕴。旅程结束了，这些经历却令人难忘，回到家里，留在心里的是永恒的美好回忆。

我们的旅行始于一个周日的早晨。导游本在内罗毕接到我们。那天我们开车行驶了6个小时，并且在接下来的一周里，我们的每天都将在车上度过，将会穿越赤道两次，在颠簸的肯尼亚公路上行驶一千多英里。

"那么，我们将在一起度

---

1 result in　导致，此处可不译出
2 patchwork ['pætʃwəːk]　n.　修补工作（拼凑的东西，混杂物），此处引申为"丰富多彩的感受"
3 sublimely [sə'blaɪmlɪ]　adv.　高尚地，卓越地
4 safari [sə'fɑːrɪ]　n.　旅行，特指野外旅行
5 crumbling [krʌmblɪŋ]　adj.　破败的
6 infrastructure ['ɪnfrəstrʌktʃə]　n.　基础设施
7 ahead of　= in front; in advance，在前面，在前头
8 equator [ɪ'kweɪtə]　n.　赤道

to Ben, "That means we will become friends."

"We are already friends," he said, smiling, in a comment typical of the friendliness of the culture.

Before long, we were out of Nairobi and off into rural Kenya. Only occasionally during the next week would we run into⁹ a small city, at places like Nakuru. We drove north through rolling foothills¹⁰ of green trees and red soil — my lasting images of Kenya. Just as I will forever associate Greece with¹¹ the colors of blue and white, Kenya evokes¹² vistas¹³ of green and red.

One of the biggest things I noticed as we drove was the number of people on the streets. Everywhere, even in what seemed to be the middle of nowhere between towns, we passed people walking or biking. Even on long stretches of empty highway, where in the United States you would encounter nothing but¹⁴ other vehicles, in Kenya, there are dozens of people just going about their daily lives. We saw women walking with huge loads of wood tied to their backs, young boys tending herds of cows, a person steering¹⁵ a donkey-driven cart. Near the tribal¹⁶ areas, there were local tribes' people tending their cattle, or doing laundry in a stream, or just

---

9 run into 偶然遇到
10 foothill ['futhɪl] n. 山麓小丘
11 associate with = connect with, 联合，联系
12 evoke [ɪ'vəuk] v. 唤起，引起
13 vista ['vɪstə] n. 展望，回想
14 nothing but = only 仅仅，只不过
15 steer [stɪə] v. 引导，驾驶
16 tribal ['traɪbl] adj. 部落的，种族的

过六天，"我对本说，"我们会成为朋友的。"

"我们已经是朋友了。"本笑着说道，他的话语中带着肯尼亚文化中典型的友善可亲。

不久以后，我们就驶出了内罗毕，来到了肯尼亚的乡村。在接下来的一周里，我们也只是偶尔才会进入像纳库鲁这样的小镇。我们开车向北，穿过连绵起伏的小山，山上长满绿树，郁郁葱葱，褚红的土壤覆盖着小山，我对肯尼亚一直就是这种印象。就像我总是把希腊与湛蓝和洁白两种颜色联系在一起一样，肯尼亚总是唤起我对翠绿和褚红的遐想。

旅途中我注意最多的就是道边行人，即使是在城镇间前不着村后不着店的地方，我们也随处可见徒步或是骑车的人。甚至在绵长空旷的高速公路上，都可以见到很多人在从容步行，这对他们来说就是日常生活；而在美国的高速公路上，你只能看见川流不息的车流。我们看到妇女背着大捆柴火走在路上，孩子们赶着成群的牛去放牧，还有一个人在赶着他的驴车。在附近聚居的部落地区，当地的居民有的看护牛群，有的在溪边洗衣服，还

out walking with a spear in hand.

Our drive took us past banana trees and coffee plantations, past vast wheat-colored fields lined by acacia[17] trees, past goats and cows wandering the sides of the road. We came across small towns, or sometimes small concentrations of ramshackle[18] shops along the way. We saw an open market, with food and clothing laid outside on carpets, surrounded by hundreds of people shopping for goods. In the cities, it was more of the same, although the buildings and stores were bigger and more sturdily[19] constructed. Wherever we stopped, people descended on the van begging us to buy something from them.

Two other things were quite noticeable as we drove. One was the matatus, which are Kenya's version of public transportation, big vans, with enough room to squeeze[20] in twelve or so people shoulder to shoulder. They are very colorful, all individually decorated and named, and ever-present along the roadways. They are a cherished part of Kenyan culture, even though the drivers are known to be somewhat wild and dangerous.

The other prominent[21] feature was the prevalence of Christianity. Many of the matatus were decorated with signs — "Lover of the Lord", "God is the Answer". Churches and Christian centers were ubiquitous[22] throughout the country.

---

17 acacia [əˈkeɪʃə]   n.   阿拉伯橡胶树
18 ramshackle [ˈræmˌʃækl]   adj.   摇摇欲坠的
19 sturdily [ˈstɜːdɪlɪ]   adv.   此处意为"体面地"
20 squeeze [skwiːz]   v.   挤
21 prominent [ˈprɒmɪnənt]   adj.   显著的，突出的
22 ubiquitous [juːˈbɪkwɪtəs]   adj.   到处存在的，遍在的

有的手执长矛而行。

我们的车穿过香蕉林、咖啡园，穿越了广袤的麦田，田间点缀着成行的橡胶树；道路两旁，牛羊迈着悠闲的步子。车子经过一个个小镇，我们有时也会看到多处破旧的小商店。我们见到了一个小集市，食品和衣物放置在外面的毯子上面，四周围了数百位购物的顾客；城市里也差不多是这样，只不过楼层更高些，店铺也更宽敞体面些。不论我们在哪里停下，人们都会从装货车上下来请我们去他们那儿买点儿什么东西。

在旅途中，有另外两件值得注意的事。其一就是马塔杜，这是肯尼亚人的公交工具，一种大型货车，若是挤一些，可以容纳12个人左右。这些车五颜六色，装饰和名称也极具个性，乘客在路边随叫随停。尽管司机开起车来有点狂野和危险，它们却是肯尼亚文化中值得珍视的一部分。

另一个突出的特点就是基督教盛行。很多马塔杜上都漆着像"爱上帝"，"上帝就是答案"这样的标记，教堂和基督教中心在这个国家也无所不在。我也渐渐习惯了看到这里

I became accustomed to[23] seeing "miracle" a lot.

It was actually good to have so much to occupy our eyes on the trip because the road was rough, making it impossible to write more than brief notes. Sometimes it was even difficult to read. The roads were just a series of potholes[24] that were sometimes surrounded by pavement. The drivers constantly had to veer from one side of the road to the other, sometimes driving on the dirt shoulder for miles at a time to avoid the worst pothole. And the dust — we were plagued[25] by it, blowing in through the bottom of the van or through small openings in the window.

There was a string of these contrasts along the way and throughout the week. We were frustrated by the crumbling infrastructure, the potholes, and the dust. But we were enthralled[26] by the landscape, the culture, and the richness of the land. We were annoyed by the constant begging and selling of souvenirs[27] whenever we stopped. When we weren't besieged[28] by people who wanted our money, we were delighted by the friendliness of the people, their smiles, and their easygoing nature. We couldn't separate one from[29] the other, so we just took it all in. It's part of the mosaic[30] that is Kenya.

From *Two Laps Around the World: Tales and Insights from a Life Sabbatical* (2007)

---

23 accustomed to　习惯于，"to" 为介词，后面接名词或动名词
24 pothole ['pɒthəʊl]　n.　（路面的）坑洼，坑洞
25 plague [pleɪg]　v.　折磨，使……苦恼
26 enthral [ɪn'θrɔːl]　v.　= fascinate，迷惑，迷醉
27 souvenir [ˌsuːvə'nɪə]　n.　旅游纪念品
28 besiege [bɪ'siːdʒ]　v.　围攻，包围
29 separate from　此处意为 "使分离，使分开"
30 mosaic [məʊ'zeɪɪk]　n.　镶嵌细工，此处引申为 "多姿多彩的文化"

的很多 "奇迹"。

其实我们应该庆幸，有如此之多的美景可以欣赏，但是因为路途颠簸，除了能简要记点笔记，几乎什么也写不了。有时读书都困难。一路上都坑坑洼洼的，偶尔才有平坦的道路出现。司机不得不经常转向，从公路一侧绕到另一侧，有时为了绕开一个大坑，要在满是尘土的路肩上一口气跑上好几英里。令我们困扰的是满街的尘土——从车的底部或窗户的小小缝隙吹进来的都是灰尘。

这种强烈的反差贯穿我们这一周旅程的始末。我们因这里基础设施破败、道路坑坑洼洼、满天尘土而烦恼；但是我们又为这里美丽的风景、丰富的文化、富饶的土地而着迷。一路上只要停下来，乞讨和叫卖纪念品的声音就不绝于耳，这让我们极其恼火。当围在我们身边的不是乞讨的人而是普通的肯尼亚人时，我们很喜欢他们的友善、他们的笑容和他们的随和的天性。我们无法把这两方面分开，于是也就照盘全收，这是肯尼亚多姿多彩文化的一部分。

含英咀华

　　位于非洲东部的肯尼亚，景色秀丽，一望无际的辽阔草原让人心旷神怡，在那里生活着成千上万的野生动物。读者可以跟随作者的描述领略非洲独特的热带风情和当地居民淳朴的民风。

多彩都市
各具风姿

First Impressions of the Capital of
Vienna
首都维也纳第一印象

Paris — The Beautiful City
美丽之城——巴黎

Zurich
苏黎世

Here Is New York
这里是纽约

Bayard Taylor

贝亚德·泰勒

贝亚德·泰勒（1825~1878），美国诗人、小说家、游记作家，出生在宾夕法尼亚州的一个农场主家庭。1844年他随表兄及几个朋友前往欧洲旅行，他们游遍了英国、德国、意大利。《旅行中的风景》（*Views Afoot; or, Europe seen with a Knapsack and Staff, 1846*）一书中囊括了他在欧洲游历的两年间写的所有文章，受到了读者的高度赞扬，并且在接下来的13年中多次再版。

First Impressions of the Capital of Vienna

首都维也纳第一印象

I have at last seen the thousand wonders of this great capital, this German Paris, this connecting-link between the civilization of Europe and the barbaric[1] magnificence of the East. It looks familiar to be in a city again whose streets are thronged[2] with people and resound with[3] the din and bustle[4] of business. It reminds me of the never-ending crowds of London or the life and tumult[5] of our scarcely less active New York. The morning of your arrival we sallied out[6] from our lodgings in the Leopoldstadt[7] to explore the world before us. Entering the broad Praterstrasse, we passed down to the little arm[8] of the Danube which separates this part of the new city from the old. A row of magnificent coffee-houses occupy the bank, and numbers of persons were taking their breakfasts in the shady porticos[9]. The Ferdinand's Bridge, which crosses the stream, was filled with people; in the motley[10] crowd we saw the dark-eyed Greek and Turks[11]

我终于目睹了这个拥有"德国巴黎"之称，连接着欧洲文明和东方狂野壮丽景观的伟大首都数以千计的奇迹。在这个城市中，一切看起来都是那么熟悉，大街上挤满了人，充满着商业的喧嚣与忙乱。这使我想起了伦敦的人山人海和纽约几乎从未停止过的喧闹。你们到达的早晨，从利奥波尔德斯塔特城的公寓出发去探索面前的这个世界。我们进入了宽阔的普拉特大街，穿过了将新旧城区分割开的多瑙河上的一个小港湾。一排排华丽的咖啡厅占满了河岸，很多人都在荫凉的门廊下享用早餐。横跨小河的费迪南德桥上挤满了人；混杂的人群中有黑眼睛的希腊人，头戴穆斯林头巾身着

1 barbaric [bɑːˈbærɪk] *adj.* 原始的，此处引申为"狂野"
2 throng [θrɒŋ] *v.* 挤满
3 resound with = (of a place) be filled with sound，指（某处）回荡着声音
4 din and bustle 喧闹与忙乱
5 tumult [ˈtjuːmʌlt] *n.* din or uproar produced by this，喧闹声
6 sally out = set out somewhere，出发
7 Leopoldstadt *n.* 利奥波尔德斯塔特，位于维也纳城中心，是维也纳的第二大街区
8 arm = thing that is shaped like or operate like an arm，这里指港湾
9 portico [ˈpɔːtɪkəʊ] *n.* roof supported by columns，柱廊
10 motley [ˈmɒtlɪ] *adj.* 混杂的
11 Turk [tɑːk] *n.* 土耳其人

in their turbans[12] and flowing robes. Little brown Hungarian boys were going around selling bunches of Lilies, and Italians with baskets of oranges stood by the sidewalk.

The throng became greater as we penetrated into[13] the old city. The streets were filled with carts and carriages, and, as there are no side-pavements, it required constant attention to keep out of[14] their way. Splendid shops fitted up with[15] great taste occupied the whole of the lower stories, and goods of all kinds hung beneath the canvas[16] awnings[17] in front of them. Almost every store or shop was dedicated to[18] some particular person or place, which was represented on a large panel by the door. The number of these paintings added much to the splendor of the scene; I was gratified to[19] find, among the images of kings and dukes, one dedicated "To the American," with an Indian chief in full costume.

The Altstadt, or "old city," which contains about sixty thousand inhabitants, is completely separated from the suburbs, whose population, taking the whole extent within the outer barrier, numbers nearly half a million. It is situated on

长袍的土耳其人。棕色皮肤的匈牙利小男孩到处叫卖着成束的百合花，挎着装满橘子的篮子的意大利人也站在人行道上。

当我们进入老城区时人群变得更加密集。大街上到处都是手推车、马车，由于道路两侧没有人行道，所以需要时刻注意给那些车让出路来。弥漫着迷人气味的豪华商店占据了所有高楼的低层，它们前面的帆布遮阳篷下挂满了各种各样的货物，基本上每一家店铺都有专人或在专门的地方来经营，门旁的巨大广告牌上描绘出了自家店铺的特点。大量的油彩画使场面变得更加壮丽；在那些国王和公爵的画像中，我很高兴找到了一幅写着"献给美国人"的画，画里是身着全套服装的印第安首领。

阿尔茨堡，或称作"老城"，拥有大约六万居民，与郊区完全地隔离开来，而整个郊区，包括外城在内，有近五十万人。城市坐落在多瑙河的分流上，城里有好多公共长廊、花园和步行街，长度从四分之一英里到半英里不等，被称作"格雷西"。这在过去属于城市的防御工事，但是由于

12　turban ['tə:bən]　n.　（穆斯林的）缠头巾
13　penetrate into　= make a way into something，进入
14　keep out of　= avoid，躲开
15　fit up with　= supply somebody with the necessary equipment, clothes, food，供给某人必要的设备、衣物、食品，此处引申为"弥漫着"
16　canvas ['kænvəs]　n.　帆布
17　awning ['ɔ:nɪŋ]　n.　遮阳篷
18　dedicate to　= devote to，献给
19　be gratified to　= be pleased to

a small arm of the Danube and encompassed[20] by a series of public promenades[21], gardens and walks, varying from a quarter to[22] half a mile in length, called the "Glacis." This formerly belonged to the fortifications[23] of the city, but as the suburbs grew up so rapidly on all sides, it was changed appropriately to a public walk. The city is still surrounded with a massive wall and a deep wide moat[24], but, since it was taken by Napoleon in 1809, the moat has been changed into a garden with a beautiful carriage-road along the bottom around the whole city.

It is a beautiful sight to stand on the summit of the wall and look over the broad Glacis, with its shady roads branching[25] in every direction and filled with inexhaustible streams of people. The Vorstaedte, or new cities, stretch in a circle, around beyond this; all the finest buildings front[26] on the Glacis, among which the splendid Vienna Theater and the church of San Carlo Borromeo[27] are conspicuous[28]. The mountains of the Vienna forest bound the view, with here and there a stately castle on their woody summits.

Every afternoon the beauty and nobility of Vienna whirl through the cool groves in their gay

四周的郊区发展很快，它们相应地变成了公共散步场所。这座城被高大的城墙和又宽又深的护城河环绕，但自从1809年被拿破仑占领以来，护城河被改造成了一个拥有环绕城市的美丽车道的花园。

站在城墙的最高处俯视整个城市，美丽的景色尽收眼底，浓密树荫覆盖的道路四通八达，人潮涌动。佛尔施塔德或新城，以环形向周围扩展；所有精美的建筑都位于"格雷西"的前面，辉煌的维也纳剧场和圣卡罗大教堂独树一帜。维也纳山上的森林映入眼帘，绿树葱葱的山顶上到处都是庄严的城堡。

每天下午，幽雅高贵的维也纳人坐在华丽的马车上穿梭在凉爽的树荫下，人行道上熙熙攘攘，心旷神怡的小院里摆满了桌椅，客人们在此谈笑风生。而在周日或假日时，更是会有上千人聚在这里。林间

---

20 encompass [ɪn'kʌmpəs] *vt.* 围绕，此处译为"布满"
21 promenade [ˌprɒmɪ'nɑːd] *n.* public place for walking，公共散步场所，此处译为"步行街"
22 vary from...to... = change according to some factors，变化
23 fortification [ˌfɔːtɪfɪ'keɪʃ(ə)n] *n.* 防御工事
24 moat [məʊt] *n.* 护城河
25 branch [brɑːntʃ] *v.* divide into small division，分支
26 front *v.* 面向，朝向
27 San Carlo Borromeo 圣卡罗·博罗门，是米兰大主教
28 conspicuous [kən'spɪkjuəs] *adj.* 显著的，此处译为"独树一帜"

多彩都市 各具风姿

equipages[29], while the sidewalks are thronged with pedestrians, and the numberless tables and seats with which every house of refreshment is surrounded are filled with merry guests. Here on Sundays and holidays the people repair[30] in thousands. The woods are full of tame deer, which run perfectly free over the whole Prater. I saw several in one of the lawns lying down in the grass, with a number of children playing around or sitting beside them. It is delightful to walk there in the cook of the evening, when the paths are crowded and everybody is enjoying the release from the dusty city. It is this free social life which renders Vienna so attractive to foreigners and draws yearly thousands of visitors from all parts of Europe…

One of the most interesting objects in Vienna is the imperial armory[31]. We were admitted through tickets previously procured[32] from the armory direction; as[33] there was already one large company within, we were told to wait in the court till our turn came. Around the wall, on the inside, is suspended the enormous chain which the Turks stretched across the Danube at Buda in the year 1529 to obstruct[34] the navigation. It has eight thousand links and is

到处都是温驯小鹿，它们在普拉特自由自在地奔跑，我看到有几只躺在草坪上，一群孩子围绕在它们身边玩耍或休憩。傍晚时分，在小湖边散步是一件很美妙的事情，那时小路上也人头攒动，每个人都在享受城市繁忙之余的闲暇时光。正是这种自由的生活方式使得维也纳对外国人如此具有吸引力，每年都吸引了数以千计来自欧洲各地的游客来此旅游参观。

维也纳最有趣的地方之一就是帝国军械库。我们提前从军械库得到了票，所以可以进入；因为有一个大团队在里面，我们被告知要在大厅稍作等待，直到轮到我们时才能进去。沿着内墙悬挂着巨大的链条，这是土耳其人在1529年为了阻断航海，在布达横贯多瑙河上挂的，共有8000个链环，大约有一英里长。大厅里有很多大炮，形状各异、大小不一，很多是在攻克其他国家

---

29 equipage ['ɪkwɪpɪdʒ] *n.* 马车
30 repair *v.* 此处译为，"放松，休息"
31 armory ['ɑːmərɪ] *n.* 军械库
32 procure [prəʊ'kjuə] *v* obtain something esp. with care or effort，取得某物
33 as 此处连接的是原因状语从句
34 obstruct [əb'strʌkt] *v.* 阻隔

nearly a mile in length. The court is filled with cannon of all shapes and sizes, many of which were conquered from other nations. I saw a great many which were cast during the French Revolution[35], with the words "Liberté! Egalité!" upon them, and a number of others bearing the simple letter "N."…

时得到的。我看到了一枚法国大革命时期的大炮，上面刻着"自由！平等！"，另外一些上面刻着简单的"N."……

From *Views Afoot* (1846)

---

35 the French Revolution: 法国大革命，是1789年至1799年间在法国发生的一场革命。这场革命共分三个阶段：一是君主立宪派统治时期；二是吉伦特派统治时期；三是雅各宾派统治时期。在这次革命中，代表资产阶级的民主党人和共和党人一起摧毁了法国的封建统治，传播了资产阶级自由民主的进步思想，对世界历史的发展有很大影响。法国大革命是资产阶级革命时代最大最彻底的一次革命，它动摇了欧洲封建统治的基础

含英咀华

　　维也纳位于阿尔卑斯山北麓多瑙河畔，坐落在维也纳盆地中。它是奥地利的首都，同时也是欧洲最古老和最重要的文化、艺术和旅游城市之一。选文中作者先从总体上描绘出对维也纳的印象，那里"大街上挤满了人，充满着商业的喧嚣与忙乱"。接着作者带我们细致地游览了维也纳的街道、店铺甚至帝国军械库。字里行间中，我们都能体会出他似火的热情，感受到他对维也纳的如醉如痴。

Anne Warwick

安·华威

安·华威（1456~1485），出生于华威城堡，她是家里的小女儿，她短暂的一生被用作政治的工具，14岁时父亲将她许配给威尔士的王子爱德华——英王亨利六世的继承人。1485年因患肺结核病死于威斯敏斯特，并埋葬在那里。她的主要作品有《世界上最值得去的地方——纽约、巴黎、维也纳、马德里和伦敦的现代生活》（*The Meccas of the World: The Play of Modern Life in New York, Paris, Vienna, Madrid and London*）。

Paris — The Beautiful City

美丽之城——巴黎

The most prejudiced[1] will not deny that Paris is beautiful; or that there is about her streets and broad, tree-lined avenues graciousness at once dignified[2] and gay. Stand, as the ordinary tourist does on his first day[3], in the flowering square before the Louvre; in the foreground are the fountains and bright tulip-bordered paths of the Tuileries — here a glint[4] of gold, there a soft flash of marble statuary[5], shining through the trees; in the center the round lake where the children sail their boats. Beyond[6] spreads the wide sweep of the Place de la Concorde[7], with its obelisk[8] of terrible significance, its larger fountains throwing brilliant jets of spray; and then the trailing, upward vista[9] of the Champs Elysées[10] to the Great Triumphal Arch; yes, even to the most

即使是最挑剔的人也不能否认巴黎是美丽的，而且同样会认可那宽阔的、绿树成荫的大道所表现出的富华安逸，这种富华让巴黎艳丽生辉。来到巴黎的第一天，站在卢浮宫前鲜花盛开的广场中，你会发现前面是人工喷泉和种满郁金香的杜乐丽小道，一会儿这儿有一道闪亮的金光，一会儿那儿有一束柔和的大理石雕像反射的光芒穿过树缝照耀下来。在广场中央的圆形湖中，孩子们划着小船。远望可以看到广阔的协和广场和意义非凡的方尖纪念碑，硕大的喷泉向外喷洒出晶莹的水花，继续向前走，你便可以欣赏到从香榭丽舍大道到凯

---

1 the most prejudiced   the+adj. 这一结构指一类人，最挑剔的人
2 dignified ['dɪgnɪfaɪd] adj. 有威严的
3 as the ordinary tourist does on his first day   这句是插入语
4 glint [glɪnt] n. 闪光，闪烁
5 statuary ['stætʃuərɪ] n. 雕像
6 beyond = at or to a more distant point, 更远处
7 spreads the wide sweep of the Place de la Concorde   此句是倒装句
8 obelisk ['ɒbəlɪsk] n. 方尖纪念碑
9 vista ['vɪstə] n. 景色，景致
10 the Champs Elysées   香榭丽舍大道。街道的名字香榭丽舍（Champs Elyseés）是由田园（Champs，音"尚"）和乐土（Etyseés，音"爱丽舍"）两词构成，故其中文译名又为"爱丽舍田园大道"或"香榭丽舍田园大道"。东起协和广场西至星形广场（即戴高乐广场），地势西高东低，全长约1800米，宽100米，是一条集高雅与繁华、浪漫与流行于一身的世界上最具光彩与盛名的道路。道路两旁商贾云集，既可在其中消遣娱乐，又可采买购物，同时也可以欣赏这个有着百年历史的人间第一美丽大道的万种风姿

indifferent, Paris is beautiful.

To the subtler of appreciation, she is more than[11] beautiful; she is impressive. For behind the studied elegance of architecture, the elaborate[12] simplicity[13] of garden, the carefully lavish[14] use of sculpture and delicate spray, is visible the imagination of a race of passionate creators — the imagination, throughout, of the great artist. One meets it at every turn and corner, down dim passageways, up steep hills, across bridges, along sinuous[15] quays; the master hand and its "infinite capacity for taking pains." And so marvelously do its manifestations of many periods through many ages combine to enhance on another that one is convinced that the genius of Paris has been perennial[16]; that St. Genevieve, her godmother, bestowed it as an immortal gift when the city was born.

From the earliest days every man seems to have caught the spirit of the man who came before, and to have perpetuated[17] it; by adding his own distinctive yet always harmonious contribution to the gradual development of the whole. One built a stately avenue; another erected a church at the end; a third added a garden on the other side of the church, and terraces[18] leading[19] up to it; a fourth and fifth cut

旋门沿途的美丽景色。是的，即便对那些最冷漠的人来说，巴黎也是最具魅力的。

经过更细致的欣赏之后，你会发现巴黎真是美极了，她是动人的。因为在严谨典雅的建筑，精心设计、简约质朴的花园，对雕像和对水花的考究使用背后，显示出了一个富有创造激情的民族的想象力——彻彻底底的艺术家式的伟大想象力。任何一个人都可以在任何一个拐角和角落发现这种创造力，下至昏暗的过道，上至陡峭的小山，穿过桥梁，沿着弯曲有致的码头，你能体会到那创造杰作的手所承载的巨大潜力。在不同时代的不同时期，这种想象力同样具有非凡的表现，这些因这种伟大想象力而诞生的杰作交相辉映，向我们证实，巴黎的智慧是永恒的。而这样的智慧，是巴黎圣吉纳维夫圣母在这座城市诞生之时就赐予它的一份不朽的礼物。

从早期开始每个人们似乎就已经领会了前人的思想，并

11 more than   = very
12 elaborate [ɪˈræbərət]   adj. 精心的
13 simplicity [sɪmˈplɪsətɪ]   n. 单纯，简朴，此处译为"简约质朴"
14 lavish [ˈlævɪʃ]   adj. 丰富的，此处引申为"考究"
15 sinuous [ˈsɪnjuəs]   adj. 弯弯曲曲的
16 perennial [pəˈreniəl]   adj. 四季不断的，此处引申为"永恒的"
17 perpetuate [pəˈpetʃueɪt]   v. 使不朽，此处引申为"永久传承下去"
18 terrace [ˈterəs]   n. 梯田
19 leading   = be a route or means of access，通往

streets that should give from the remaining two sides into other flowery squares with their fine edifices. And so from every viewpoint, and from every part of the entire city, today we have an unbroken series of vistas — each one different and more charming than the last.

History has lent its hand to[20] the process, too; and romance — it is not an insipid[21] chain of flower-beds we have to follow, but the holy warriors of Saint Louis[22], the roistering[23] braves of Henry the Great, the gallant[24] Bourbons[25], the ill-starred[26] Bonaparte. These as they passed have left their monuments; it may be only in a crumbling old chapel[27] or ruined tower, but there they are, eloquent of days that are dead, of a spirit that lives forever staunch in the heart of the fervent[28] French people.

It comes over one overwhelmingly sometimes, in the midst of the careless gaiety[29] of the modern city, the old, ever-burning spirit of rebellion and savage strife[30] that underlies[31] it all, and that can spring to[32] the surface now on certain memorable days, with a vehemence[33] that

20 lend one's hand to ＝ help
21 insipid [ɪn'sɪpɪd] adj. 枯燥乏味的，无吸引力的
22 Saint Louis n. 圣路易斯
23 roistering ['rɔɪstərɪŋ] adj. noisy merrymaking，喝酒喧哗的
24 gallant [gælənt] adj. 英勇的
25 Bourbon ['buəbən] n. 波旁皇族，政治上之极端保守分子
26 ill-starred ['ɪl'stɑːd] adj. 注定要倒霉的，不幸的
27 chapel ['tʃæpəl] n. 小礼拜堂
28 fervent ['fɜːvənt] adj. passionate，热情的
29 gaiety ['geɪətɪ] n. 愉快
30 strife [straɪf] n. 争吵，此处引申为"叛乱"
31 underlie exist beneath
32 spring to ＝ jump quickly，这里指突然出现
33 vehemence ['viːəməns] n. 热烈，激情

通过融入自己独特而又和谐的作品使整体逐步发展，从而把这种思想永久地传承了下来。一个人修了一条雄伟的大道，另一个人在大道的尽头建立了一座教堂，第三人又在教堂的旁边建了一座花园，连接着片片梯田。第四个、第五个人又把街道两旁剩下的空间变成了矗立着宏伟建筑、鲜花盛开的广场。所以，从每一个视角，从整座城市的每一个角落，我们今天都可看到一系列连续的景致，每一个景致都不尽相同，一个比一个更具魅力。

历史也同样见证着这样的过程。浪漫不是一系列枯燥乏味的花坊，让我们必须去追随。浪漫是圣路易斯的圣骑，是亨利一世时期敢于喝酒喧嚣的勇士，是英雄的波旁王朝，是注定要失败的拿破仑·波拿巴。随着他们的逝去，留下的是他们的丰碑。浪漫，可能仅存于一间快要坍塌的小教堂中或是一座废弃的古塔中，但它们意味深长，纪念着在那里曾经逝去的光阴，留下一种精神永远地、坚定地扎根于热情的法国人民心中。

这种精神有时会势不可挡地席卷而来，完全湮没在现代城市欢乐氛围之中的古老而炽烈的反抗精神和野蛮叛乱在某

is terrifying. Look across the Pont Alexandre[34], at the serene gold dome of the Invalids, surrounded by its sleepy bar-racks. Suddenly you are in the fires and awful slaughter of Napoleon's wars. The flower of France is being pitilessly[35] cut down for the lust[36] of one man's ambition; and when that is spent, and the wail of[37] the widowed country pierces heaven with its desolation, a costly asylum[38] is built for the handful of[39] soldiers who are left — and the great Emperor has done his duty!

Or you are walking through the Cité, past the court of the Palais de Justice. You glance in, carelessly—memory rushes upon[40] you — and the court flows with blood, "so that men waded through[41] it, up to the knees!" In the tiny stone-walled room yonder[42], Marie Antoinette sits disdainfully composed before her keepers; her face is white with the sounds she hears, as the friends and followers are led out to swell that hideous river of blood.

A pretty, artificial city, Paris; good for shopping, and naughty amusements, now and then. History? Oh yes, of course; but all that's so dry and uninspiring, and besides it happened so long ago.

些纪念日中也会强烈地迸发出来。看看那亚历山大三世桥，安宁平静的金色荣军院穹顶，被酣睡的兵营包围。顿时你会身感处于战火之中，处于拿破仑时代的残酷杀戮中。"法国"这朵浪漫之花被一个人的野心欲望所折断。当这种代价付出后，孤寂的城市用它的悲凉划破了天空，为没有战死的伤兵建一座昂贵的庇护所便是这位伟大的君主所尽的职责！

或者你可能正穿梭于城市，走过立法大楼，你瞥了一眼，一些模糊的记忆浮现在脑海中，似乎看到勇士在鲜血染红的庭院中艰难跋涉。在更远处的一间石头砌的小屋里，玛丽·安托瓦尼特皇后在她的守护者面前沉着而又高傲地坐着，响声不绝于耳，她面色苍白，因为她的朋友和追随者都身陷可怕的血泊之中。

一个人工雕饰的美丽之

---

34 the Pont Alexandre 亚历山大三世桥。亚历山大三世桥坐落在风光明媚的塞纳河上，这座金碧辉煌的桥是巴黎最美丽的桥梁。桥头两端雕刻着希腊女神像和许多法国名人的雕像。桥长107米，宽40米。大桥将两岸的香榭丽舍与荣军院连接起来。左岸两座立柱上有代表文艺复兴时期与路易十四时期的法国标志。右岸两座立柱上有象征古代法兰西和现代法兰西的标志。桥的每一个入口都竖着高高的角柱

35 pitilessly ['pɪtɪlɪslɪ] adv. 冷酷地

36 lust n. strong desire，欲望

37 wail of = shrill cry of pain or grief，尖叫

38 asylum [ə'saɪləm] n. 庇护所

39 the handful of = a group of

40 rush upon = come with great speed

41 wade through = walk with an effort，努力地走，此处译为"跋涉"

42 yonder ['jɒndə] adj. 远处的

Did it? In your stroll along the Rue Royale[43], among the jewelers' and milliners' shops and Maxim's, glance up at the Madeleine, down at the obelisk in the Place de la Concorde. Little over a hundred years ago, this was the brief distance between life and death for those who one minute were dancing in the "Temple of Victory," the next were laying their heads upon the block of the guillotine[44].

From *The Meccas of the World: The Play of Modern Life in New York, Paris ,Vienna, Madrid and London* (1913)

城——巴黎，有时也会是购物的天堂、喧哗嬉戏的好去处。它的历史呢？当然有，但那些都太枯燥也不鼓舞人心，且早已久远。

难道不是吗？在你沿着巴黎皇家路闲逛时，在珠宝商或是百万富翁经营的商店里，抬头瞥一眼玛德莲教堂，低头看看协和广场上的方尖纪念碑。你就会领悟到，这就是在百年前那些前一分钟还在"胜利之庙"跳舞，下一刻就被送上断头台的人所面临的生与死之间的短暂距离。

43 the Rue Royale 巴黎皇家路，是一条拱廊的商店街
44 guillotine ['gɪlətɪːn, gilə'tiːn] *n.* 断头台

含英咀华

巴黎是法国的首都和最大的城市，也是法国的政治文化中心。它有着"梦幻之都"的美誉，从很早以前就是艺术家、作家、思想家和冒险家最想一探究竟的地方。在巴黎市中心漫步，不管在哪里，无论是狭小蜿蜒的街道，还是令人惊叹的教堂、富丽堂皇、令人难以置信的17世纪文艺复兴宫殿，拿破仑时期辉煌的遗迹，19世纪由奥斯曼规划的树木参天包罗万象的大道，都可以印证这一点。选文中作者的文笔清新，就像一个不紧不慢的导游，带着读者从卢浮宫到亚历山大三世桥再到立法大楼一点点品味着巴黎"动人的"景致，也让读者感受到了法国人的文化和他们"富有激情的创造力"。

W. D. McCrackan
W. D.迈克克兰肯威

W. D. 迈克克兰肯，毕业于哈佛大学圣三一学院（*Trinity College, Harvard*），对于政治学和社会学颇有研究，是一位思想家，著有《瑞士共和政体的崛起》（*The Rise of the Swiss Republic, 1892*）一书。

Zurich

苏黎世

If you arrive in Zurich after dark, and pass along the river-front[1], you will think yourself for a moment in Venice. The street lamps glow responsively across the dark Limmat[2], or trail their light from the bridges. In the uncertain darkness, the bare house walls of the farther side put on[3] the dignity of palaces. There are unsuspected architectural glories in the Wasserkirche and the Rathhaus, as they stand partly in the water of the river. And if, at such times, one of the long, narrow barges[4] of the place passes up stream, the illusion is complete; for, as the boat cuts at intervals through the glare of gaslight it looks for all the world like a gondola[5] …

Zurich need not rely upon any fancied resemblance of this sort for a distinct charm of its own[6]. The situation of the city is essentially beautiful, reminding one, in a general way, of that of Geneva, Lucerne, or Thun — at the outlet of a lake, and at the point of issue of a swift river. Approaching from the lakeside, the twin towers of the Grossmünster loom[7] upon the light,

假如你黄昏时分到达苏黎世，徘徊在河畔，你会感觉仿佛身处威尼斯。路灯照亮利马河的每一个角落，灯光从桥上向四处漫延开来。在模糊的黑夜中，远处那些未加装饰的房屋墙壁披上了宫殿般的庄严和肃穆。毋庸置疑，部分矗身水中的水教堂和市政厅是值得称耀的建筑。若在此刻，有狭窄的驳船逆流而上，这幻影将更加完整；因为当小船在煤气灯昏暗的光影间穿梭的时候，像极了威尼斯的小船贡得拉……

苏黎世不需要依赖任何这种虚幻的相似性来体现自己，这个城市本身就具有它独特的魅力。在湖的出口处，在河口，都会使人联想起日内瓦、卢塞恩或是杜安。从湖边慢慢靠近，格罗斯大教堂的双

---

1 river-front 临河建筑区，河边地区，此处译为 "河畔"
2 Limmat *n.* 利马河，瑞士境内的一条河流
3 put on = wear，此处译为 "披上……"
4 barge [bɑ:dʒ] *n.* 驳船
5 gondola ['gɔndələ] *n.* （意大利威尼斯的）小划船
6 a distinct charm of its own 独特的魅力
7 loom [lu:m] *v.* 隐约出现，隐约可见

capped by ugly rounded tops, like miters; upon the left, the simple spires[8] of the Fraumünster and St. Peter's. A conglomeration[9] of roofs denotes the city houses. On the water-front, extensive promenades[10] stretch, crescent[11] shaped, from end to end, cleverly laid out, tho[12] as yet too new to quite fulfil their mission of beauty. Some large white buildings form the front line on the lake — notably the theater, and a few hotels and apartment houses. Finally, there where the River Limmat leaves the lake, a vista of[13] bridges open into the heart of the city — a succession of arches and lines that invite[14] inspection.

Like most progressive cities of Europe, Zurich has outgrown its feudal accouterments[15] within the last fifty years. It has razed[16] its walls, converted its bastions[17] into playgrounds, and, pushing out on every side, has incorporated[18] many neighboring villages, until today it contuins more than ninety thousand inhabitants. The pride of modern Zurich is the Bahnhof-strasse, a long street which leads from the railroad station to the lake. It is planted with trees, and counts as the one, and only boulevard[19] of the city.

塔在灯光的映衬下忽隐忽现，罩着丑陋的圆形的屋顶，酷似僧人的帽子；左边是尖顶的圣母教堂和圣·彼得大教堂。聚集的、一层层的屋顶便是城市中的房屋了。水面前方，广阔的散步区延伸着，向前伸展形成新月形，首尾相接，整齐地排开，它们还太新显示不出其美感所在。一些大的白色建筑在湖边形成一条线——著名的剧院、宾馆和公寓。在利马河逐渐远离湖的区域，一连串的桥横跨在市中心——那一连串的桥洞和航线吸引了人们的视线。

像欧洲大多数的现代化城市一样，苏黎世在过去的五十什摆脱了封建的束缚。推翻了旧城墙，将堡垒变成了广场，城市向各个方向扩展，合并了周围的村庄，直到今天拥有九万多居民。[注：1902年的人口达到152

---

8 spire ['spaɪə] *n.* 尖顶
9 conglomeration [kən.glɒmə'reɪʃn] *n.* 聚集，凝聚
10 promenade [,prɒmə'nɑːd] *n.* public place for walking，公共散步场所
11 crescent ['kresnt] *n.* 新月，新月形
12 tho though的缩略形式，虽然，尽管
13 a vista of long series of scenes，一连串景色
14 invite [ɪn'vaɪt] *vt.* increase the likelihood of，引起，招致
15 accouterment [ə'kuːtəmənt] *n.* = equipment，配备，此处引申为"束缚"
16 raze [reɪz] *vt.* destroy completely，彻底破坏，摧毁
17 bastion ['bæstɪən] *n.* 堡垒
18 incorporate [ɪn'kɔːpəreɪt] *v.* 合并
19 boulevard ['buːləvɑːd] *n.* 林荫大道

Unfortunately, a good view of the distant snow mountains is very rare from the lake promenade, altho[20] they appear with distinctness upon the photographs sold[21] in the shops.

Early every Saturday the pleasant women come trooping in[22], with their vegetables, fruits, and flowers, to line the Bahnhof-strasse with carts and baskets. The ladies and kitchen-maids of the city come to buy; but by noon the market is over. In a jiffy[23], the street is swept as clean as a kitchen floor, and the women have turned their backs on[24] Zurich. But the real center of attraction in Zurich will be found by the traveler in that quarter where stands the Grossmünster, the church of which Zwingli[25] was incumbent[26] for twelve years.

It may well be called the Wittenberg church of Switzerland. The present building dates from the eleventh and twelfth centuries; but tradition has it that the first minster[27] was founded by Charlemagne[28]. That ubiquitous[29] emperor certainly manifested great interest in Zurich. He has been represented no less than three times in various parts of the building. About midway up

000] 班郝夫大道是现代苏黎世的骄傲，它是一条连接火车站和湖边的大街。道路两旁种满了树，宛若一体，是城市里唯一的一条林荫大道。不幸的是，在湖边散步时很难看到远处雪山的美丽景色，虽然这种景色在商店出售的照片里清晰可见。

每个周六的早晨，兴奋的农妇成群结队地推着手推车，挎着篮子，带着她们的蔬菜、水果和鲜花来到班郝夫大道出售。城里的主妇和仆女们前来购买；但是到中午时分，市场就结束了，一会儿，街道就被清扫得像厨房的地板一样干净，女人们对苏黎世就都失去了兴趣。但是苏黎世真正吸引游客的地方是格里斯大教堂，茨温利在这里当了12年的牧师。

它是被称作瑞士威登堡的教堂。现在的建筑可以追溯

---

20 altho   = although的缩略形式，虽然，尽管
21 sold   此处为过去分词作定语
22 troop in   = come or go in large numbers，成群结队而行
23 jiffy ['dʒɪfɪ]   n.   瞬间
24 turn one's back on   = avoid or reject someone or something，避开或拒绝
25 Zwingli   n.   茨温利（1484~1531，瑞典宗教改革家）
26 incumbent [ɪn'kʌmbənt]   n.   领圣职的俸禄的牧师
27 minster ['mɪnɪstə]   n.   修道院的附属教堂
28 Charlemagne: n.   查理曼（742~814），即查理大帝，法兰克王国加洛林王朝国王（768~814），神圣罗马帝国皇帝（800~814），称查理一世
29 ubiquitous [ju:'bɪkwɪtəs]   adj.   present everywhere，到处存在的

one of the towers, his statue appears in a niche, where pigeons strut[30] and prink[31] their feathers, undisturbed. Charlemagne is sitting with a mighty two-edged sword upon his knees, and a gilded crown upon his head; but the figure is badly proportioned[32], and the statue is a good-natured, stumpy[33] affair, that makes one smile rather than admire. The outside of the minster still shows traces if the image breakers of Zwingli's time, and yet the crumbling north portal remains beautiful, even in decay. As for[34] the interior, it has an exceedingly bare and stript[35] appearance; for, altho there is good, solid stonework in the walls, the whole has been washed a foolish, Philistine[36] white. The Romanesque[37] of the architectural is said to be of particular interest to connoisseurs[38], and the queer archaic[39] capitals must certainly attract the notice even of ordinary tourists. …

Zurich is, at the present time, undoubtedly the most important commercial city in Switzerland, having distanced[40] both Basel and Geneva in this direction. The manufacturing of silk, woolen, and linen fabrics has flourished here since the end of the thirteenth century. In modern

到11到12世纪；但传说是查理曼大帝设立了第一座教堂。这位具有无上权力的皇帝当然对苏黎世有浓厚的兴趣，他的雕像在这座建筑的不同部分至少出现了三次。在塔的中间部位，他的雕像放在神龛上，鸽子们在这里迈步，梳理它们的羽毛，悠闲自在。查理曼大帝的膝上放着威武的双刃剑，头戴镀金的皇冠；但是这座雕像的体态不成比例，雕像面容和蔼，身材矮胖，只会让人付诸一笑而不会崇拜。教堂的外面仍然可看到茨温利时代的历史痕迹，北面有些裂痕、有些风化，却仍很美丽。至于内部，变得异常光秃；墙虽然是坚硬的石头，却全部都被刷成愚蠢庸俗的白色。据说很多鉴赏家都对这里的罗马式建筑非常感兴趣，即使是普通游客，也会被那奇特古老的柱顶所吸引。

目前，苏黎世无疑是瑞士

---

30 strut [strʌt] v. 昂首阔步地走
31 prink [prɪŋk] vt. 打扮，装饰
32 proportioned [prəˈpɔːʃənd] adj. 成比例的（相称的）
33 stumpy[ˈstʌmpɪ] adj. 矮胖的
34 as for with regard to
35 stript [strɪpt] adj. 剥落的
36 philistine [ˈfɪlɪˌstiːn] adj. 平庸的，庸俗的
37 Romanesque [ˌrəʊməˈnesk] n. 罗马式建筑
38 connoisseur [ˌkɒnəˈsɜː] n. 鉴赏家
39 archaic [ɑːˈkeɪɪk] adj. 古代的，老式的
40 distance [ˈdɪstəns] v. 远远超过，遥遥领先于……

times, however, cotton and machinery have been added as staple articles of manufacture. Much of the actual weaving is still done in outlying parts of the Canton, in the very cottages of the peasants, so that the click of the loom is heard from open windows in every village and hamlet.

But modern industrial processes are tending continually to[41] drive the weavers from their homes into great centralized factories, and every year this inevitable change becomes more apparent. It is certainly remarkable that Zurich should succeed in turning out cheap and good machinery, when we remember that every ton of coal and iron has to be imported, since Switzerland possesses not a single mine, either of the one or the other.

From *Teutonic Switzerland* (1894)

最重要的商业城市，在这方面遥遥领先于巴赛尔和日内瓦。自从13世纪末，丝绸、羊毛、亚麻纤维制造业就在这里繁荣、兴盛。而今，棉纺织和机器制造成为主要的制造业。实际上大部分纺织业仍然位于州县郊区的农院里，因此每村每户打开窗就能听到织布机的咔嗒声。

但是现代工业过程正处于由家庭作坊逐步向工厂集中转变的过程中，这一趋势逐年明显。瑞士没有任何矿产资源，每一吨煤和钢铁都得依赖进口，考虑到这一点，苏黎世能够生产出物美价廉的机械产品真是太了不起了。

---

41 tend to = be likely to behave in a certain way，倾向，趋向

含英咀华

苏黎世是瑞士的第一大城市，甚至很多人都认为这里是瑞士的首都。选文中作者从各个角度对苏黎世进行了描述，先从它的美景开始介绍，让你觉得仿佛"身处威尼斯一般"；接着，又把视角延伸到了那里记载着历史的教堂和古迹上，因为苏黎世的悠久历史甚至可以追溯到罗马时代；最后，作者又把笔墨放在了苏黎世的商业和工业上，用实例来说明它既是一个历史悠久的古城又是一个充满现代化气息的城市。

Elwyn Brooks White
埃尔文·布鲁克斯·怀特

埃尔文·布鲁克斯·怀特（1899~1985），美国当代著名散文家、评论家，以散文闻名于世，其文风冷峻清丽、辛辣幽默、自成一格。1918年至1921年在康奈尔大学就读，期间曾担任《西雅图时报》(The Seattle Times) 等多家媒体的记者。1924年回到纽约，当了一位广告撰稿人。1927年，他来到《纽约客》(The New Yorker) 杂志社做编辑工作，随后的11年里，他为杂志写了大量的散文和诗歌。1938年至1943年间，作为《哈珀斯》(Harper's Magazine)杂志的专栏作家，怀特为"个人观点"专栏撰写了大量的散文。这些"怀特式"的散文在1942年结集出版，被评论界认为是怀特最优秀的一本散文集。怀特的主要作品有《小老鼠斯图尔特》(Stuart Little, 1945)、《天鹅的喇叭》(The Trumpet of the Swan, 1970) 等，其中最为世人称道的一篇是《林湖重游》(Once More to the Lake, 1941)。

Here Is New York

On any person who desires queer, New York will bestow the gift of loneliness and the gift of privacy. It is this largess that[1] accounts for the presence within the city's walls of a considerable section of the population; for the residents of Manhattan are to a large extent[2] strangers who have pulled up stakes somewhere and come to town, seeking sanctuary[3] or fulfillment or some greater or lesser grail[4]. The capacity to make such dubious[5] gins[6] is a mysterious quality of New York. It can destroy an individual, or it can fulfill him, depending a good deal on luck. No one should come to New York to live unless he is willing to be lucky.

New York is the concentrate of art and commerce and sport and religion and entertainment and finance, bringing to a single compact arena the gladiator, the evangelist[7], the promoter, the actor, the trader, and the merchant. It carries on its lapel the unexpungeable[8] odor of the long past, so that no matter where you sit in

1 It is this largess that   这里是强调句结构
2 to a large extent   =to the degree specified，很大程度上
3 sanctuary ['sæŋktʃuərɪ]   n. 圣所，此处引申为"梦想的家园"
4 grail [greɪl]   n. 圣杯，此处引申为"抱负"
5 dubious ['djuːbɪəs]   adj. 可疑的
6 gin [dʒɪn]   n. 陷阱，此处引申为"可能"
7 evangelist [ɪ'vændʒəlɪst]   n. 布道者
8 unexpungeable [ʌnɪks'pʌndʒəbl]   adj. 不可去除的，此处译为"挥之不去"

这里是纽约

假使有人求取孤独和退隐这样奇怪的奖品，纽约会大方地让他达成心愿。正是因为这种大方的气质，各方人士都汇集到纽约。曼哈顿的居民大多都是外乡人，他们从很远的地方搬到这里，为的就是探寻梦想的家园、实现自身的价值或某些或大或小的抱负。纽约的神秘之处恰恰在于创造了各种看似不可能的可能。它可以毁灭一个人，也可以让这个人飞黄腾达，这主要全由运气主导。假如一个人不愿意祈求好运，那他最好就不要来纽约生活。

纽约浓缩了艺术、商业、体育、宗教、娱乐和金融的精髓。在这片袖珍的土地上，角斗士、布道者、推销商、演员、证券投机者和商人等纷纷亮相，展示着自己的本领。它处处都显露出了挥之不去的传统气息，因此不管你坐在纽约的哪个地方，你都可以感受到伟大的时代和各种丰功伟绩、千奇百怪的人物及事件所带来的震撼。此时在32.2摄氏度的

New York you feel the vibrations[9] of great times and tall deeds, of queer people and events and undertakings. I am sitting at the moment in a stifling hotel room in 90-degree[10] heat, halfway down an air shaft, in midtown. No air moves in or out of the room, yet I am curiously affected by emanations[11] from the immediate surroundings. I am twenty-two blocks from where Rudolph Valentino lay in state, eight blocks from where Nathan Hale was executed, five blocks from the publisher's office where Ernest Hemingway hit Max Eastman on the nose, four mile from where Walt Whitman sat sweating out editorials for the Brooklyn Eagle, thirty-four blocks from the street Willa Cather lived in when she came to New York to write books about Nebraska, one block from where Marceline used to clown on the boards of the Hippodrome, thirty-six blocks from the spot where the historian Joe Gould kicked a radio to pieces in full view of[12] the public, thirteen blocks from where Harry Thaw shot Stanford Whites, five blocks from where I used to usher at the Metropolitan Opera and only 112 blocks from the spot where Clarence Day the Elder was washed off his sins in the Church of the Epiphany (I could continue this list indefinitely[13]); and for that matter I am probably occupying the very room that any number of exalted and somewise

---

9 vibration [vaɪˈbreɪʃn] n. 震动、颤动, 此处引申为 "震撼"
10 90-degree 此处为华氏90度, 相当于32.2摄氏度
11 emanation [ˌeməˈneɪʃən] n. 散发, 发出
12 in full view of = completely visible, 全都看得见
13 indefinitely [ɪnˈdefɪnətlɪ] adv. 无限地, 无穷地

高温下, 我正坐在纽约城中一间燥热的宾馆里, 在这间悬在半空中的房间里, 空气静止了一般, 但我的情绪却不明来由地被周围散发的某种东西所影响。我清楚, 自己所在的地方离鲁道夫·瓦伦蒂诺的长眠之地有22个街区; 离纳森·黑尔英勇的牺牲处有8个街区; 离当年欧内斯特·海明威拳打马克斯·伊斯曼的出版大楼有5个街区; 离沃尔特·惠特曼奋笔疾书为 "布鲁斯之鹰" 撰写评论的住所有4英里; 离维拉·凯瑟搬来纽约从事内布拉斯加系列作品写作时所住的大街有34个街区; 离马赛林过去表演杂耍的马戏场仅有一街之隔; 离当年历史学家裘·古尔德在众人面前脚踢收音机的地方有36个街区; 离哈里·肖枪击斯坦福·怀特的地点有13个街区; 离我以前作引导员的大都会歌剧院有5个街区; 离当年克拉伦斯·戴的忏悔之所——显圣殿, 也仅112个街区 (仅举几个例子)。正是由于这些原因, 此时, 我或许就待在那些尊贵而值得怀念的人们曾待过的地方。或许, 在那些酷热、阴沉的午后, 他们中的一些人——虽然寂寞无

memorable characters sat in, some of them on hot, breathless afternoons, lonely and private and full of their own sense of emanations from without.

When I went down to lunch a few minutes ago I noticed that the man sitting next to me (about eighteen inches away along the wall) was Fred Stone. The eighteen inches were both the connection and the separation that New York provides for its inhabitants. My only connection with Fred Stone was that I saw him in *The Wizard of Oz* around the beginning of the century. But our waiter felt the same stimulus from being close to a mail from Oz, and after Mr. Stone left the room the waiter told me that when he (the waiter) was a young man just arrived in this country and before he could understand a word of English, he had taken his girl for their first theater date to *The Wizard of Oz*. It was a wonderful show, the waiter recalled — a man of straw, a man of tin. Wonderful! (And still only eighteen inches away.) "Mr. Stone is a very hearty eater," said the waiter thoughtfully, content with[14] this fragile participation in destiny, this link with Oz.

New York blends the gin of privacy with the excitement of participation, and better than most dense communities it succeeds in insulating[15] the individual (if he wants it, and

---

14 content with = satisfied with，心满意足
15 insulating ['ɪnsjuleɪtɪŋ] *adj.* 绝缘的，此处引申为"远离干扰"

聊——却曾经和我现在一样在这周围的景色中徜徉。

几分钟前我下楼吃饭时，发现在我旁边（大约18英寸外挨墙的地方）坐着的是弗雷德·斯通。18英寸的距离，纽约提供给它的居民是在给人亲近感的同时，又仿佛会拒人于千里之外。我和弗雷德·斯通唯一的联系便是大概本世纪初的时候，我曾在《绿野仙踪》中看过他的表演。而我们的服务生则因为近距离地接触到了"稻草人"先生的信件，也感受到了同样的"鼓舞"。当斯通先生离开饭店后，这名服务生告诉我，当自己还是个年轻小伙，刚到纽约，对英语一窍不通时，他和女朋友第一次去歌剧院约会，当时放映的影片就是《绿野仙踪》。服务生回忆说，演出很美妙，剧中那个微不足道的稻草人被演得活灵活现。服务生（仍然保持只有18英寸的距离）若有所思地说："斯通先生吃得可真多。"他因为终于和"稻草人"先生沾上了一点关系而沾沾自喜。

纽约是一个让人既可以独处，也可以与他人分享快乐的地方。与世界上其他的大都市

almost everybody wants or needs it) against all enormous and violent and wonderful events that are taking place every minute. Since I have been sitting in this miasmial[16] air shaft, a good many rather splashy[17] events have occurred in town. A man shot and killed his wife in a fit of[18] jealousy. It caused no stir outside his block and got only small mention in the papers. I did not attend. Since my arrival, the greatest air show ever staged in all the world took place in town. I didn't attend and neither did most of the eight million other inhabitants, although they say there was quite a crowd. I didn't even hear any planes except a couple of westbound commercial airliners that habitually use this air shaft to fly over. The biggest oceangoing ships on the North Atlantic and departed. I didn't notice them and neither did most other New Yorkers. I am told this is the greatest seaport in the world, with 650 miles of waterfront[19], and ships calling[20] here from many exotic lands, but the only boat I've happened to notice since my arrival was a small sloop tacking[21] out of the East River night before last on the ebb tie when I was walking across the Brooklyn bridge. I heard the Queen Mary blow one

---

16 miasmial [mɪˈæzməl] *adj.* 毒气的，此处引申为"空气混浊的"
17 splashy [ˈsplæʃi] *adj.* 引人注目的
18 a fit of = short period of an intense feeling，一股，一阵
19 waterfront [ˈwɔːtəfrʌnt] *n.* 水边的码头区，滨水地区
20 calling 这里指船进港
21 tack [tæk] *v.* 此处指"迎风破浪"

相比，纽约有一个优势，那就是虽然这里时时刻刻都发生着一些或惊天动地或暴力残忍或美妙无比的事情，它却能确保让每一个人（如果这个人想的话，我想人们大都希望如此）远离干扰。自从我踏进这空气混浊的房间起，城里已经发生了很多重大的事件。一名男子出于妒忌，用枪杀死了他的妻子。除了事发公寓，其他地方并未引起什么轰动，报上也只草草写了几行文字。我也没有在意。自我来这儿以后，纽约举办过全球最盛大的航空展。尽管我听别人说，现场人山人海，可我没去参加，纽约八百多万人口中的大部分人也都没参加。除了几架平日里常常从屋顶上掠过向西飞去的商业飞机，我居然没听到其他飞机的声音。在北大西洋上航行的世界上最大的远洋船来了又去了，我没有看到过这些船，绝大多数纽约人也没有。人们告诉我，纽约港是全球最大的海港，码头区长达六百五十英里，进港的船只来自世界各地。然而，自从我来了以后，我只见过一艘船，那是前天晚上走过布鲁克林大桥时，一艘在退潮时沿东河迎风破浪的

midnight, though, and the sound carried the whole history of departure and longing and loss. The lions[22] have been in convention. I've seen not one Lion. A friend saw one and told me about him. (He was lame, and was wearing a bolero[23].) At ballgrounds and horse parks the greatest sporting spectacles have been enacted. I saw no ballplayer, no race horse. The governor came to town. I heard the siren[24] screamed, but that was all — there was to that an eighteen-inch margin[25] again. A man was killed by a falling cornice[26]. I was not a party to the tragedy, and again the inches counted heavily...

From *The New Yorker* (1949)

单桅小帆船。的确，有一天子夜，我曾经听过"玛丽女王"的汽笛声，那声音富含了整个历史的伤感、渴望和失落。那些社会权贵们已经开过了集体会议，但我一个权贵也没有看到。一位朋友倒是看到了其中的一位，还向我描绘了他的外貌（此人腿有残疾，身穿一件西班牙式的敞胸短上衣）。纽约的球场和马场上，以前曾上演过规模宏大的赛事，可我没看到棒球手，也没有看到赛马。州长光顾这儿，我听到过警笛长鸣，但也仅仅是到此为止——这次又是18英寸的距离阻断人们的联系。一个人被掉下的门楣砸死。此事与我毫无干系，那18英寸的距离又一次扮演了卑劣的角色……

---

22 lions　这里指社会权贵们，非"狮子"
23 bolero [bə'leərəu]　*n.*　女用短上衣
24 siren ['saɪərən]　*n.*　警报器
25 margin ['mɑ:dʒɪn]　*n.*　边缘
26 cornice ['kɔ:nɪs]　*n.*　门楣

含英咀华

　　在纽约这片袖珍的土地上，浓缩了艺术、商业、体育、宗教、娱乐和金融的精髓。与世界上其他的大都市相比，纽约的神秘之处恰恰在于它创造了各种看似不可能的可能。还记得曹桂林先生曾经这样写道，"如果你爱他，就把他送到纽约，因为那里是天堂；如果你恨他，就把他送到纽约，因为那里是地狱……"。

缤纷城市
缤纷印象

A Guest's Impression of New England
新英格兰的访客印象

Cracow
克拉科夫

Edinburgh
爱丁堡

Florence Eighty Years Ago
八十年前的佛罗伦萨

Geneva
日内瓦

Marseilles
马赛

St. Andrews
圣安德鲁斯

Venice
威尼斯

Sight-seeing in Melbourne
观光墨尔本

William Faulkner

威廉·福克纳

威廉·福克纳(1897~1962)，美国现代著名小说家，生于美国密西西比州新奥尔巴尼的一个庄园主家庭。福克纳的作品最大的外在特点是绵延婉转、结构极为繁复的长句子和反复斟酌推敲后选取的精巧词汇，他与风格简洁明了、干脆利落的海明威是两个极端。他的作品中有南方人特有的幽默感，深入刻画了黑人与白人的地位、相处、矛盾等敏感问题，生动描绘出了惟妙惟肖的南方人形象。他笔下的故事情节浸染着人物的复杂心理变化，细腻的感情描写穿插其中。他一生多产，一共写了19部长篇小说与近百篇短篇小说，其中15部长篇与绝大多数短篇的故事都发生在约克纳帕塔法县，称为约克纳帕塔法世系。其中最具代表性的作品是《喧哗与骚动》(The Sound and the Fury, 1929)，福克纳的其他重要作品还有《押沙龙，押沙龙！》(Absalom, Absalom!, 1936)、《我弥留之际》(As I Lay Dying, 1930)、《八月之光》(Light in August, 1932)等。

A Guest's Impression of New England

新英格兰的访客印象

It is not the country which impressed this one. It is the people — the men and women themselves so individual, who hold individual integration and privacy as high and dear as they do[1] liberty and freedom; holding theses so high that they take it for granted that all other men and women are individuals, too, and treat them as such, doing this simply by letting them alone with absolute and complete dignity and courtesy[2].

Like this, one afternoon (it was October, the matchless Indian summer of New England), Malcolm Cowley and I were driving through back roads in western Connecticut and Massachusetts. We got lost. We were in what a Mississippian would call mountains[3] but which New Englanders call hills; the road was not getting worse yet just hillier[4] and lonelier and apparently going nowhere save upward, toward a range of[5] hills. At last, just as we were about to turn back, we found a house, a mailbox, two men, farmers or in the costume of farmers —sheep-lied coats and caps with earflaps[6] tied over the crown —

这一片土地并没有给我留下深刻的印象，反倒是生活在这片土地上的人让我久久不能忘怀——因为这里的男人和女人们都有自我意识。如同追求解放和自由一样，他们高尚而虔诚地对待自己的个性完整和私生活自由。这种观念是如此的根深蒂固，以至于他们认为其他人理所当然也同样是一个独立的个体，也应受到同等的对待，即拥有绝对而且完全的自尊和尊严。

举一个例子，一天下午（当时是十月份，无与伦比的新英格兰阳春天气），我和马尔科姆·考利正开着车在康涅狄克州和马萨诸塞州西部偏僻的公路上行驶。走了一段路后，我们迷了路。困住我们的地方，密西西比州人会把它叫做高山，而新英格兰人则把它称为丘陵。路还不是太难走，只是变得越来越陡峭偏僻，很明显这是通往山顶的路。经过许多小山后，正当我们要掉转车头往回走的时候，却发现了一座房子，一个邮筒，看到邮

1 do v. 这里是代替前面的动词hold，译为"追求"
2 courtesy ['kɜːtəsɪ] n. 尊严
3 what a Mississipian would call mountains 这里是名词性从句
4 hilly ['hɪlɪ] adj. 多小山的，丘陵，此处引申为"陡峭"
5 a range of = a row of
6 earflap ['ɪəflæp] n. （附于帽侧，可放下护耳御寒的）耳扇，耳罩，帽耳

standing beside the mailbox, and watching us quietly and with perfect courtesy as we drove up and stopped.

"Good afternoon," Cowley said.

"Good afternoon," one of the men said.

"Does this road cross the mountain?" Cowley said.

"Yes," the man said, still with that perfect courtesy.

"Thank you," Cowley said and drove on, the two men still watching us quietly — for perhaps fifty yards, when Cowley braked[7] suddenly and said, "Wait," and backed[8] the car down to the mailbox again where the two men still watched us. "Can I get over it in this car?" Cowley said. "No," the same man said. "I don't think you can." So we turned around and back the way we came.

That's what I mean. In the West, the Californian[9] would have been a farmer only by hobby, his true dedication[10] and calling being that of a car trader, who would assure us that our car could not possibly make the crossing but that he had not only a car that could make it, but the only car west of the Rocky Mountains that could do it; in the Central States and the East we would have been given directions to circumvent[11] the mountain, based on[12] obscure third-

---

7 brake [breɪk] v. 刹车
8 back v. move backward, 后退
9 Californian [ˌkælɪˈfɔːnjən] n. 加州人，加利福尼亚州人
10 dedication [ˌdedɪˈkeɪʃn] n. 奉献，这里指他们全身心投入干的事，"认可的"
11 circumvent [ˌsɜːkəmˈvent] v. 躲开，绕行
12 base on 此处意为"参照"

筒旁边还站着两个男人。他们是农民，或者说穿得很像是农民——一身羊皮袄，帽子两侧的耳扇系在雀帽顶上。他们什么也没说，只是十分礼貌地看着我们把车停下来。

"下午好！"考利喊道。

"下午好！"其中一人回答道。

"这条路能通往山上吗？"考利问。

"是的。"那人回答道，态度仍然是客客气气的。

"谢谢。"说完，考利继续发动汽车向前开，那两个人仍一声不响地看着我们。大约走了50码，考利冷不防地把车停下来说："等一下。"他把车倒回到邮筒旁边，那两个人居然还在看着我们。"我开着这辆车能过去吗？"考利问道。

"不能，"还是刚才说话的那个人，"我想你开不过去。"我们只好掉头原路返回。

这就是我要表达的意思。在美国西部，加利福尼亚人务农仅仅是因为一种业余爱好，他们真正认可的职业是做汽车生意。加利福尼亚人会肯定地告诉我们：我们的车根本没有翻山而过的可能，且他不但拥有一辆可以翻越的车，并且

count road forks[13] and distant houses with lightning rods on the northeast chimney and creek crossings. If you looked carefully you could discern the remains of bridges vanished these forty years ago which Gabriel[14] himself could not have followed; in my own South the two Mississippians[15] would have adopted[16] us before Cowley could have closed his mouth and put the car in motion[17] again, saying one of them (the other would already be getting into the car): "Why sure, it won't be ang trouble[18] at all; Jim here will go with you and I'll telephone across[19] the mountain for my nephew to meet you with his truck where you are stuck; it'll pull you right on through and he'll even mechanic waiting with a new crankcase[20]."

But not the New Englander, who respects your right to privacy and free will by telling, giving you only and exactly what you asked for, and no more. If you want to try to take your car over that road, that's your business and not his to ask you why. If you want to wreck it and spend the night on foot to the nearest lighted window or disturbed watchdog, that's your

---

是在落基山脉以西唯一一辆可以翻越山脉的车子。在美国的中部和东部各州，人们会为我们指路，告诉我们如何绕过山区，告诉我们参照的路标是从某个地方数起的第三条拐弯处，或是远处某些房子东北角烟囱上的避雷针，或是一些小河的渡口。如果你在那儿仔细查看，还可以目睹40年前就消失的桥梁和它们留下的痕迹，这些路线恐怕连《圣经》中的大天使加百列也不知来由。而换在南方，用不着考利说完话，重新发动汽车，那两个密西西比州人就会跑上前来帮忙。其中一个会说（另一个正在上车）："啊，这根本不值得担心，吉姆会和你们一起去。然后，我再给山那边的侄子打个电话，告诉他开卡车到你们过不去的地方等着。卡车会把你们的车拖上去。没准他还会带上汽车修理工和新的工具箱去等你们呢！"

但这却不是新英格兰人的作风。他们会十分尊敬你的隐私权和个人意愿。他回复你的或者给你的和你所需要的丝毫不差，不多不少。如果你想尝试沿着那一条路把车开过去，那是你自己的事情，他没有权

---

13 fork ['fɔːt]　n.　分岔，岔路口
14 Gabriel ['geɪbrɪəl]　n.　加百列（七大天使之一，报喜天使）
15 Mississippian [ˌmɪsɪ'sɪpɪən]　n.　密西西比州人
16 adopt [ə'dɒpt]　v.　采用，收养，接受
17 put...in motion　= cause something to start moving，此处为"发动汽车"
18 won't be any trouble　此处意为完全没问题，不值得担心
19 across [ə'krɒs]　= on the other side
20 crankcase ['kræŋkkeɪs]　n.　曲轴箱，此处为"修理箱"

business, too, since it's your car and your legs. You had wanted to know if the car could cross the mountain, you would have asked that. Because he is free, private, not made so by the stem and rockbound[21] land — the poor thin soil and the hard long winters — on which his lot[22] was cast, but on the contrary: having elected deliberately of his own volition[23] that stem land and weather, because he knew he was tough enough to cope with them; having been bred by the long tradition which sent him from old worn-out Europe so he could be free; taught him to believe that there is no valid reason why life should be soft and docile[24] and amenable, that to be individual and private is the thing and that the man who cannot cope with any environment anywhere had better not clutter[25] the earth to begin with.

To stand out against[26] that environment which has done its worst to him, and failed, leaving him not only superior to it but its master too. He quits it occasionally of course, but he takes it with him, too. You will find it in sunglasses and straw sandals[27] and his shirt-tail[28] outside his pants. But open the aloha bed-jacket and scratch him a little and you will

利去问为什么。如果你想丢下车子，在漆黑的夜晚向最近处的灯光徒步行走或者吵醒了某户人家的看门狗，那也是你自己的事，因为汽车和双腿都是你的财产，都由你支配。如果你想知道这辆汽车是否可以驶过山区的话，那你就应该直接地问他。因为他享有自由和隐私的权利。新英格兰人思想自由，崇尚隐私，这种性格并不是由他命中注定、赖以生存的严酷、岩石遍地的环境——土壤贫瘠，冬季寒冷漫长——造就的，相反是他自己选择了这片土地，他清楚自己坚韧的性格足以应对逆境。远离哺育他长大的悠久腐朽的欧洲文化，他自由自在；他坚信生活不可能也不应该轻松安逸，最重要的是个人独立和个人的隐私权利。一个人的一生如果不能随时随地应付艰苦的环境，那他还不如不生活在这片土地上。

环境的恶劣注定要以失败告终，他的坚韧不屈不仅让他未向周围的环境低头，反而却让他成了环境的主人。当然偶尔他也会离开一段时间，但是环境的烙印却深深地刻在了他们身上并一直伴随着他们。这能从他们戴着的太阳镜、穿着

21 rockbound *adj.* 被岩石包围的（多岩的）
22 lot ＝person's fortune, destiny or share，命运
23 volition [vəˈlɪʃ(ə)n] *n.* 意志，决心
24 docile [ˈdəʊsaɪl] *adj.* 温顺的，此处引申为"轻松"
25 clutter [ˈklʌtə] *v.* fill or cover something in an untidy way，此处引申为"生活"
26 stand out against ＝ continue to resist，坚持抵抗
27 sandal [ˈsændl] *n.* 凉鞋
28 shirt-tail *n.* 衬衫下摆

find thin soil and the rocks and the long snow and the man who hadn't at all been driven from his birthplace because it had beaten him at last, but who had left because he himself was the victor and the spirit was gone with his cooling and slowing blood, and now is simply using that never-never land of mystics and astrologers[29] and fire-worshippers and raw-carrot friends as a hobby for his declining years.

From Essay: *A Guest's Impression of New England* (1954)

的草鞋、露在裤子外面的衬衫下摆中看出来。然而，你只要撩起他的花衬衫，摸摸他的身子，你就会发现那贫瘠的土壤和岩石还有长年的积雪留下的印记。他离开家乡，并不是因为他屈服于环境，而是因为他战胜了环境。而留下来是人因为那种勇敢的精神已经随着逐渐冷却的热血，以及逐渐减慢的流动，悄然而去了。而现在，在那个神秘主义者、占星家、拜火教徒和红毛妖怪的虚幻世界中，他仅仅是在做一些晚年的消遣娱乐而已。

---

29 astrologer [əˈstrɒlədʒə]　*n.*　占星家

含英咀华

　　选文中作者并未把笔墨倾注在对新英格兰美景的描绘上，而是描写了生活在这片土地上的人，文中的故事情节浸染着人物的复杂心理变化，细腻的感情描写也穿插其中。

Ménie Muriel Dowie

梅尼·墨里埃尔·多维

梅尼·墨里埃尔·多维（1867~1945），英国杰出的作家、旅行家，出生于利物浦，在英国利物浦、德国斯图加特和法国接受过教育。她二十岁左右时一直在游历，1895年发表了第一部小说《高卢》(Gallia)，小说出版后曾因为其中的性描写一度引起争议，这部小说也使她成为新女性作家之一。在1899年和1901年她又分别发表了另外两部小说。1941年她移居美国，1945年在亚利桑那州去世，享年78岁。

Cracow

Cracow[1], old, tired and dispirited[2], speaks and thinks only of the ruinous[3] past. When you drive into Cracow from the station for the first time, you are breathless, smiling, and tearful all at once[4]; in the great Ring-platz — a mass of old buildings — Cracow seems to hold out her arms to you — those long sides that open from the corner where the cab drives in. You do not have time to notice separately the row of small trees down on one side, beneath which bright-colored women-figures control their weekly market; you do not notice the sort of court-house[5] in the middle with its red roof, cream-colored galleries[6] and shops beneath; you do not notice the great tall church at one side of brick and stone most perfectly time-reconciled, or the houses, or the crazed paving, or the innocent little groups of cabs — you only see Cracow holding out her arms to you, and you may lean down your head[7] and weep from pure instinctive sympathy. Suddenly a choir[8] of trumpets[9] breaks out[10] into a chorale[11]

1 **Cracow** *n.* 克拉科夫，位于波兰南部维斯瓦河上游左岸，距华沙约250公里，是波兰第三大城市，波兰最大的文化、科学、工业与旅游中心，曾是波兰的首都，作为历史名城和文化中心而闻名
2 **dispirited** [dɪs'pɪrɪtɪd] *adj.* 沮丧的，缺乏生机的
3 **ruinous** ['ruːɪnəs] *adj.* 毁坏的，衰败的
4 **all at once** = suddenly 突然
5 **court-house** *n.* 法院大楼；县政府大楼
6 **gallery** ['gæləri] *n.* 画廊
7 **lean down one's head** = lower one's head，低下头
8 **choir** [kwaɪə] *n.* 唱诗班
9 **trumpet** ['trʌmpɪt] *n.* 喇叭声，此处引申为"音乐声"
10 **break out** 突然发生，此处意为"传来"
11 **chorale** [kɒ'rɑː] *n.* 赞美诗

克拉科夫

古老、陈旧、缺乏生机的克拉科夫述说与回忆着它那已经没落的历史。当你第一次乘车从车站驶进克拉科夫时，你将会为它那过去的辉煌惊叹、微笑，同时为它现在的没落而突然痛心；一大群旧式的建筑围成了一个环状广场，当出租车从角落里沿路驶进广场时，克拉科夫似乎正在张开她的双臂欢迎你的到来。你无暇顾及路边成行的树木，在那之下是光鲜亮丽的女人们在每周一次的集市上操控着市场；你无暇顾及中间那红屋顶的法院大楼，在那里面是乳酪色的画廊与商店；你无暇顾及路边那些被时间磨洗得近乎完美的砖石做的宏伟而高大的教堂，还有那些房子、出现裂纹的石路或者那些单调的一组组的出租车。你只会看到克拉科夫张开她的双臂欢迎你，你也许会低下头出于本能的同情而落泪。突然，从大教堂的塔里传来了唱诗班的赞美诗，其内在的忧伤令我永生难忘；这恰到好处的曲调是如此的苍老与疲惫；

from the big church tower; the melancholy[12] of it I shall never forget — the very melody seemed so old and tired, so worn and sweet and patient, like Cracow. Those trumpet notes have mourned[13] in that tower for hundreds of years. It is the *Hymn of Timeless Sorrow* that[14] they play, and the key to which they are attuned in Cracow's long despair. Hush! That is her voice, the old town's voice, high and sad — she is speaking to you.

Dear Cracow! Never again it seems to me, shall I come so near to the deathless hidden sentiment[15] of Poland[16] as in those first moments. It would be no use to[17] tell her to take heart, that there may be brighter days coming, and so forth. Lemberg[18] may feel so, Lemberg that has the feelings of any other big new town, the strength and the determination; but Cracow's day was in the long ago, as a gay capital, a brilliant university town full of princes, of daring, of culture, of wit. She has outlived[19] her day, and can only mourn over what has been and the times that she has seen; she may be always proud of her character, of the brave blood that has made scarlet[20] her streets, but she can never be happy remodeled as an

---

12 melancholy ['melənkəlɪ] *n.* 忧沉，悲哀，愁思
13 mourn [mɔːn] *v.* 呜咽，哀鸣
14 It is…that 这是一个强调句
15 sentiment ['sentɪmənt] *n.* 感情，情绪
16 Poland ['pəʊlənd] *n.* 波兰
17 be no use to 无益于做某事
18 Lemberg *n.* 伦贝格，现在的利沃夫（乌克兰西部城市）
19 outlive [,aʊt'lɪv] *vt.* 比……活得长
20 scarlet ['skɑːlət] *adj.* 肥斐色的，深红色的，此处为宾语
　　　　　　　　　　　"her streets"的补足语，即"… has
　　　　　　　　　　　made her streets scarlet…"

如此的憔悴、甜美与包容，就同这座城市一样。那些诗乐已经在塔里哀鸣了数百年。他们演奏的是《亘古不变的悲痛圣歌》，那是在克拉科夫的长期没落中谱成的。请肃静！那是她的声音，一个古老城镇的声音，如此的高亢与悲伤——她正在对你诉说。

亲爱的克拉科夫！在最初的一段时间里，我对波兰不灭的、深藏的感情来得如此强烈，以至于我觉得它不会再来第二次了。单纯地叫她重新振作起来、告诉她光明就在眼前等等是毫无用处的。这对伦贝格也许会有效，伦贝格有着和其他新兴大城镇一样的力量与决心；但是作为一个快乐的首都，一个充满着贵族气质、骑士勇气、文化底蕴与圣贤智慧的璀璨的大学之城，克拉科夫的时代已经过去了。这个时代已经不属于她了，现在能做的只是追悼那些曾经的辉煌以及她所见证的历史；她也许常常会为自己的个性而骄傲、为染红街道的勇敢者的鲜血而骄傲，但她永远不会为成为奥地利的驻军城镇而快乐。而在以人民意志为建国基石的新波兰——有一天这块基石也许会

Austrian garrison[21] town, and in the new Poland — the Poland whose foundation stones are laid in the hearts of her people, and that may yet be built some day — in that new Poland there will be no place for aristocratic[22], high-bred Cracow.

During my stay in the beautiful butter-colored palace that is now a hotel, I went round the museums, galleries, and universities, most if not all of which are free to the public. It would be unfair to give the idea that Cracow has completely fallen to decay[23]. This is not the case. Austria has erected some very handsome buildings; and a town with such fine pictures, good museums, and two universities, can not be complained of[24] as moribund[25]. At the same time, I can only record faithfully my impression, and that was that everything new, everything modern, was hopelessly out of tone[26] in Cracow; progress, which, though desirable, may be a vulgar thing, would not suit her, and does not seem at home in her streets.

All the stars were shining, and little red-yellow lights in the castle windows were not much bigger. Above the whisper of the willows on its bank came the deep, quiet murmur of the Vistula[27], and every now and then, over the several towers of the solemn old palaces and the spires[28] of the church

重建——在那不幸的新波兰将会容不下贵族出身、血统优越的克拉科夫。

当我停留在那曾是辉煌宫殿的旅馆期间，我参观了附近的博物馆、画廊和大学，它们大多数是对民众免费开放的。认为克拉科夫已经完全陷入衰落是不公平的，事实并非如此。奥地利人曾经建造过一些非常漂亮的建筑；并且一个城镇有如此美丽的景致、如此优良的博物馆和两所大学，不能被抱怨是衰败的、腐朽的。但与此同时，我只能忠实地记录我的印象：现在这里所有的事物都是新颖的，所有的事物都是现代化的，很难和克拉科夫的格调相一致；进步虽然是人们所渴望的，但也许是件粗俗的事物，并不适合克拉科夫，这让她变得有点不伦不类。

天上的星星在闪烁，城堡的窗户里透出微弱的红黄色光。有时河堤上的柳树在微微耳语。在那旧时庄严的宫殿的

---

21 garrison ['gærɪsn]   n.   守备队，驻军
22 aristocratic [ˌærɪstə'krætɪk]   adj.   贵族的，贵族气派的
23 decay [dɪ'keɪ]   v.   衰退，衰落
24 complain of   固定搭配，意为"抱怨"
25 moribund ['mɒrɪbʌnd]   adj.   垂死的，前面省略"being"
26 out of tone   此处指"与……不相容"
27 Vistula ['vɪstjʊlə]   n.   维斯杜拉河（波兰中部河流）
28 spire ['spaɪə]   n.   尖顶

where Poland has laid her kings, and so recently the king of the poets, the stars were dropping from their places, like sudden spiders, letting themselves down into the vast by faint yellow threads that showed a moment after the star itself was gone.

Later, as I looked from the open gallery of the train that was taking me away, I could not help thinking that, just a hundred years ago, Wawel[29]'s star was shining with a light bright enough for all Europe to see; but even as the stars fell that night and left their places empty, so Wawel's star has fallen and Poland's star has fallen too.

From *Seeing Europe with Famous Authors* (2006)

塔顶、那宏伟教堂的塔尖、波兰国王曾居住的地方，而现在是诗圣的居所。星宿正在陨落，就像敏捷的蜘蛛，划过一道微黄色的弧线，落向那茫茫的洪荒，一瞬间就不见了。

后来，在离开的火车上，我望着窗外的风景，忍不住在想，仅在一百年前，瓦维尔宫殿像一颗明星，光芒照亮了整个欧洲，但现在这里边星星已经陨落了，只留下空空的宫殿。瓦维尔宫没落了，整个波兰也没落了。

---

29 Wawel　　n　瓦维尔宫，建立在克拉科夫市维斯杜拉河畔的石灰岩山岗上，是波兰最古老的宫殿之一

含英咀华

克拉科夫市位于波兰南部离华沙约300公里的维斯杜拉河河畔，是波兰最大的文化、科学、工业与旅游中心。作者用许多美妙的形容词来表达对这座城市的喜爱，把对这座古都的感情表现得淋漓尽致。

Robert Louis Stevenson

罗伯特·路易斯·史蒂文森

罗伯特·路易斯·史蒂文森(1850~1894)，苏格兰小说家、诗人、游记作家，是新浪漫主义和英国文学的代表人物。史蒂文森从小就对文学情有独钟，因此向父亲要求学文学，结果未获批准，作为折中，他改学了法律。1875年毕业后他成为一名律师，但仍抽空从事文学创作。1878年他出版了第一本游记《内河航程》（*An Inland Voyage, 1878*）。一年后，又出版了《骑驴漫游记》（*Travels with a Donkey in the Cévennes, 1879*）。从此，他放弃律师业务，潜心写作，在短短的一生中写下了大量的散文、游记、随笔、小说和诗歌。

Edinburgh

Venice, it has been said, differs from all other cities in the sentiment which she inspires. The rest may have admirers[1]; she only, a famous fair one, counts lovers in her train. And, indeed, even by her kindest friends, Edinburgh is not considered in a similar sense[2]. These like her for many reasons, not any one of which is satisfactory in itself. They like her whimsically[3], if you will, and somewhat as a virtuoso[4] dotes upon[5] his cabinet. Her attraction is romantic in the narrowest meaning of the term. Beautiful as she is[6], she is not so much beautiful as interesting. She is preeminently[7] Gothic, and all the more so since she has set herself off[8] with some Greek airs, and erected classic, temples on her erys. In a word, and above all, she is a curiosity.

The palace of Holyrood[9] has been left aside in the growth of Edinburgh, and stands gray and silent in a workman's quarter and among breweries[10] and

---

1 admirer [əd'maɪərə(r)]   *n.* 仰慕者
2 in a sense   = if the statement, etc is understood in a particular way，在某种意义上
3 whimsically ['(h)wɪmzɪklɪ]   *adv.* 古怪地，此处引申为"疯狂地"
4 virtuoso [ˌvɜ:tʃu'əʊsəʊ]   *n.* 艺术品鉴赏家
5 dote upon   = dote on, show (too) much fondness for somebody or something，溺爱
6 beautiful as she is   此处为倒装结构
7 preeminently [ˌpri(:)'emɪnəntlɪ]   *adv.* 卓越地，此处译为"出类拔萃"
8 set off   = make something appear more attractive by contrast，（通过对比）使某事物更有吸引力
9 The palace of Holyrood   在苏格兰爱丁堡的属于英国皇家的宫殿,女皇每年有固定时间在这里居住，特别是在夏天的时间
10 brewery ['bru:ərɪ]   *n.* 啤酒厂

爱丁堡

据说，威尼斯因她所散发出的独特风情而与众不同。别的城市也有众多的仰慕者；她只是一个出名的城市，火车上尽是她的崇拜者。事实上，即使是她最友好的朋友爱丁堡的韵味与她截然不同。每个人都有喜爱她的理由，但这些理由本身没有一个能让人满意。人们疯狂地爱着这座城市，如果你愿意，可以像一位艺术品鉴赏家溺爱他的收藏品一样爱着这座城市。她的魅力在于她的浪漫。爱丁堡确实美丽，但与其说她有魅力还不如说她更让人感兴趣。她哥特式的风格出类拔萃，不仅如此，她还散发着一股希腊的气息，她的沙漠上矗立着古典的神殿。总之一句话，她令人心驰神往。

在爱丁堡发展的历史进程中，荷里路德宫被人们淡忘了，灰头土脸地坐落在工人广场里，夹杂在一些酿酒厂和煤气厂中间。她是一座拥有许多历史回忆的宫

gas-works. It is a house of many memories. Great people of yore[11], kings and queens, buffoons[12] and grave ambassadors, played their stately farce[13] for centuries in Holyrood. Wars have been plotted, dancing has lasted deep into the night, and murder has been done in its chambers. There Prince Charlie held his fantom[14] levees[15], and in a very gallant[16] manner represented a fallen dynasty for some hours. Now, all these things of day are mingled with the dust, the king's crown itself is shown for six pence to the vulgar[17]; but the stone palace has outlived these changes. For fifty weeks together, it is no more than a show for tourists and a museum of old furniture; but on the fifty-first, beholds the palace reawakened and mimicking[18] its past.

The Lord Commissioner, a kind of stave[19] sovereign[20], sits among stage courtiers[21]; a coach and six and clattering escort come and go before the gate; at night, the windows are lighted up, and its near neighbors, the workmen, may dance in their own houses to the palace music. And in this the palace is typical. There is a spark among the embers[22]; from time to time the old volcano smokes. Edinburgh has but partly abdicated[23], and

11 yore [jɔ:] *n.* 往昔，昔日
12 buffoon [bə'fu:n] *n.* 小丑
13 farce [fɑ:s] *n.* 闹剧
14 fantom ['fæntəm] *n.* 阴影，此处引申为"飘摇的"
15 levee ['levɪ] *n.* （旧时帝王的）早朝
16 gallant ['gælənt] *adj.* 华丽的，此处引申为"大气，硬朗"
17 vulgar ['vʌlgə(r)] *adj.* （俗语）平民，百姓
18 mimicking ['mɪmɪkɪŋ] *n.* 模仿，此处引申为"再现"
19 stave [steɪv] *n.* 梯级
20 sovereign ['sɒvrɪn] *n.* 元首
21 courtier ['kɔ:tɪə] *n.* 朝臣
22 ember ['embə] *n.* （pl.）余烬
23 abdicate ['æbdɪkeɪt] *v.* 放弃

殿。昔日的伟人们，国王、皇后、小丑、严肃的大使们就在这个宫殿中演绎他们长达几个世纪的闹剧。这里曾是秘密策划战争的地方，这里曾歌舞升平直至深夜，这里也曾经发生过卧室谋杀案。查理王子力挺着飘摇的皇室，用一种十分大气硬朗的方式代表着一个业已腐朽坍塌的王朝最后的尊严。现在，所有的这些历史已经混入了历史的尘土，就连国王的王冠也被以六便士明码标价展示给平民百姓。但是这座石头筑的宫殿经受住了历史的沧海桑田。一年中有50个星期，它只是为游客们展出老式家具的博物馆；但是在其余的时间里，它再度复苏，重现了过去的辉煌。

隶属统治阶层的王室专员坐在朝臣席位上，四轮的大马车还有一行六人的护卫队吵闹着、喧哗着，在宫殿门前来来去去。到了晚上，宫殿里灯火通明，而宫殿旁边住的工人，也许正和着从宫里传出的音乐在自己家里翩翩起舞。在这方面，这座宫殿是很典型的，仿佛是燃烧完的灰烬中的一点火星，仍然可以使古老的火山时

still wears, in parody[24], her metropolitan trappings. Half a capital and half a country town, the whole city leads a double existence: it has long trances[25] of the one and flashes of the other; like the king of the Black Isles, it is half alive and half a monumental marble. There are armed men and cannon in the citadel overhead; you may see the troops marshaled[26] on the high parade; and at night after the early winter even-fall, and in the morning before the laggard[27] winter dawn, the wind carries abroad over Edinburgh the sound of drums and bugles. Grave judges sit bewigged in what was once the scene of imperial deliberations. Close by, in the High Street perhaps, the trumpets may sound about the stroke of noon; and you see a troop of citizens in tawdry[28] masquerade[29]; tabard above, heather-mixture trousers below, and the men themselves trudging in the mud among unsympathetic[30] bystanders. The grooms of a well-appointed circus tread[31] the streets with a better presence. And yet these are the Heralds[32] and Pursuivants[33] of Scotland, who are about to proclaim a new law of the United Kingdom before two score boys, and thieves, and hackney[34] coachmen…

---

24 parody ['pærədɪ]   n.   拙劣的模仿
25 trance [trɑ:ns]   n.   昏迷，昏睡
26 marshal ['mɑ:əl]   v.   gather，聚焦
27 laggard ['lægəd]   adj.   缓慢的
28 tawdry ['tɔ:drɪ]   adj.   showy or gaudy but without real value，俗丽的
29 masquerade [,mæskə'reɪd]   n.   false show，假装
30 unsympathetic ['ʌn,sɪmpə'θetɪk]   adj.   无情的
31 tread [tred]   = walk
32 herald ['herəld]   n.   传令官
33 pursuivant ['pə:sɪvənt]   n.   随从
34 hackney ['hæknɪ]   n.   出租汽车

不时地喷出一点浓烟。爱丁堡已经基本上从历史舞台的中心退位了，却依然假装还披着她首都城市的外衣。它现在以双重身份存在，半首都半乡村；它长时间地处于一种昏睡的状态，而又会不时地闪现出另一种状态的火花，就像黑岛的国王，一半是活体而另一半只是一块有纪念意义的大理石而已。在你头顶上的城堡要塞处有武装起来的人们和大炮，你会看到军队在游行。在初冬甚至是晚秋的夜里，在漆黑漫长的冬日黎明前的清晨，寒风携着战鼓和军号的声音掠过爱丁堡的上空。神色凝重戴着假发的法官坐在曾是皇家议事的地方。也许就是在附近的繁华商业街上，小号吹响了午间的号子，这时，你会看到一群穿着俗丽的假装游行的市民，他们上身穿着粗布大衣，下身穿着杂色毛线织的裤子，自顾自地艰难地在泥淖中前行，而旁边则是漠不关心的看客。配备齐全的马戏团的马倌在大街上行走则更有些看头。而这些苏格兰的皇家传令官和皇室随从，他们即将在四十个男童、流氓和出租马车夫面前正式宣

The east of new Edinburgh is guarded by a craggy[35] hill, of no great elevation, which the town embraces. The old London road runs on one side of it; while the New Approach, leaving is on the other hand, completes the circuit…Of all places for a view, this Calton Hill is perhaps the best; since you can see the Castle, which you lose from the Castle, and Arthur's Seat, which you can not see from Arthur's Seat. It is the place to stroll[36] on one of those days of sunshine and east wind which are so common in our more than temperate summer. The breeze comes off the sea, with a little of the freshness, and that touch of chill, peculiar to[37] the quarter, which is delightful to certain very ruddy organizations, and greatly the reverse to the majority of mankind. It brings with it a faint, floating haze, a cunning decolorizer[38], altho not thick enough to obscure out lines near at hand. But the haze lies more thickly to wind-ward at the far end of Musselburgh Bay; and over the Links of Aberlady and Berwick Law and the hump of the Bass Rock it assumes the aspect of a bank of thin sea fog.

Immediately underneath, upon the south, you command the yards of the High School, and the towers and courts of the new Jail — a large place, castellated[39] to the extent of folly, standing by itself on the edge of a steep cliff, and often joyfully hailed[40] by tourists as the Castle. In the one, you

布英国的新法律……

新爱丁堡的东面隐约可见一座陡峭而崎岖但海拔并不算高被小镇环绕的山峰。旧伦敦的公路在山的一边飞驰而过，另一面则是新干线，组成了环状的环山公路……在众多可以观看风景的地点中，卡尔顿山可能是最好的。在山上你看得到爱丁堡城堡，在城堡中你却很难望得到卡尔顿山；你看得到"亚瑟王宝座"，从亚瑟王宝座却难以看到卡尔顿山。在气候温和的夏天，阳光明媚，和风煦煦，此地正是一个休闲漫步的好地方。从海上吹来的柔风，带着一丝清新气息，那种冰冷的触感是这个地区特有的。这里给某些红色组织以快乐，然而对大多数人而言却是相反的。海风带来的是一层薄薄的、缓缓流动的薄雾，一切变得含混而失去颜色，虽然这雾并不足以模糊视线。但是在穆塞尔堡海湾尽头，雾顺着风吹来的方向变得愈来愈浓；它在整个阿伯莱迪群岛、贝里克罗峰和巴斯怪石的上空漂浮，我们看到了薄雾笼罩海岸的样子。

朝着南面俯瞰，你将看到一座中学的操场、塔和一座新监狱的庭院———座像城堡的装饰性建筑某种意义上愚蠢地矗立在

---

35 craggy ['krægɪ] *adj.* 多峭壁的，此处译为"陡峭的"
36 stroll: [strəʊ] *v.* **walk in a leisurely walk**，散步
37 peculiar to = belong only to somebody，独特
38 decolorizer [dɪ'kləraɪzə] *n.* 脱色剂
39 castellated ['kæstəleɪtɪd] *adj.* 造成城形的
40 hail [heɪl] *v.* 致敬，此处引申为"惊叹"

may perhaps see female prisoners taking exercise like a string of nuns; in the other, schoolboys running at play, and their shadows keeping step with them. From the bottom of the valley, a gigantic chimney rises almost to the level of the eye, a taller and a shapelier[41] edifice than Nelson's Monument. Look a little farther and there is Holyrood Palace, with its Gothic frontal and ruined abbey[42], and the red sentry pacing smartly to and fro before the door like a mechanical figure in a panorama[43]. By way of an outpost, you can single out the little peak-roofed lodge, over which Rizzio's murderers made their escape[44], and where Queen Mary herself, according to gossip, bathed in[45] white wine to retain her loveliness.

Behind and overhead lies the Queen's Park[46]; and thence, by knoll[47] and rocky bulwark[48] and precipitous[49] slope, the eye rises to the top of Arthur's Seat, a hill for magnitude, a mountain in virtue of its bold design. This upon your left. Upon the right, the roofs and spires of the Old Town climb one above another to where the citadel[50] prints its broad bulk and jagged crown of bastions[51] on the western sky…Perhaps it is now one in the afternoon;

41 shapely ['ʃeɪplɪ]   adj.   形状美好的，此处引申为 "雄伟壮观"
42 abbey ['æbɪ]   n.   修道院
43 in a panorama   = view of a vide area，全景
44 make their escape   = escape
45 bathed in   = wet or bright all over with something，沐浴
46 behind and overhead lies the Queen's Park: 此处为倒装结构
47 knoll [nəʊl]   n.   小山
48 bulwark ['bʊlwək]   n.   壁垒
49 precipitous [prɪ'sɪpɪtəs]   adj.   陡峭的
50 citadel ['sɪtədəl]   n.   城堡，要塞
51 bastion ['bæstɪən]   n.   堡垒

悬崖边缘，这常常引来游客们的阵阵惊叹。在某个地方，你也许还会看见正在放风的女囚，像一群修女。在其他的地方，上中学的男孩子们正在戏耍玩闹，背后拖着他们长长的身影。在山谷的底部，是一个几乎与目光平齐的巨人般的烟囱和一座比尼尔森纪念碑更雄伟壮观的大厦。再往这稍远的地方看去，就是神圣的荷里路德宫，有着哥特式风格的外貌，还有破败的修道院，穿着红衣的哨兵在大门口来回踱步，乍看像一个机器人。在一个前哨旁的小路上，你会看到一座尖顶小屋，李吉欧的杀人犯们就是从那里逃走的，据传言，玛丽皇后也正是在那里用白葡萄酒沐浴以保持她的美丽。

后上方是王后公园，紧接着，经过小山岗、石头壁垒、和陡峭的斜坡，我们的目光到达了亚瑟王宝座的顶部。亚瑟王宝座，就它的大小而言我们可以称之为小丘，而从它的气势来看则可被称为山。这是在你的左侧。而在你的右侧，老城区的房顶和塔顶一座比一座高，直到那城堡的庞大身躯和层次分明的城堡顶遮住了西方的天空……也许此刻恰巧是一个下午，而偏偏就是这一刻，

and at the same instant of time, a ball rises to the summit of Nelson's flagstaff close at hand, and, far away, a puff of[52] smoke, followed by a report, bursts from the half-moon battery at the Castle. This is the time-gun by which people set their watches, as far as the sea coast or in hill farms upon the Pentlands. To complete the view, the eye enfilades Prince's Street, black with traffic, and has a broad look over the valley between the Old Town and the New; here, full of railway trains and stepped over by the high North Bridge upon its many columns, and there, green with trees and gardens…

From *Picturesque Notes on Edinburgh* (1879)

一个圆球升到尼尔森教堂旗竿的顶端，近在咫尺，远处，在半月形的城堡炮台上，则突然升腾出一股烟，紧接着是一声爆裂。这是人们用来调整时间的报时炮，远到海岸和佩特兰山的农场的人们都可以看到。最后我们把目光投向车水马龙的王子街，尽览新城和旧城之间的山谷：这里到处是火车轨道，由众多柱子支撑的北部高架桥横跨其上；而另一处，则是绿树成荫和花园……

52 a puff of: amount of smoke, steam, etc sent., out at one time，一缕（烟）

含英咀华

爱丁堡是一个历史悠久、风景秀丽的文化城市，它依山傍水，地貌多姿，素有"北方雅典"之称。它也是苏格兰的首府和医疗、司法、银行保险、核能及电子研究的中心。从选文中读者不仅能体会到爱丁堡之美，还能体味到作者的语言之美。作者使用了大量的修饰性词语，而这些辞藻却少有重复，读者在沉浸于作者精彩的措词的同时，也感受着爱丁堡的"令人心驰神往"的美景。

William Cullen Bryant
威廉·柯伦·布莱恩特

威廉·柯伦·布莱恩特(1784~1878)，是第一位美国土生土长的诗人，他引导美国诗歌摆脱了古典主义模式的僵硬束缚，使之进入了一个简朴清新的时期。他的旅行书简记载了他多次旅欧见闻。在旅行书简风行一时的年代，布莱恩特的旅行书简深受广大读者的喜爱。他的主要作品有《致水鸟》(To a Waterfowl, 1815)、《死亡随想》(Thanatopsis, 1817)、《诗选》（Poems, 1821）、《泉》(The Fountain, 1842)、《白蹄鹿》(The White-Footed Deer, 1844)、《似水流年》(The Flood of Years, 1878)。

Florence Eighty Years Ago

八十年前的佛罗伦萨

There is a great deal of prattle[1] about Italian skies; the skies and clouds of Italy, so far as I have had an opportunity of judging, do not present so great a variety of beautiful appearances as our own; but the Italian atmosphere is far more uniformly fine than ours. Not to speak of[2] its astonishing clearness, it is pervaded by a certain warmth of color which enriches every object. This is more remarkable about the time of sunset, when the mountains put on an aerial aspect, as if they belonged to another and fairer world; and a little after the sun has gone down, the air is flushed[3] with a glory which seems to transfigure[4] all that it encloses.

Many of the fine old palaces of Florence, you know, are built in a gloomy and grand style of architecture, of[5] a dark-colored stone, massive and lofty, and overlooking narrow streets that lie in almost perpetual[6] shade. But at the hour of which I am speaking, the bright warm radiance reflected from the sky to the earth, fills the darkest lanes, streams into the most shadowy nooks[7], and makes the prison-like

描写意大利天空的美文无数；如果给我机会让我对此做出评价，我会说意大利的天空和云朵虽不及美国的那样多姿多彩，但意大利的空气却平添了一丝清新淡雅，更别说它那令人惊叹的万里晴空了。空气中弥漫着一种色彩所带来的暖意，这种色彩让世间万物顿显生机勃勃。日落则更是一个不寻常的时刻，绵绵山峰在天空的映衬下使人感觉像置身于另一个更美妙的仙境！太阳下山了，渐行渐远，空气中漫延着落日的灿烂，仿佛将它周围的一切都美化了！

佛罗伦萨大多数杰出古老的宫殿都采用灰暗而宏伟的建筑风格，由深色的石头堆砌而成，巨大而巍峨，似永远在俯瞰其阴影下的街道。我的话音未落，一束明亮而温暖的光芒

---

1 prattle [ˌprætl] *n.* talk at length esp. about unimportant things，闲聊，此处译为 "美文"
2 not to speak of = not worth mentioning，更不用说
3 flushed [flʌʃt] *adj.* (be flushed with sth.) 兴奋的，充满喜悦的，此处引申为 "漫延着"
4 transfigure [trænsˈfigə] *v.* 美化
5 of = a style of
6 perpetual [pɔˈpetʃuəl] *adj.* 永恒的，永久的
7 nook [nʊk] *n.* 角落，隐蔽处

structures glitter as with a brightness of their own.

It is now nearly the middle of October, and we have had no frost. The strong summer heats which prevailed when I came hither[8], have by the slowest gradations[9] subsided[10] into an agreeable autumnal temperature. The trees keep their verdure, but I perceive their foliage growing thinner, and when I walk in the Cascine on the other side of the Arno[11], the rustling of the lizards, as they run among the heaps of crisp[12] leaves, reminds me that autumn is wearing away, tho the ivy which clothes the old elms has put forth[13] a profuse[14] array[15] of blossoms, and the walks murmur with bees like our orchards in spring. As I look along the declivities[16] of the Apennines[17], I see the raw earth every day more visible between the ranks of olive-trees and the well-pruned maples which support the vines.

If I have found my expectations of Italian scenery, in some respects, below the reality; in other respects, they have been disappointed. The forms of the mountains are wonderfully picturesque, and

8 hither ['hɪðə]   adv.   to or towards this place，到此处
9 gradation [grə'deɪʃn]   n.   gradual change from one thing to another，渐变
10 subside [səb'saɪd]   v.   sink to a lower or to the normal level，下降
11 Arno: ['ɑːhəʊ]   n.   亚诺河（位于在意大利中部）
12 crisp [krɪsp]   adj.   易碎的
13 put forth   = (trees and plants)send out or produce (buds, shoots)，（花草树木）长出（花蕾或发芽）
14 profuse [prə'fjuːs]   adj.   很多的，丰富的，此处引申为"饱满的"
15 array [ə'reɪ]   n.   一系列，此处译为"一串串"
16 declivity [dɪ'klɪvɪtɪ]   n.   斜坡
17 the Apennines   亚平宁山脉，意大利亚平宁半岛（又称意大利半岛）的主干山脉，是阿尔卑斯山脉主干南伸的部分。西起濒海的阿尔卑斯山脉附近的卡迪蓬纳山口，向南呈弧形延伸至西西里岛以西的埃加迪群岛

就从天空直射到地面，射进黑暗的巷道里，流入阴冷的角落中，连那些酷似监狱的一座座建筑也闪闪发光起来。

现在已近十月中旬，却未见霜冻。我到这儿时，炎热的酷夏正渐渐进入温和的暖秋。树木依然郁郁葱葱，但可以感觉到它们的叶子已开始变得稀稀落落。当我沿着亚诺河河岸走向另一边的卡席尼散步时，耳边传来了蜥蜴爬行的沙沙声，它们好像在成堆的脆叶上奔跑，似要提醒我，秋天正一步步离我们远去。虽然缠绕在老榆树身上的常青藤绽放出一串串饱满的花朵，种植园在与蜜蜂低语，仿佛迈进春天的果园。顺着亚平宁的斜坡一眼望去，成排的橄榄树和精心修剪的爬满青藤的枫树之间，片片裸露的土壤日渐清晰。

我发现我心中期待的意大利风景，在某些方面，不如现实美丽；而在另外一些方面让人倍感失落。一座座风景如画的山峦，透过那浓雾观看，愈加雄伟壮丽了，再对比山旁那一座座由于时间流逝而脆弱得不堪一击的建筑，这山更显得令人崇敬了。如果人类想刻意

their effect is heightened[18] by the rich atmosphere through which they are seen, and by the buildings, imposing from their architecture or venerable[19] from time, which crown the eminences[20]. But if the hand of man has done something to embellish[21] this region, it has done more to deform it. Not a tree is suffered to retain its natural shape, not a brook to flow in its natural channel. An exterminating[22] war is carried on against the natural herbage[23] of the soil. The country is without woods and green fields; and to him who views the vale[24] of the Arno "from the top of Fiesole," or any of the neighboring heights, grand as he will allow the circle of the mountains to be, and magnificent the edifices with which the region is adorned, it appears, at any time after mid-summer, a huge valley of dust, planted with low rows of the pallid and thin-leaved olive, or the more dwarfish[25] maple on which vines are trained.

The simplicity of nature, so far as can be done, is destroyed; there is no fine sweep of forest, no broad expanse of meadow or pasture ground, no ancient and towering trees clustered[26] about the villas, no rows of natural shrubbery[27] following the course of the brooks and rivers. The streams, which are often but the beds of torrents dry during the

美化它，还不如说那是在损毁它。一棵棵树不再保有自然的形状，一条条小溪不再沿着自然的河道流淌，一场灭绝天然牧场的战争已经打响。这个城市将没有树木，没有绿色的田野；从索莱顶部或任何一个周边高地向亚诺山谷望去，山峦的轮廓可以说得上是雄伟，点缀其间的建筑可以说是壮丽，但在仲夏的任何时间显现在眼前的却是布满沙尘的峡谷，其间散布的只有零星树叶、毫无生气的一排排低矮橄榄树，或更多矮小的攀爬着藤本植物的枫树。

目前朴素的大自然已经遭到了破坏，再也看不到绵延的森林、广袤的草原、遍地的牧草，再也看不到依偎着别墅的古老而高耸的树木、伏在溪流和小河两岸的成行的灌木丛。急流处的河床经常在夏天干枯，被局限在一个用石头砌成的墙和护堤笔直的河槽中；天然的斜坡也都被改造成了梯田，面目全非。树木因不断的修剪而低矮地趴在亚平宁半山腰，由于耕地的限制，那里到山顶是一堆光秃秃的石头，没有植被和土壤。

18 heighten ['haɪtn] v. 加强
19 vunerable ['vʌnərəbl] adj. 庄严的；脆弱的；敏感的
20 eminence ['emɪnəns] n. 显赫，此处引申为"令人崇敬"
21 embellish [ɪm'belɪʃ] v. 装饰，此处引申为"美化"
22 exterminate [ɪk'stɜːmɪneɪt] v. **destroy completely**，彻底毁灭
23 herbage ['hɜːbɪdʒ] n. 草本
24 vale [veɪl] = valley
25 dwarfish ['dwɔːfɪʃ] adj. 矮小的
26 clustered ['klʌstəd] 过去分词作定语
27 shrubbery ['ʃrʌbərɪ] n. 灌木丛

summer, are confined in[28] straight channels by stone walls and embankments; the slopes are broken up[29] and disfigured by terraces; and the trees are kept down by constant pruning[30] and lopping[31], until half way up the sides of the Apennines, where the limit of cultivation is reached, and thence to the summit is a barren steep of rock, without herbage or soil. The grander features of the landscape, however, are fortunately beyond the power of man to injure; the lofty mountain-summits, bare precipices[32] cleft with chasms[33], and pinnacles[34] of rock piercing the sky, betokening[35], far more than any thing I have seen elsewhere, a breaking up of the crust of the globe in some early period of its existence. I am told that in May and June the country is much more beautiful than at present and that owing to[36] a drought it now appears under disadvantage...

Florence, from being the residence of the Court, and from the vast number of foreigners who throng to[37] it, presents during several months of the year an appearance of great bustle[38] and animation. Four thousand English and American, friend tells me, visit Florence every winter, to say nothing of[39] Russia, the number of visitors

幸运的是，这壮丽的风景，绝非是人类的力量所能破坏的，高傲的山峰，濒临深渊的光秃悬崖，还有直入云霄的岩石，这一切都预示着在早期形成阶段地壳破裂的痕迹，而这远远超过了我在别处见过的任何景色。据说五月和六月的景色远比现在的绮丽，那是因为现在正处于干旱期……

作为皇宫的所在地，大批外国人蜂拥而至，佛罗伦萨一年当中的好几个月都呈现出喧闹和生机勃勃的气息。一位美国朋友告诉我，每年冬天来佛罗伦萨旅游的英美人达四千人更不用说俄罗斯人了，其人数在逐年增加，甚至连佛罗伦萨画廊的回声都学会了怎样去重复斯拉夫人的古怪口音。让我来为你讲述那一个明朗的十月的某一

28 confine in＝ confine to   keep something in a restricted space，局限在
29 break up   = separate
30 prune ['pruːn]   *n.* 修剪
31 lop [lɒp]   *n.*   cut branches,twigs off（a tree），剪去
32 precipice ['presəpɪs]   *n.*   断崖
33 chasm ['kæzəm]   *n.*   裂口
34 pinnacle ['pɪnəkl]   *n.*   高峰
35 betoken [bɪ'təʊkən]   *v.*   预示
36 owing to   = because of
37 throng to   move in a crowd, 蜂拥而至
38 bustle ['bʌsl]   *n.*   喧闹
39 to say nothing of   更不用说

from the latter country is every year increasing, and the echoes of the Florence gallery have been taught to repeat the strange accents of the Slavonic. Let me give you the history of a fine day in October, passed at the window of my lodgings on the Lung Arno, close to the bridge.

Waked by the jangling[40] of all the bells in Florence and by the noise of carriages departing loaded with travelers, for Rome and other places in the south of Italy, I rise, dress myself, and take my place at the window. I see crowds of men and women from the country, the former in brown velvet jackets, and the latter in broad-brimmed straw hats, driving donkeys loaded with panniers[41] or trundling hand — carts before them, heaped with[42] grapes, figs, and all the fruits of the orchard, the garden, and the field. They have hardly passed, when large flocks of sheep and goats make their appearance, attended[43] by shepherds and their families, driven by the approach of winter from the Appenines, and seeking the pastures of the Maremma[44], a rich, but, in the summer, an unhealthy tract on the coast.

The men and the boys are dressed in knee-breeches, the women in bodices, and both sexes wear capotes[45] with pointed hoods, and felt hats with conical[46] crowns; they carry long staves[47] in

天的经历吧，那时我住在亚诺河边，一所邻桥的寓所里。

那些装满了游客、要离开佛罗伦萨赶到罗马及意大利南部其他地方的马车，一路上喧哗着，叮当作响，连同佛罗伦萨的其他铃声一起将我吵醒，我起了床，穿好衣服，站在窗边。我看见一大群来自乡村的男男女女，男的穿着褐色丝绒的夹克，女的戴着宽大的草帽，赶着驴车，车上装满了挂篮；手推车上面堆着葡萄、无花果等所有来自果园、花园和田野里的水果。他们还没有走过去时，一大群绵羊和山羊出现了，由牧羊人和他的家人照看着，被亚平宁冬天的逐步驱赶着，去寻找马雷马那肥沃的牧场，但在夏天，这牧场则会变作海岸边贫瘠的土地。

男人们和男孩子们都穿着马裤，女人们穿着紧身衣；他们都穿着有尖顶风帽的斗篷，戴着顶部为圆锥形

---

40 jangling ['dʒæŋglɪŋ] *adj.* 吵闹的
41 pannier ['pænɪə] *n.* 挂篮
42 heap with = load or place something in a pile on someone，装满
43 attend [ə'tend] *v.* take care of，本句中过去分词表示被动
44 Maremma [mə'remə] *n.* 马雷马牧场
45 capote [kə'pəut] *n.* 有帽子的斗篷
46 conical ['kɒnɪkl] *adj.* cone-shaped，圆锥形的
47 stave [steɪv] *n.* any of the curved pieces of wood forming the side of a barrel or tub，桶板

their hands, and their arms are loaded with kids and lambs too young to keep pace with[48] their mothers. After the long procession of sheep and goats and dogs and men and women and children, come horses loaded with cloths and poles for tents, kitchen utensils, and the rest of the young — lings of the flock...

From *Letters of a Traveler* (1834)

的毡帽，手里拿着长棍，怀抱还不能走路的孩子或小羔羊。一大队的山羊、绵羊、小狗、男人、女人和小孩的队伍经过，紧跟着装满了支帐篷的布、杆和厨房用具的马群，后面紧跟着一大群年轻人……

48 keep pace with: = move forward at the same rate，意为"跟上"

含英咀华

　　佛罗伦萨是意大利中部的一个城市，位于亚平宁山脉中段的西麓盆地中。选文中作者先阐明了自己想像中佛罗伦萨的样子，之后又描写了他所看到的实景，而这现实"有些让人失望"，因为"淳朴的大自然已经遭到了破坏"，所以人们"再也看不到绵延的森林，再也望不见广袤的草原，再也见不到遍地的牧草，依偎着别墅古老而高耸的树木，伏在溪流和小河两岸的成行的灌木丛。"这的确是一种遗憾，尽管这里缺少了大自然的淳朴，但这里依然有人类的文明，有"灰暗而宏伟的建筑"，有佛罗伦萨独有的气息。

Francis H. Gribble

弗郎希斯·亨利·古利伯

弗郎希斯·亨利·古利伯（1862~1946），出生在英国德文郡的巴恩斯特普尔小镇。他的著作有《乔治·桑和她的情人们》（*George Sand and Her Lovers, 1907*）、《谢利的浪漫生活及续篇》（*The Romantic Life of Shelley and the Sequel, 1911*）、《日内瓦湖》（*The Lake of Geneva, 1909*）。

Geneva

Straddling[1] the Rhone, where it issues from the bluest lake in the world, looking out upon green meadows and wooded hills, backed by[2] the dark ridge of the Salève, with the "great white mountain" visible in the distance, Geneva has the advantage of an incomparable site; and it is, from a town surveyor's point of view, well built. It has wide thoroughfares[3], quays[4], and bridges; gorgeous public monuments and well-kept public gardens; handsome theaters and museums; long rows of palatial[5] hotels; flourishing suburbs; two railway-stations, and a casino. But all this is merely the façade[6] — all of it quite modern; hardly any of it more than half a century old. The real historical Geneva — the little of it that remains — is hidden away in the background, where not every tourist troubles to look for it.

It is disappearing fast. Italian stonemasons[7] are constantly engaged in driving lines through it. They have rebuilt, for instance, the old Corraterie, which is now the Regent Street of Geneva, famous for its confectioners'[8] and booksellers' shops;

1 straddle ['strædl] v. 跨坐，把两腿叉开，这里引申为河流 "横跨"
2 back by = face something at the back
3 thoroughfare ['θʌrəfeə] n. 通路，大道
4 quay [ki:] n. 码头
5 palatial [pə'leɪʃl] adj. 宏伟的
6 façade [fə'sa:d] n. = outward appearance，外表，这里引申为 "表面现象"
7 stonemason ['stəunmeɪs(ə)n] n. 石工，石匠
8 confectioner [kən'fekʃənə(r)] n. 糖果店

日内瓦

发源于世界最蓝湖泊的隆河穿城而过，前望翠绿的草地和林木茂密的小山，背依萨雷布山深色的山脊，并有"大白山"雄峙远方，所有这些都构成了日内瓦无与伦比的自然地理优势。即使从一个城市检验员的角度来看，日内瓦也是一座建设优良的城市。城市拥有宽阔的大道、码头和桥梁；绚丽多姿的公共纪念碑和整齐保存良好的公共花园；气派的剧院、博物馆；鳞次栉比的豪华酒店；蓬勃发展的郊区；两个火车站以及一个大赌场。然而这些还都只是一些表面现象，即城市的一切都现代感十足；几乎没有什么东西的历史超过半个世纪。真正历经沧桑的日内瓦——日内瓦仅存的一点——都隐藏在了背后，而这些又不是每个游客都愿意费力去探寻的。

日内瓦这座城市的特色正在迅速消失。意大利的石匠们一直在这座城市中进行着改造。例如，他们已经重建了以

they have destroyed, and are still destroying, other ancient slums, setting up white buildings of uniform ugliness in place of the picturesque but insanitary[9] dwellings of the past. It is, no doubt, a very necessary reform, tho one may think that it is being executed in too utilitarian[10] a spirit. The old Geneva was malodorous[11], and its death-rate was high. They had more than one Great Plague there, and their Great Fires have always left some of the worst of their slums untouched[12]. These could not be allowed to stand in an age which studies the science and practices the art of hygiene[13]. Yet the traveler who wants to know what the old Geneva was really like must spend a morning or two rambling among them before they are pulled down.

The old Geneva, like Jerusalem, was set upon a hill, and it is toward the top of the hill that the few buildings of historical interest are to be found. There is the cathedral — a striking object from a distance, tho the interior is hideously bare. There is the Town Hall, in which, for the convenience of notables carried in litters, the upper stories were reached by an inclined plane instead of a staircase. There is Calvin's old Academy, bearing more than a slight resemblance to certain of smaller colleges at Oxford and Cambridge. There, too, are to be seen a few mural tablets, indicating the residences of past celebrities. In such a house Rousseau was

古老的科哈德里,也就是现在以糖果店和书店闻名的摄政大街。当然,他们也毁掉了并且现在还正在毁掉着一些老式的破旧房子,转而建造了一些难看的样式相同的白色大楼来取代过去那些虽然有特色却不卫生的旧房子。虽然有人认为这种变革带有很强的功利性,但这种变革确是非常必要的。从前的日内瓦非常脏乱,而且死亡率很高。历史上曾暴发过多次瘟疫,大火烧得只剩断壁残垣。而这样的破房子在研究科学和践行卫生的时代是不能被人们所接受的。那些想了解从前的日内瓦的游客就不得不在它们被拆毁之前花一两个早晨到这些地方漫游。

如耶路撒冷一样,古日内瓦建立在山顶之上。山上还可以看见几处名胜古迹,有一个大教堂——尽管内部空无一物,从远处望去还是显得很引人注目。城中市政厅为方便达官贵人通向较高楼层特设固定升降机而非楼梯。从前的加尔文学院也在市中,风气与哈

9 insanitary [ɪn'sænətərɪ] *adj.* 不卫生的,有碍健康的
10 utilitarian [ˌjuːtɪlɪ'teərɪən] *adj.* 功利的,实利的
11 malodorous [mæ'ləʊdərəs] *adj.* 脏乱的
12 slums untouched 这里指残垣断壁
13 hygiene ['haɪdʒiːn] *n.* 卫生

born; in such another house — or in an older house, now demolished, on the same site — Calvin died. And toward these central points the steep and narrow, mean streets — in many cases streets of stairs — converge[14].

As one plunged into[15] the streets one seems to pass back from the twentieth century to the fifteenth, and need not exercise one's imagination very severely in order to picture the town as it appeared in the old days before the Reformation. The present writer may claim permission to borrow his own description from the pages of "Lake Geneva and Its Literary Landmarks":

"Narrow streets predominated[16], tho there were also a certain number of open spaces — notably at the markets, and in front of the Cathedral, where there was a traffic in those relics and rosaries which Geneva was presently to repudiate[17] with virtuous[18] indignation[19]. One can form an idea of the appearance of the narrow streets by imagining the oldest houses that one has seen in Switzerland all closely packed together — houses at the most three stories high, with gabled roofs, ground-floors a step or two below the level of the roadway, and huge arched doors studded with[20] great iron nails, and looking strong enough to resist

---

14 converge [kən'vɜːdʒ] v. 聚合，集中于一点（或一块）
15 plunge into = fall into something suddenly，进入，来到
16 predominate [prɪ'dɒmɪneɪt] v. 成为主流
17 repudiate [rɪ'pjuːdɪeɪt] v. 拒绝履行
18 virtuous ['vɜːtʃuəs] adj. 有品德的，善良的，贞洁的
19 indignation [,ɪndɪg'neɪʃn] n. 愤怒，愤慨，义愤
20 studded with = decorate with many studs, precious stones，用许多饰钮、宝石装饰表面

佛、剑桥规模较小的学院如出一辙。还有一些壁画，它们暗示了那里曾是名人的居所。卢梭就诞生在其中的一间房里。也是在其中一间房——或是其中一间更老的房屋，现在已经被拆除，但还是在原址——加尔文于其中去世。朝向这些中心处，陡峭、狭窄、拥挤的街道——多数情况下是带有台阶的大道，在此交汇。

进入这些街道就好像从20世纪回到了15世纪，不需要刻意想像就能描述出小镇在宗教改革之前的古老年代中的样子。当代作家可能要借用《日内瓦湖及其文学的里程碑》中的语句来对它加以描述：

"日内瓦狭窄的街道在城市中占据主导地位，但宽敞的地方也很多——最显著的就是在市场，大教堂前。这些历史遗迹前如果通车的话，日内瓦人都会进行和平的抵制。人们如果在脑海中想像一下瑞士最古老、最拥挤的房子，就会浮现日内瓦狭窄的街道的样子——那些瑞士的老房子最高为三层、尖顶，第一层楼低于路面一两个台阶，门呈拱形并镶有巨大的钢钉，看起来坚实得能够抵挡得住猛烈的攻击。

a battering-ram. Above the doors, in the case of the better houses, were the painted escutcheons[21] of the residents, and crests were also often blazoned[22] on the window-panes. The shops, too, and more especially the inns, flaunted[23] gaudy[24] signboards with ingenious[25] devices. The Good Vinegar, the Hot Knife, the Crowned Ox, were the names of some of these; their tariff is said to have been five pence a day for man and beast." ...

In the first half of the sixteenth century occurred the two events which shaped the future of Geneva; Reformation theology[26] was accepted; political independence was achieved. Geneva it should be explained, was the fief[27] of the duchy[28] of Savoy; or so, at all events[29], the Dukes of Savoy maintained, the citizens were of the contrary opinion. Their view was that they owed allegiance[30] only to their Bishops, who were the Viceroys of the Holy Roman Emperor; and even that allegiance was limited by the terms of a Charter granted in the Holy Roman Emperor's name by Bishop Adhémar de Fabri. All went fairly well until the Bishops began to play into the hands of the Dukes; but then there was friction[31], which rapidly became acute. A revolutionary party — the Eidgenossen,

如果房子更好一些，门的上方还会有绘制的房主的盾形图像，窗玻璃上也会有鸟冠式样的家徽作装饰。同样，像商店特别是酒馆这样的地方，会用一些巧妙的设施使其店牌更加飘扬醒目。好醋、热门刀、冠牛等就是其中一些典型的名字。这些地方的收费标准通常是人、畜每天5便士。"……

16世纪上半叶，日内瓦爆发了改变其未来的两件大事，即宗教改革理论被广泛接受和政治上实现了独立。需要指出的是，日内瓦当时属于萨依公爵封地，尽管公民都反对但萨依公爵封地还是保留了下来。在日内瓦人们的观念中，他们只忠诚于主教，即圣罗马帝国国王的总督，即使是这种忠诚被在圣罗马帝国国王的名义下由法里大主教所颁布的大宪章中的条款所限制。在大主教让公爵有可乘之机之前还是万事顺利的。但之后出现了分歧，

21 escutcheon [ɪsˈkʌtʃən] *n.* 饰有纹章的盾
22 blazon [ˈbleɪzn] *v.* 以家徽装饰
23 flaunted [ˈflɔːntɪd] *adj.* 飘扬的
24 gaudy [ˈgɔːdɪ] *adj.* 俗丽的
25 ingenious [ɪnˈdʒiːnɪəs] *adj.* 巧妙的
26 theology [θɪˈɒlədʒɪ] *n.* 神学
27 fief [fiːf] *n.* 封地
28 duchy [ˈdʌtʃɪ] *n.* 公爵领地
29 at all events = whatever happens; in any case，无论如何
30 allegiance [əˈliːdʒəns] *n.* 忠诚
31 friction [ˈfrɪkʃən] *n.* 分歧

or Confederates — was formed. There was a Declaration of Independence and a civil war.

So long as the Genevans stood alone, the Duke was too strong for them. He marched into the town in the style of a conqueror, and wreaked his vengeance[32] on[33] as many of his enemies as he could catch. He cut off the head of Philibert Berthelier, to whom there stands a memorial on the island in the Rhone; he caused Jean Pecolat to be hung up in an absurd posture in his banqueting-hall, in order that he might mock at his discomfort while he dined; he executed, with or without preliminary torture, several less conspicuous[34] patriots[35]. Happily, however, some of the patriots — notably Besançon Hugues — got safely away, and succeeded in concluding treaties of alliance between Geneva and the cantons of Berne and Fribourg.

The men of Fribourg marched to Geneva, and the Duke retired. The citizens passed a resolution that he should never be allowed to enter the town again, seeing that[36] "he never came there without playing the citizens some dirty trick or other;" and, the more effectually to prevent him from coming, they pulled down their suburbs and repaired their ramparts, one member of every household being required to lend a hand for the purpose.

Presently, owing to religious dissensions, Friboutg withdraw from the alliance. Berne, however,

且日益激烈。此时，一个革命性的政党——同盟党，便应运而生了。随后通过了独立宣言并爆发了内战。

如果日内瓦人彼此孤立，那么公爵对他们来说就太强大了。他以胜利者的姿态向城镇进军，并对抓到的敌人进行报复。他砍掉了菲利普的头颅，现在隆岛上还有一座纪念菲利普的墓碑。他抓住了吉恩·皮克拉并把他以一种极其荒谬的姿势吊死在自己的宴会大厅内，以使自己可以在吃饭时嘲笑吉恩这种不雅的姿态。他还或用酷刑或直接杀害了一些爱国人士。但令人欣慰的是，一些不是很明显的爱国人士——如博桑松·胡格斯——成功地逃脱并与伯尔尼以及弗里堡各州缔结了盟约。

弗里堡的勇士进军日内瓦，公爵撤退了。日内瓦人民决定禁止公爵踏入城中一步。人们认为"他来城中只会给人民带来灾难"。为了更有效地阻止公爵进城，人们毁掉了城郊，修复了城墙。为此，每个家庭都要派出一员给予帮助。

32 vengeance ['vendʒəns]　n.　复仇
33 wreak on　= carry out (revenge or vengeance) on someone, 向某人报仇
34 conspicuous [kən'spɪkjuəs]　adj.　显著的，显而易见的
35 patriot ['peɪtrɪət]　n.　爱国者
36 seeing that　= in view of the fact that

adhered to[37] it, and in due course, responded to the appeal for help by setting an army of seven thousand men in motion. The route of the seven thousand lay through the canton of Vaud, then a portion of the Duke's dominions, governed from the Castle of Chillon. Meeting with no resistance save at Yverdon, they annexed[38] the territory, placing governors of their own in its various strongholds. The Governor of Chillon fled, leaving his garrison to surrender; and in its deepest dungeon[39] was found the famous prisoner of Chillon, François de Bonivard. From that time forward Geneva was a free republic, owing allegiance to no higher power.

From *Geneva* (1909)

目前，由于宗教分歧，弗里堡从联盟撤回。而伯尔尼还继续忠实于同盟，回应到在需要的时候，建立了七千名士兵组成的部队进行支援。七千人的部队穿越了沃德州，穿越了公爵曾统治的西庸城堡的一部分。他们在伊华东并未遇到任何抵抗，吞并了土地，设置了一个又一个要塞。西庸城堡的总督逃跑了，他手下的驻军缴械投降；在最深的地牢里发现了著名的西庸城堡囚犯弗朗索瓦德。从那时起日内瓦便成了自由共和国，不效忠任何至高权力。

---

37 adhere to　　= remain faithful to something
38 annex [ə'neks]　　v.　吞并
39 dungeon ['dʌndʒən]　　n.　地牢，土牢

含英咀华

日内瓦是一个历史悠久的国际都市，也是世界钟表之都，它以深厚的人道主义传统、多彩的文化活动、重大的会议和展览会、令人垂涎的美食、清新的市郊风景及众多的游览项目和体育设施而闻名于世。选文中作者用清新的文笔细致地描绘了日内瓦的自然景观和人文景观，其中不乏对历史的回顾。品读本文，宛如与作者一同游历这里的一山一湖，一草一木。

Charles Dickens

查尔斯·狄更斯

查尔斯·狄更斯，作者介绍见 "*In and About the City*"。

Marseilles

So we went on, until eleven at night, when we halted at the town of Aix (within two stages of Marseilles) to sleep. The hotel, with all the blinds and shutters closed to keep the light and heat out, was comfortable and airy next morning, and the town was very clean; but so hot, and so intensely light, that when I walked out at noon it was like coming suddenly from the darkened room into crisp[1] blue fire. The air was very clear, that distant hills and rocky points appeared within an hour's walk; while the town immediately at hand[2] — with a kind of blue wind between me and it — seemed to be white and hot, and to be throwing off[3] a fiery air from its surface.

We left this town toward evening, and took the road to Marseilles. A dusty road it was; the houses shut up close; and the vines powdered white. At nearly all the cottage doors, women were peeling and slicing[4] onions into earthen bowls for supper. So they had been doing last night all the way from Avugnon. We passed one or two shady dark châteaux, surrounded by trees, and embellished[5] with cool basins of water, which were the more

马赛

就这样我们继续走了下去，直到午夜11点我们到了埃克斯（与马赛相距两站路）才停下来休息。旅馆所有的窗帘和百叶窗都紧闭着以阻挡热气和强光，所以第二天早上，旅馆空气凉爽而舒适。小镇很干净，但是炎热无比，阳光强烈，以至于中午外出时宛如从一个黑屋子步入烈火之中。空气清新，远处的山岗看来步行一个小时即可到达，而小镇近在咫尺，在我和小镇之间略微夹杂着一丝微风，似乎炽热难耐，地面上还散发着火辣辣的热气。

直到晚上，我们才离开小镇前往马赛，道路上尘土飞扬，路边的房屋房门紧闭，藤木像涂过粉一样泛着白光。几乎所有的农舍门前，妇女们都在剥切洋葱，并将其放在陶碗之中以备晚餐之用。从亚维

---

1 crisp [krɪsp]　*adj.*　(of the weather or air) dry and cold 干冷的
2 at hand　= near, close by
3 throw off　这里指散发出
4 slice [slaɪs]　*v.*　切成薄片
5 embellish [ɪmˈbelɪʃ]　*v.*　装饰

refreshing to behold[6], from the great scarcity[7] of such residences on the road we had traveled.

As we approached Marseilles, the road began to be covered with[8] holiday people. Outside the public-houses were parties smoking, drinking, playing draughts and cards and (once) dancing. But dust, dust, dust, everywhere. We went on, through a long, straggling[9], dirty suburb, thronged with[10] people; having on our left a dreary[11] slope of land, on which the country-houses of the Marseilles merchants, always staring[12] white, are jumbled[13] and heaped without the slightest order; backs, fronts, sides, and gables[14] toward all points of the compass; until, at last, we entered the town.

I was there, twice, or thrice afterward, in fair weather and foul[15]; and I am afraid there is no doubt that it is a dirty and disagreeable place. But the prospect, from the fortified heights, of the beautiful Mediterranean, with its lovely rocks and islands, is most delightful. There heights are a desirable retreat, for less picturesque reasons — as an escape from a compound of vile smells perpetually[16] arising from a great harbor full of

农来的一路上发现她们都是如此。途中，我们经过了一两处灰色的庄园，庄园周围长满了树木，门外还装饰着一些装满了凉水的盆子，给我们极度困乏的旅途带来了一股清新。

当我们靠近马赛时，路上到处可见度假的人们。酒吧外很多人在抽烟、喝酒、下着国际象棋、打着纸牌，时不时还跳起了舞。但是尘土、尘土，到处都是尘土。我们一直往前走，路过了幽长零乱且挤满了人群的市郊地区，左边有一片沉寂的斜坡。马赛商人的住所被建在这里，一律是刺眼的白色，毫无秩序杂乱地堆积在两边，前、后、左、右甚至山坡，遍布所有的方位。最后，我们进了城。

后来我去过那里两三次，碰到过好天气也碰到过坏天气。无疑这是一个肮脏且令人生厌的地方。但站在高处

---

6 behold [bɪ'həʊld] *v.* 看，注视
7 scarcity ['skeəsɪtɪ] *n.* 稀少
8 be covered with 此处是"充满，挤满"
9 straggling ['stræɡlɪŋ] *adj.* 四散的，零落的
10 throng with = fill (a place) with a crowd，（人群）挤满（某处）
11 dreary ['drɪərɪ] *adj.* 沉闷的
12 staring ['steərɪŋ] *adj.* 刺眼的
13 jumbled *adj.* 混乱的，乱七八糟的
14 gable ['ɡeɪbl] *n.* 山墙，三角墙
15 foul [faʊl] *adj.* 天气恶劣的
16 perpetually [pə'petʃuəlɪ] *adv.* 持久地

stagnant[17] water, and befouled[18] by the refuse[19] of innumerable ships with all sorts of cargoes, which, in hot weather, is dreadful in the last degree.

There were foreign sailors, of all nations, in the streets; with red shirts, blue shirts, buff shirts, tawny[20] shirts, and shirts of orange color; with red caps, blue caps, green caps, great beards, and no beards; in Turkish turbans[21], glazed English hats, and Neapolitan[22] headdresses[23]. There were the townspeople sitting[24] in clusters on the pavement, or airing themselves on the tops of their houses, or walking up and down the closest and least airy of boulevards[25]; and there were crowds of fierce-looking people of the lower sort, blocking up the way, constantly.

In the very heart of all this stir and uproar, was the common madhouse; a low, contracted miserable building, looking straight upon the street, without the smallest screen or courtyard; where chattering madmen and madwomen were peeping out, through rusty bars, at[26] the staring faces below, while the sun, darting[27] fiercely aslant[28] into their little cells, seemed to dry up[29] their brains, and

远远望去，美丽的地中海风光无限，可爱的石子、美丽的岛屿，是最令人欢愉的。这些海拔高的地方是理想的隐居处，就原因说来似乎有点亵渎这如画的风景，只因能远离那充满了死水并被那些装满各种货物的船只排放的垃圾所污染的港口所持续泛起的坏透了的臭气，这在热天尤其令人无法忍受。

街上随处可见来自各国的水手，有穿红衬衫的、蓝衬衫的、浅黄色衬衫的、茶色衬衫的，还有穿橘黄色衬衫的；有戴红帽子的，有戴蓝帽子的，还有戴绿色帽子的；有留着茂密胡须的，有没有胡须的；有围着土耳其头巾的，戴着英式帽子的，还有裹着那不勒斯头饰的。城里的人们或成群结队地坐在路面上，或坐在屋顶上纳凉，或者悠闲地在附近为数不多的林荫大道上走来走去，也有面容狰狞素质低的人群不时堵塞道路。

这所有的喧哗和骚动的中心是精神病院，那是一座低矮的充满了痛苦的小楼，正对着街道，没有任何的屏风和庭院的阻隔，在那里喋喋不休的疯男疯女们透过生锈的铁栅栏，

17 stagnant ['stægnənt]   adj.   不流动的
18 befoul [bɪ'faʊl]   v.   弄脏，污损
19 refuse [rɪ'fjuːz]   n.   垃圾，废弃物
20 tawny ['tɔːnɪ]   adj.   茶色的
21 turban ['tɜːbən]   n.   (穆斯林的)缠头巾
22 Neapolitan [nɪə'pɒlɪtən]   n./ adj.   那不勒斯人（的）
23 headdress ['heddres]   n.   饰头巾，头发编梳的式样
24 sitting   这里是现在分词结构修饰名词作状语
25 boulevard ['buːləvɑːd]   n.   林荫大道
26 peeping at   =look cautiously，窥视
27 dart [dɑːt]   v.   投射，这里指 "阳光照射"
28 aslant [ə'slɑːnt]   adj.   斜的
29 dry up   = become completely dry

worry them, as if they were baited by a pack of dogs.

We were pretty well accommodated at the Hôtel du Paradis, situated[30] in a narrow street of very high houses, with a hairdresser's shop opposite, exhibiting in one of its windows two full-length waxen[31] ladies, twirling[32] around and around; which so enchanted the hairdresser himself, that he and his family sat in armchairs and in cool undresses, on the pavement outside, enjoying the gratification of the passers-by, with lazy dignity. The family had retired to rest when we went to bed, at midnight; but the hairdresser (a corpulent[33] man, in drab[34] slippers) was still sitting there, with his legs stretched out before him, and evidently couldn't bear to have the shutters put up.

Next day we went down to the harbor, where the sailors of all nations were discharging and taking in cargoes of all kinds: fruits, wines, oils, silks, stuffs, velvets, and every manner of merchandise. Taking one of a great number of lively little boats with gay-striped awnings[35], we rowed away, under the sterns of great ships, under tow-ropes and cables against and among other boats, and very much too near the sides of vessels that were faint with oranges, to the "Marie Antoinette," a handsome steamer bound for Genoa, lying near

凝视着楼下陌生的面孔，阳光斜射进他们狭小的囚室中，仿佛要晒干他们的大脑，恐惧感笼罩其全身，宛如被一群狗所激怒一般。

我们在幸福旅馆很好地安顿了下来，这家旅馆位于一条满是高楼的狭窄街区，它的对面是一家发廊，其中一个窗口展示着两个跟真人身高一样的蜡像女郎，在那里不停地旋转，理发师总是会陶醉在她们的舞动之中。他和家人衣着随便地坐在石板上的扶手椅上，慵懒地盯着过往的行人，眼中充满了满足。当我们午夜开始休息的时候，他们一家人也就寝休息了。但是理发师（一个肥胖、穿着褐色拖鞋的男人）依旧坐在那里，双腿伸向前方，显然他不能忍受这关上百叶窗后闷热的屋子。

第二天，我们来到了港口，各国的水手都忙着卸货和处理各种货物：水果、油、丝绸、食物、天鹅绒和其他各式商品。在众多欢快色彩条纹的篷船里，我们选了一艘前行，

30 situated　过去分词作定语
31 waxen ['wæksn] adj.　蜡制的
32 twirl [twɜ:l] vt.　快速转动（扭转）
33 corpulent ['kɔ:pjulənt] adj.　肥胖的
34 drab [dræb] adj.　褐色的
35 awning ['ɔ:nɪŋ] n.　甲板上的天篷

the mouth of the harbor.

By and by, the carriage, that unwieldy "trifle from the Pantechnicon," on a flat barge[36], bumping against everything, came stupidly alongside; and by five o'clock we were steaming out in the open sea. The vessel was beautifully clean; the meals were served under an awning on deck; the night was clam and clear; the quiet beauty of the sea and sky was unspeakable.

From *Picture from Italy* (1844)

穿梭在威严的货轮和用绳索彼此相连的小船之间，最近一艘船舷的两侧涂成橙色。船驶到了玛丽·安托瓦内特时，只见一艘开往热那亚的高大货轮静静地停在港口附近。

不久，货车车厢——笨拙的"家具搬运车"，在驳船上撞击着所有的东西，歪歪扭扭地从旁边驶过。5点钟，我们驶进了大海，游轮是美丽而干净的，在甲板的遮阳伞下我们享用美食；夜是宁静而清新的，静谧的大海和天空显现出一种不可言说的美。

36 barge [bɑːdʒ] *n.* 驳船

含英咀华

本文节选自狄更斯的《意大利美景》(*Pictures from Italy*)中的第三章"从阿维尼翁到热那亚"(*Avignon to Genoa*)。在这本游记中，狄更斯重点描述了一路上的所见所闻和当地的风俗文化，用很少的笔墨介绍了意大利著名的宫殿和教堂，意大利之行是他创作生涯中的重要一环。由于狄更斯前往意大利时取道法国，因此该书前面部分还涉及法国风光的描写。选文记载了作者对法国马赛的观感。细读这一选段，从旅馆到小镇，从路边的人群到港口各国的水手，每一处描写都显示出狄更斯生动与幽默的写作手法。

塞缪尔·约翰逊

塞缪尔·约翰逊(1709~1784)，英国作家、批评家，英国文学史上重要的诗人、散文家、传记家和健谈家，他编纂的《英文词典》(*A Dictionary of the English Language, 1755*)对英语发展具有重大贡献，1765年出版了经他校订的《莎士比亚戏剧集》(*The Plays of William Shakespeare*)。他被尊称为当时文坛的一代盟主，他对小说、诗歌等文学作品的评论，即使是只言片语，也被众口宣传，当作屑金碎玉。在约翰逊时代，文化氛围已经在向浪漫主义方向发展了，人们已不再视"三一律"(*the three unities: action, place, time*)为经典。与德莱登、伏尔泰相比，约翰逊是更为宽容的新古典主义者。

St. Andrews

圣安德鲁斯

At an hour somewhat late we came to St. Andrews, a city once archiepiscopal[1]; where that university still subsists[2] in which philosophy was formerly taught by Buchanan, whose name has as fair a claim to immortality as can be conferred[3] by modern latinity[4], and perhaps a fairer than the instability of vernacular[5] languages admits.

We found, that by the interposition[6] of some invisible friend, lodgings[7] had been provided for us at the house of one of the professors, whose easy civility[8] quickly made us forget that we were strangers; and in the whole time of our stay we were gratified[9] by every mode of kindness, and entertained with all the elegance of lettered hospitality.

In the morning we rose to perambulate[10] a city, which only history shows to have once flourished[11], and surveyed the ruins of ancient magnificence, of which even the ruins cannot long be visible, unless some care be taken to preserve

我们到达圣安德鲁斯时已经很晚了。这座城市曾经一度是大主教的天下。现在城市中依然有大学存在，布坎南曾在那所大学中讲授哲学。自然地，他的名字可以像现代拉丁语一样永远不被湮没，而且可能比地方语的不稳定性所能接受更加自然。

在一些"隐形的"朋友的帮助下，我们在一个教授家里找到了住处。教授随和有礼，很快我们就忘记了我们的陌生人身份。而我们在他家所住的时间里，他都尽力热情地招待，我们对他有修养的殷勤款待感到很满足也很快乐。

清晨，我们在城市中漫步，只有从历史中才能了解这里曾经的繁荣。我们在一些遗

---

1 archiepiscopal [ˌɑːkɪ'pɪskəpəl] *adj.* 大主教的
2 subsist [səb'sɪst] *v.* 生存，此处意为"存在"
3 confer [kən'fɜː] *v.* 赠予，协议
4 latinity [lə'tɪnɪtɪ] *n.* 拉丁语的使用，拉丁语式
5 vernacular [və'nækjələ] *adj.* 地方的，用地方语写成的
6 by the interposition of 插入，干涉，这里 = with the help of, 引申为"在……的帮助下"
7 lodging ['lɒdʒɪŋ] *n.* 寄宿处
8 civility [sɪ'vɪlətɪ] *n.* = politeness, 礼貌
9 gratify ['grætɪfaɪ] *v.* = satisfy, 使满足
10 perambulate [pə'ræmbjuleɪt] *v.* 漫步
11 flourish ['flʌrɪʃ] *v.* 繁荣，茂盛

them; and where is the pleasure of preserving such mournful[12] memorials? They have been till very lately so much neglected, that every man carried away the stones who fancied that he wanted them.

The cathedral[13], of which the foundations may be still traced, and a small part of the wall is standing, appears to have been a spacious and majestic[14] building, not unsuitable to the primacy of the kingdom. Of the architecture, the poor remains can hardly exhibit, even to an artist, a sufficient specimen[15]. It was demolished, as is well known, in the tumult[16] and violence of Knox' reformation.

Not far from the cathedral, on the margin of the water, stands a fragment of the castle, in which the archbishop anciently resided. It was never very large, and was built with more attention to security than pleasure. Cardinal Beatoun is said to have had workmen employed in improving its fortifications[17] at the time when he was murdered by the ruffians[18] of reformation, in the manner of which Knox has given what he himself calls a merry narrative.

The city of St. Andrews, when it had lost its archiepiscopal pre-eminence, gradually decayed: One of its streets is now lost; and in those that remain, there is silence and solitude of inactive indigence[19] and gloomy depopulation.

---

12 mournful ['mɔːnfəl] *adj.* 悲恸的，悲哀的
13 cathedral [kə'θiːdrəl] *n.* 大教堂
14 majestic [mə'dʒestɪk] *adj.* 宏伟的，庄严的
15 specimen ['spesɪmən] *n.* 样本，标本
16 tumult ['tjuːmʌlt] *n.* 骚动，暴乱
17 fortification [ˌfɔːtɪfɪ'keɪʃn] *n.* 防御工事，尤指堡垒、要塞城墙等
18 ruffian ['rʌfɪən] *n.* 恶棍，无赖，此处意为"革命暴徒"
19 indigence ['ɪndɪdʒəns] *n.* 贫穷

址中找寻这里曾经的辉煌，但即使这些是遗迹，它们也都快要消失了，除非专门采取措施对它们进行保护；那么维护这些令人悲伤的纪念品的乐趣何在呢？它们直到最近才被重视起来。从前每个想从这里得到一砖一瓦的人都到这里肆意乱拿。

大教堂的地基可能仍有迹可寻，墙的一小部分仍然矗立着，显示出这曾经是一座雄伟壮丽的建筑，完全符合王国的至高无上。由于这座建筑现存部分太少，所以即使对艺术家来说它也不足以成为建筑标本。众所周知，这座教堂是在诺克斯改革暴乱时被毁坏的。

离大教堂不远，在河边还存有城堡的残迹，这里曾是大主教居住的地方。它一直都很小，建筑时考虑更多的是安全而不是美观舒适。据说比唐红衣大主教曾雇人改进其防御措施，就在那时，他被一群革命暴徒以诺克斯给他所谓的得意的办事方式给谋害了。

当圣安德鲁斯失去了它神圣的大教堂后，就逐渐衰败了：其中的一条街道消失了；那些保留下来的也在沉默和孤独的闲置中被穷困和黯淡销毁。

Saint Andrews seems to be a place eminently[20] adapted to study and education, being situated in a populous, yet a cheap country, and exposing the minds and manners of young men neither to the levity[21] and dissoluteness[22] of a capital city, nor to[23] the gross luxury of a town of commerce, places naturally unpropitious[24] to learning; in one the desire of knowledge easily gives way to[25] the love of pleasure, and in the other, is in danger of yielding to[26] the love of money.

The students however are represented as at this time not exceeding a hundred. Perhaps it may be some obstruction[27] to their increase that there is no Episcopal[28] chapel[29] in the place. I saw no reason for imputing their paucity to the present professors; nor can the expense of an academical education be very reasonably objected. A student of the highest class may keep his annual session[30], (or as the English call it), his term, which lasts seven months, for about fifteen pounds, and one of lower rank for less than ten; in which board, lodging, and instruction are all included.

The chief magistrate[31] resident in the

圣安德鲁斯人口众多而消费颇低，似乎是一个极其适合学习和教育的地方，在这里学生的思想和生活方式既不像首都城市的人们那样轻率和放荡，也不像商业小镇的人们那样奢华，商业小镇这些地方自然不适合学习；一方面对知识的渴求容易被享乐的追求所取代，另一方面，容易陷入盲目追求金钱的危险中。

然而，据说那里的学生数量不超过一百人。也许这里没有主教的礼拜堂是它数量不能得以增长的障碍。我看不出有什么理由可以把学生的数量少归因于现在的教授们；学术教育的费用也没理由遭到什么合理的反对。最高年级的学生学习一个阶段（英语中称做一学期）的时间为7个月，在这期间大约花费15英镑，稍低年级的还不到10磅，包括食宿和学习费用。

学校的首席驻扎长官职

20 eminently ['emɪnəntlɪ] *adv.* 突出地(著名地)，这里引申为 "极其"
21 levity ['levətɪ] *n.* 轻浮，轻率
22 dissoluteness ['dɪsəlu:tnɪs] *n.* 放荡，淫荡
23 expose...to... 使暴露，后面两个短句中的 "to" 前面都省略了 "exposing"
24 unpropitious ['ʌnprə'pɪʃəs] *adj.* 不适合的
25 give way to = be replaced by，被代替
26 yield to 顺从，屈服于
27 obstruction [əb'strʌkʃn] *n.* 障碍，妨碍
28 episcopal [ɪ'pɪskəpl] *adj.* 主教的，主教管辖的
29 chapel ['tʃæpl] *n.* 小礼拜堂
30 session ['seʃn] *n.* 期限
31 magistrate ['mædʒɪstreɪt] *n.* 长官

university, answering to our vice-chancellor[32], and to the rector[33] magnificus on the continent, had commonly the title of Lord Rector; but being addressed only as Mr. Rector in an inauguratory[34] speech by the present chancellor, he has fallen from his former dignity of style. Lordship was very liberally annexed[35] by our ancestors to any station or character of dignity: They said, the Lord General, and Lord Ambassador; so we still say, my Lord, to the judge upon the circuit[36], and yet retain in our Liturgy[37] the Lords of the Council.

In walking among the ruins of religious buildings, we came to two vaults over which had formerly stood the house of the sub-prior. One of the vaults was inhabited by an old woman, who claimed the right of[38] abode[39] there, as the widow of a man whose ancestors had possessed the same gloomy mansion for no less than four generations. The right, however[40] it began, was considered as established by legal prescription, and the old woman lives undisturbed. She thinks however that she has a claim to something more than sufferance; for as her husband's name was Bruce, she is allied to royalty, and told Mr. Boswell that when there were persons of quality in the place, she was distinguished by some

位相当于我们的副校长或是欧洲大陆的教区长。通常情况下，他们应该被称为教区长阁下，但他在本届校长就职演说时被称作教区长先生，这就意味着他已经不再具有以前的高职位了。先辈们对任何体面的职位都称作阁下，他们说将军阁下、大使阁下。因此我们会称巡回审判法官为"尊敬的阁下"，但是在我们的礼拜仪式上保留了议院阁下这个称呼。

在宗教性建筑的残骸中行走时，你会发现两个地下室，那里曾经是副修道院的房屋所在。其中一个房间里居住的是一位老妇人，她作为一个男人的遗孀对这块土地享有居住权，这阴暗的房屋已在那个男人的家族中传承了超过四代。不管这一居住权最初以何种方式获得，它在当时还是合法的，且老妇人的居住并未受到任何干扰。然而她认为她拥有的不应该仅仅是这种对她房屋的默认拥有权，因为她的丈夫

32 vice-chancellor ['vaɪs'tʃɑ:nsələ] *n.* 大学副校长
33 rector ['rektə] *n.* 教区院长
34 inauguratory [ɪ'nɔ:gjərətərɪ] *adj.* = inaugural就职的, 开始的
35 annex [ə'neks] *v.* 附加, 添带
36 circuit ['sɜ:kɪt] *n.* 巡回（审判）
37 liturgy ['lɪtɪdʒɪ] *n.* 礼拜形式, 典礼
38 claim the right of 此处意为"声称有权利"
39 abode [ə'bəʊd] *n.* 住处, 住所
40 however [haʊ'evə(r)] = no matter how, 不论怎样

notice; that indeed she is now neglected, but she spins a thread, has the company of her cat, and is troublesome to nobody.

Having now seen whatever this ancient city offered to our curiosity, we left it with good wishes, having reason to be highly pleased with the attention that was paid us. But whoever surveys the world must see many things that give him pain. The kindness of the professors did not contribute to abate[41] the uneasy remembrance[42] of an university declining, a college alienated[43], and a church profaned[44] and hastening to the ground.

St. Andrews indeed has formerly suffered more atrocious[45] ravages[46] and more extensive destruction, but recent evils affect with greater force. We were reconciled to the sight of archiepiscopal ruins. The distance of a calamity[47] from the present time seems to preclude the mind from contact or sympathy. Events long past are barely known; they are not considered. We read with as little emotion the violence of Knox and his followers, as the irruptions[48] of Alaric and the Goths. Had the university been destroyed two centuries ago, we should not have regretted it[49]; but to see it

叫布鲁斯，所以她应该是皇室中人。而且她还告诉波斯韦尔先生当地如果有什么贵人的话，非她莫属。可事实上她确实被忽略了，但她在小猫的陪伴下纺线织布，并未给他人带来任何麻烦。

在欣赏了这座古老城市中一切能引起我们好奇的东西之后，我们深深地祝福它，并有理由为我们在这里得到的关注而高兴。但任何深入了解这个"世界"的人一定会看到令他们痛苦的东西。教授的仁慈并不能减轻大学衰退、学院疏离、教堂被亵渎并即将倒塌带给我们的痛苦回忆。

圣安德鲁斯的确曾经遭受过残暴且大面积的破坏，但近年来遭到的破坏却更加严重。我们对大教堂的废墟也只能听之任之。现在看这场已过去许久的大灾难似乎并不能使我们感同身受并引起我们心中的怜悯之情。过去的事几乎不为人所知，不被人考虑。读到关于诺克斯和他的追随者们的暴力活动就像在读阿拉里克和哥特人侵一样没有任何情感的触动。如果这所大学是在两个世纪以前被摧毁的，我们应该不会感到遗憾；但看到它在哀败

---

41 abate [ə'beɪt] v. 减弱，减轻
42 remembrance [rɪ'membrəns] n. 回忆，记忆
43 alienated ['eɪlɪəneɪtɪd] adj. 疏远的，被隔开的
44 profane [prə'feɪn] v. 亵渎，玷污
45 atrocious [ə'trəʊʃəs] adj. 残暴的
46 ravage ['rævɪdʒ] n. 破坏
47 calamity [kə'læmətɪ] n. 灾难，不幸事件
48 irruption [ɪ'rʌpʃ(ə)n] n. 突入，此处意为"入侵"
49 Had the unversity been destroyed…, we should not have regretted…
此句为虚拟语气，表示与过去事实相反的状态，从句省略
"if"，将"had"提前

pining in decay and struggling for life, fills the mind with mournful images and ineffectual wishes.

From *Journey to the Western Isles of Scotland* (1775)

中萎缩又在挣扎着生存，我们的思绪中就浸满了凄苦的景象和徒劳的希望。

含英咀华

圣安德鲁斯是苏格兰境内风景最美的海滨城镇之一，这里旖旎浪漫，春光无限。有著名的圣安德鲁斯大学，经历风雨的城堡让人感觉到这个城市历史的沧桑。本文语言使用规范，句式简单易懂，适合模仿。

Henry James

亨利·詹姆斯

亨利·詹姆斯(1843~1916)，美国小说家、文学批评家、剧作家和散文家。詹姆斯是19世纪美国现实主义文学的三大倡导者之一，他同豪威尔斯、马克·吐温一起，为美国现实主义文学的发展做出了积极贡献。詹姆斯的主要作品是小说，此外他也写了许多文学评论、游记、传记和剧本。重要的长篇小说有《美国人》(*The American, 1876~1877*)、《贵妇人的画像》(*The Portrait of a Lady, 1881*)，著名的中短篇小说有《黛西·密勒》(*Daisy Miller, 1878*)。他的作品细腻、优雅，包含着精敲细琢的词句、贴切完美的幽默、微妙至极的含蓄和耐人寻味。他的随笔为在第二次世界大战后风靡的新批评主义散文文章提供了丰富的词汇，是这一时期的典范。

Venice

It is a great pleasure to write the word; but I am not sure there is not a certain impudence[1] in pretending to add anything to it. Venice has been painted and described many thousands of times, and of all the cities of the world is the easiest to visit without going there. Open the first book and you will find a rhapsody[2] about it; step into the first picture and you will find three or four high-colored "views" of it. There is notoriously[3] nothing more to be said on the subject. Every one has been there, and every one has brought back a collection of photographs. There is as little mystery about the Grand Canal as about our local thoroughfare[4], and the name of St. Mark is as familiar as the postman's ring. It is not forbidden[5], however, to speak of familiar things, and I hold that for the true Venice-lover Venice is always in order. There is nothing new to be said about her certainly, but the old is better than any novelty[6]. It would be a sad day indeed when there should be something new to say. I write these lines with the full consciousness of having no information whatever to offer. I do not pretend to enlighten the reader; I pretend only to give a

---

1 impudence ['ɪmpjədəns]   n. 冒失，无礼
2 rhapsody ['ræpsədɪ]   n. 溢美之词，热情赞颂
3 notoriously [nəʊ'tɔːrɪəslɪ]   adv. 众所周知地
4 thoroughfare ['θʌrəfeə]   n. 通路，大道
5 be forbidden   不许，禁止
6 novelty ['nɒvltɪ]   n. 新奇，新鲜，新奇的事物

威尼斯

非常荣幸能提笔写下威尼斯这个词，但是我不确定为此添写些什么是否会有些冒昧。威尼斯曾被数以千次地描绘讲述过，它是世界上最容易不亲自前往就能让人身临其境的一个城市。翻开第一本书，你会发现它的赞美诗；当你看到第一张图片时，你会欣赏到三四幅关于它的色彩鲜艳的风景图片。众所周知，关于威尼斯已经没有什么更多可说的了。每个人都已去过那里，并都带回了很多照片。大运河就像我们附近的街道一样没有神秘感，圣马克的名字像邮差的铃声一样为人们所熟知。然而，说一些人们熟悉的事物也未尝不可，我认为对于真正的威尼斯热爱者来说她总是那么秩序井然。当然关于她并没有什么新鲜的故事，但是这种古老要比任何新鲜的故事更美妙。老实说如果关于她有了些新的故事反而会让人感到伤感。当我书写这些文字时，我清醒地意识到并没有什么信息可传达。我并不是想启发读者，只是假装

fillip to[7] his memory; and I hold any writer sufficiently justified who is himself in love with his theme.

It is a city in which, I suspect, there is very little strenuous[8] thinking, and yet it is a city in which there must be almost as much happiness as misery. The misery of Venice stands there for all the world to see; it is part of the spectacle[9] — a thoroughgoing devotee[10] of local color might consistently say it is part of the pleasure. The Venetian people have little to call their own — little more than the bare privilege[11] of leading their lives in the most beautiful of towns. Their habitations are decayed; their taxes heavy; their pockets light; their opportunities few. One receives an impression, however, that life presents itself to them with attractions not accounted for in this meagre[12] train of advantages, and that they are on better terms with[13] it than many people who have made a better bargain. They lie in the sunshine; they dabble[14] in the sea; they wear bright rags; they fall into attitudes and harmonies; they assist at an eternal conversazione[15]. It is not easy to say that one would have them other than they are, and it certainly would make an immense

---

7 give a fillip to 刺激，"fillip" = stimulus，刺激物
8 strenuous ['strenjuəs]   adj.   奋发的，有奋斗之必要的
9 spectacle ['spektəkl]   n.   值得看的东西，光景
10 devotee [ˌdevə'ti:]   n.   爱好者，热心者
11 privilege ['prɪvəlɪdʒ]   n.   特权
12 meagre ['mi:gə(r)]   adj.   贫乏的
13 be on good terms (with)   (与)……关系良好，友善
14 dabble ['dæbl]   v.   嬉水
15 conversazione [ˌkɔnvəˌsætsɪ'əʊnɪ]   n.   座谈会，此处引申为"话题"

刺激一下读者们那尘封已久的记忆；并且我认为所有钟爱自己主题的作者都会有其合理的理由来这样做。

我认为在这座城市里很少有冥思苦想，然而它一定是一个痛苦与快乐并存的地方。威尼斯的苦难显而易见；它是壮观美景的一部分———个十足的本地风景爱好者会一贯认为它是快乐的一部分。威尼斯人拥有的唯一特权便是有机会在这座最美丽的城市中生活。他们的住所破旧，税务繁重，口袋空空，机会寥寥无几。然而在外人看来，威尼斯人的生活却有着一种这种特权所不能带来的诱惑，生活于此的威尼斯人虽不似他人般志得富足，却过得更为舒心惬意。他们沐浴在阳光里；嬉戏在海水中；穿着鲜艳的衣服；沉浸在和谐快乐的气氛中；没完没了地聊天。我们很难说如果他们不是现在这个状态还会不会拥有这些，如果他们丰衣足食情况将大不相同。在威尼斯饱受饥饿之苦的人不在少数，但是若我们不能同等地意识到威尼斯人在极差的物质条件下也可以拥有浓厚的"威尼斯性情"，这就更令人痛苦了。大自然是很

difference should they be better fed. The number of persons in Venice who evidently never have enough to eat is painfully large; but it would be more painful if we did not equally perceive[16] that the rich Venetian temperament[17] may bloom upon a dog's allowance. Nature has been kind to it, and sunshine and leisure and conversation and beautiful views form the greater part of its sustenance[18]. It takes a great deal to make a successful American, but to make a happy Venetian takes only a handful of quick sensibility. The Italian people have at once the good and the evil fortune to be conscious of few wants; so that if the civilization[19] of a society is measured by the number of its needs, as seems to be the common opinion today, it is to be feared that the children of the lagoon[20] would make but[21] a poor figure in a set of comparative tables. Not their misery, doubtless, but the way they elude[22] their misery, Is what pleases the sentimental tourist, who is gratified[23] by the sight of a beautiful race that lives by the aid of its imagination. The way to enjoy Venice is to follow the example of these people and make the most of simple pleasures. Almost all the pleasures of the place are simple; this may be maintained even under the imputation[24]

16 perceive [pə'siːv] v. 感觉
17 temperament ['tempərəmənt] n. 气质，性质，性情
18 sustenance ['sʌstənəns] n. 生活资料
19 civilization [ˌsɪvɪlaɪ'zeɪʃn] n. 文明
20 lagoon [lə'guːn] n. 池塘，水池
21 but [bʌt] = only 介词，只是
22 elude [ɪ'luːd] v. 逃避，躲避
23 gratify ['grætɪfaɪ] v. 使满足
24 imputation [ˌɪmpju'teɪʃən] n. 污名，罪名

眷顾威尼斯的，阳光、闲暇、交谈、美丽的风景构成了生活的主体。造就一个成功的美国人需要投入很多，但是培养一个快乐的威尼斯人则只需一点感情。意大利人需求意识很淡薄，这是幸运的，也是不幸的。所以，如果按现今流行的观点，即通过需求量来衡量一个社会的文明程度的话，那么在污水池旁长大的孩子们在那一系列的对比表格中所占据的数字会很低。毋庸置疑，这不是他们的悲剧，但他们逃避不幸的方法却能取悦情感丰富的旅客，这样的旅客会因为见到一个美丽却需借助想像而生活的种族而感到满足。欣赏威尼斯的方法就是效仿这些人并且充分享受最简单的快乐。几乎这里的所有快乐都很简单；而这种快乐即使在精巧的谬论的诋毁中也可以维持。没有比欣赏一幅优秀的提香画作更简单的快乐了，除非是看一幅丁托列托精美的油画或在圣马克教堂散步——养成这种习惯的方式是可恶的——使疲惫的双眼在黑暗中得到片刻休息；乘小船在河中随波漂流；在阳台上小憩；在佛罗里安品咖啡。威尼斯的一天就是由这些简单的

of ingenious[25] paradox[26]. There is no simpler pleasure than looking at a fine Titian, unless it be looking at a fine Tintoret or strolling into St. Mark's, — abominable[27] the way one falls into the habit, — and resting one's light-wearied eyes upon[28] the windowless gloom; or than floating in a gondola[29] or than hanging over a balcony or than taking one's coffee at Florian's. It is of such superficial[30] pastimes that a Venetian day is composed, and the pleasure of the matter is in the emotions to which they minister[31]. These are fortunately of the finest — otherwise Venice would be insufferably dull. Reading Ruskin is good; reading the old records is perhaps better; but the best thing of all is simply staying on. The only way to care for Venice as she deserves it is to give her a chance[32] to touch you often to linger and remain and return.

From *Italian Hours* (1909)

快乐构成的。这些活动的快乐就在于它们所能提供给我们的精神的快乐。幸运的是这些都是最精美的，否则威尼斯将会呈现一种令人没法忍受的乏味状态。阅读拉斯金的作品感觉会很好；而阅读古老的记录可能更好；但最好的是就停留在威尼斯。唯一喜欢威尼斯的方法就是给她一次机会接近你，使你在威尼斯驻足、停留并重游。

---

25 ingenious [ɪn'dʒiːnɪəs] *adj.* 精致的，有独创性的
26 paradox ['pærədɒks] *n.* 自相矛盾的话
27 abominable [ə'bɒmɪnəbl] *adj.* 讨厌的，令人憎恶的
28 rest on/upon = gaze at, 凝视
29 gondola ['gɒndələ] *n.* （威尼斯的）小划船
30 superficial [,suːpə'fɪʃl] *adj.* 表面的，肤浅的
31 minister ['mɪnɪstə] *v.* （古语）提供，供给
32 give sb. a chance to do = give sb. an opportunity to do, 寻找机会

含英咀华

　　水城威尼斯位于意大利东北部亚得里亚海滨，素有"亚得里亚海明珠"之称，它既是旅游胜地，又是意大利的重要港口。从地图上看，威尼斯仿佛一颗镶嵌在美丽长靴靴腰上的水晶，在亚得里亚海的波涛中熠熠生辉。威尼斯的风情总离不开"水"，蜿蜒的水巷，流动的清波，她就好像一个漂浮在碧波上浪漫的梦，诗情画意久久挥之不去。

Mary Anne Barker

玛丽·安妮·巴克

玛丽·安妮·巴克（1831~1911），出生于牙买加，她是家里的长女。在英国完成学业，1852年嫁给皇家陆军军官乔治·罗伯特·巴克，后改名为巴克夫人。她的丈夫于1896年去世，她返回伦敦居住，于1911年3月去世。1870年她出版了第一本书，名为《新西兰的牧场生活》(Station Life in New Zealand, 1870)这是一本家信的合集。这本书非常成功，并被翻译成德语和法语。在接下来的8年里，她共写了10本书，包括《新西兰的牧场生活》的续篇《新西兰牧场的乐趣》（Station Amusements in New Zealand, 1873)。

Sight-seeing in Melbourne

观光墨尔本

We have seen a good deal of Melbourne this week; and not only of the town, for we have had many drives in the exceedingly pretty suburbs, owing to the kindness of the drivers, who have been most hospitable[1] and made our visit here delightful. We drove out to their house at Toorak three or four times; and spent a long afternoon with them; and there I began to make acquaintance with[2] the Antipodean trees and flowers. I hope you will not think it a very sweeping assertion[3] if I say that all the leaves look as if they were made of leather, but it really is so; the hot winds appear to parch up[4] everything, at all events[5], round Melbourne, till the greatest charm of foliage[6] is more or less lost; the flowers also look withered and burnt up, as yours do at the end of a long, dry summer, only they assume this appearance after the first hot wind in spring. The suburb called Heidelberg is the prettiest, to my taste — an undulating[7] country with vineyards, and a park-like appearance which, is very charming. All round Melbourne there are nice, comfortable, English-looking villas. At one of these we called to

这周在墨尔本我欣赏到很多美丽的景色，不仅是城市的景色，我们也穿梭于风光旖旎的郊区，正是因为那些热情好客、心地善良的司机，我们的旅行变得格外愉快。我们驾车去他们图雅克的房子三四次；在那我们共度了一个漫长的下午；在那我开始渐渐熟悉安提博帝恩的花草树木。如果我说所有的叶子看起来像是皮革制成的，我希望你们不要认为这是一个鲁莽的断言，但事实确实如此；不管怎样，燥热的风正在烘干墨尔本周围的一切，直到吸干绿叶所有的魅力；花也枯萎，变焦，在其他国家经过漫长干燥的夏季时才会出现这种情况，而在这里还是春天的第一缕热风。海德堡的郊区是最美的——波浪起伏的葡萄园，一幅迷人的花园景象。墨

---

1 hospitable ['hɒspɪtəbl]　*adj.*　好客的
2 make acquaintance with　此处意为"熟悉"
3 assertion [ə'sɜ:ʃn]　*n.*　= claim，断言，主张
4 parch up　烘干
5 at all events　= in any event，无论如何，不管怎样
6 foliage ['fəʊlɪdʒ]　*n.*　叶子（总称）
7 undulating ['ʌndjuleɪtɪŋ]　*adj.*　波浪起伏的

return a visit and found a very handsome house; luxuriously furnished, with beautiful garden and grounds. One afternoon we went by rail[8] to St. Kilda's, a flourishing bathing-place on the sea-coast, about six miles from Melbourne. Everywhere building is going on with great rapidity, and you do not see any poor people in the streets. If I wanted to be critical and find fault, I might object to[9] the deep gutters[10] on each side of the road; after a shower of rain[11] they are raging torrents[12] for a short time, through which you are obliged to splash[13] without regard to the muddy consequences; and even when they are dry, they entail sudden and prodigious jolts. There are plenty of Hansoms and all sorts of other conveyances[14], but I had no peace until he took me for a drive in a vehicle which was quite new to me — a sort of light car with a canopy[15] and curtains, holding four, two on each seat, dos-a-dos, and called a "jingle," — of American parentage[16], I fancy. One drive in this carriage was quite enough, however, and I contented myself with[17] Hansoms afterwards; but walking is really more enjoyable than anything else, after having been so long cooped[18] up on board ship.

We admired the fine statue, at the top of

---

8 go by rail = go by railway/ go by train，乘火车
9 object to = criticize，固定搭配，此处意为"批评"
10 gutter ['gʌtə] n. 排水沟
11 a shower of rain 阵雨
12 torrent ['tɒrənt] n. 激流，水流
13 splash [splæʃ] v. 溅湿，溅开
14 conveyance [kən'veɪəns] n. 运输，运输工具
15 canopy ['kænəpɪ] n. 天篷，遮篷
16 parentage ['peərəntɪdʒ] n. 亲子关系，出身
17 content oneself with 此处指"满足于"
18 coop [ku:p] v. 关进，这里指"拘禁"

尔本的四周都是美丽、舒适、英式风格的别墅。在这些别墅中，一个富丽堂皇的房子映入了我们的眼帘：内有奢华的家具，外有漂亮宽敞的花园和草坪。一天下午，我们乘火车去圣吉达，是离墨尔本六英里的一个海边游泳圣地。新建筑无时无刻不在拔地而起，在街上永远看不到生活窘迫的人。如果要我挑剔一点，非指出一点瑕疵，那我可能会批评一下道路两边的排水沟；阵雨过后，暂时就会水流奔腾，而你也会被无意中溅上泥土；即使地面干的时候，它们也会骤然间产生巨大的摇动。这里有很多汉萨（车夫驾驶台在后的单马双轮双座马车）和其他各种各样的交通工具，直到我坐上一种从未见过的车时，我的心才平静下来，这是一种带天篷和窗帘的轻型车，车上有四个"多斯多斯"，两个座位每个上面两个，被叫做"叮当"——我猜想是源于美国吧。坐这种车体验一次足矣，后来感觉坐在汉萨里很满足；不过在船上经过长途颠簸后，才发觉还是走路最舒服了。

在科林斯街头，矗立着一座精美的雕像，我们特别敬仰

Collins Street, to the memory of the two most famous of Australian explorers, Burke and Wills, and we made many visits to the Museum, and the glorious Free Library; we also went all over the Houses of Legislature — very new and grand. But you must not despise me if I confess to[19] having enjoyed the shops exceedingly: it was so unlike a jeweler's shop in England to see on the counter gold in its raw state, in nuggets[20] and dust and flakes[21]; in this stage of its existence it certainly deserves its name of "filthy lucre," for it is often only half washed. There were quantities of emus' eggs in the silversmiths'[22] shops, mounted in every conceivable[23] way as cups and vases, and even as work-boxes: some designs consisted of three or five eggs grouped together as a centre-piece. I cannot honestly say I admired any of them they were generally too elaborate, comprising[24] often a native (spear in hand), a kangaroo, palms[25], ferns, cockatoos[26], and sometimes an emu[27] or two in addition, as a pedestal[28] all this in frosted silver or gold. I was given a pair of these eggs before leaving England: they were mounted in London as little flower-vases in a setting consisting only of

它，这是为了纪念两个著名的澳大利亚探险家，伯克和威尔斯而建造的。之后我们又参观了很多博物馆和完全免费的图书馆，还游览了崭新宏伟的立法院。如果我承认我更喜欢这里的商店，你可千万不要鄙视我：这里的珠宝店和英国不一样，在柜台看到的是未加工的黄金，成块的、粉末状的、片状的；在这一阶段所处的状态，称它为"脏钱"的确名副其实，因为它们通常洗得不干净。在银器店里可以看到很多鸸鹋蛋，它们可裱成任何想得到的样子，例如杯子、花瓶，甚至是工具箱：有一些设计是由三五个蛋组合在一起。坦白说，我不是打心底里喜欢这里的每一件工艺品；它们太精美了，形状各异，通常由土著人（手里拿着一杆长矛）、袋鼠、棕榈树、蕨类植物构成，甚至有时候以一个或两个鸸鹋

---

19 confess to 固定搭配，"to"为介词，后面接名词或动名词，此处意为"承认"
20 nugget ['nʌgɪt] n. 金块，贵金属块
21 flake [fleɪk] n. 薄片，小片
22 silversmith ['sɪlvəsmɪθ] n. 银器匠
23 conceivable [kən'si:vəbl] adj. 想得到的，可想像的
24 comprising 现在分词短语作状语，表伴随
25 palm [pɑ:m] n. 棕榈树
26 cockatoo [ˌkɒkə'tu:] n. 蕨类植物
27 emu ['i:mju:] n. 鸸鹋
28 pedestal ['pedɪstl] n. 基架，底座

a few bulrushes[29] and leaves, yet far better than any of these florid designs; but the emu-eggs are very popular in Sydney or Melbourne, and I am told sell rapidly to people going home, who take them as a moment of their Australian life, and probably think that the greater the number of reminiscences[30] suggested by the ornament[32], the more[31] satisfactory it is as a purchase.

From *Station Life in New Zealand* (1870)

作为镀金或镀银的底座。离开英国之前别人送给我一对鸸鹋蛋：在伦敦装裱成有底座的小花瓶，只有几片香蒲和树叶，然而却胜过这里任何华丽的设计；但是鸸鹋蛋在悉尼和墨尔本很流行，别人告诉我立刻把它卖给要回家的人，他们把这作为澳大利亚美好时光纪念，可能会认为勾起越多回忆的纪念品，越值得购买。

29 bulrush ['bʊlrʌʃ] *n.* 芦苇；香蒲
30 reminiscence [ˌremɪ'nɪsns] *n.* = remembrance，回想，回忆
31 the greater ... the more "the＋比较级，the＋比较级"表示"越……越……"
32 ornament ['ɔ:nəmənt] *n.* 装饰（物）

含英咀华

如果说悉尼是南太平洋的纽约，那墨尔本则可说是伦敦。维多利亚州的首府——墨尔本是澳大利亚的第二大城市，这是个古老的城市，同时也是澳大利亚的经济、文化、金融中心。墨尔本市内树木林立，19世纪维多利亚式的建筑比比皆是，因此，她除了被誉为"花园城市"之外，更被誉为是该国最具"欧陆风味"的城市。在这篇文章里，作者形象生动地描写了这座城市独特的建筑特色及欧陆风情。